Where There's No Wine, There Can Be No Miracles:

The Power and Purpose of Teaching

Bishop Robert L. Cade
&
Dr. Maurice L. Furdge

Table of Contents

INTRODUCTION / PURPOSE 6
CHAPTER 1: MIRACLES 15
CHAPTER 2: THE FIRST MIRACLE OF JESUS: WATER INTO WINE 23
CHAPTER 3: THE MYSTERY OF TEACHING 45
CHAPTER 4: A TALE OF TWO WINES 61
CHAPTER 5: THE ROLE OF THE GOVERNOR 90
   REVELATION – PART I 90
   REVELATION - PART II 102
CHAPTER 6: TEACHING AND MIRACLES 121
   PART I – NEW TESTAMENT MIRACLES AND TEACHINGS 123
   PART II – OLD TESTAMENT MIRACLES AND TEACHINGS 136
   PART III - FAITH IN THE TEACHINGS 147
CHAPTER 7: THE RESPONSIBILITY OF THE STUDENT 165
CHAPTER 8: OBSTACLES 184
   OBSTACLE I: Sin/Lack of Repentance 189
   OBSTACLE II: Immaturity/Lack of Management ... 208
   OBSTACLE III: Lack of Communication/Prayer 219
   OBSTACLE IV: Lack of Faith 236

OBSTACLE V: Faith Contaminants 266
OBSTACLE VI: Disobedience 277
OBSTACLE VII: Ignorance 306
OBSTACLE VIII: Tradition 317
OBSTACLE IX: Unforgiveness 330
CHAPTER 9: THERE'S NO SUCH THING… 347
CHAPTER 10: THE HEART 365

ABOUT THE AUTHORS

Bishop Robert Cade, affectionately known as "Coach," is known for developing a solid TEAM and teaching people how to WIN in all aspects of life. Born and raised in Mobile, Alabama, to the late Cornelius Cade, Sr. and the late Mary Abrams, Bishop Cade graduated from Williamson High School and furthered his educational studies at Alcorn State University on a full athletic scholarship. He received a Bachelor's in Health and Physical Education and a Master's in Educational Leadership.

Bishop Cade has served as in the capacities of Head Basketball Coach, Football Coach, Track & Field Coach, Athletic Director, and Summer Camp Coordinator for more than 30 years. Throughout his coaching journey, Bishop Cade has learned the importance of knowing your opponent, strategies for VICTORY, and overcoming obstacles to WIN. Although Bishop Cade retired as a coach in the public system, he never stopped "COACHING."

Bishop Cade now serves as the Senior Pastor and Overseer of Word of Faith Ambassadors Worship and Outreach Centers, providing effective methods, strategies, and Kingdom principles, which cause those who encounter his teachings to excel in all arenas.

An advocate of gaining knowledge, Bishop continued his educational studies at Word of Faith Bible College, receiving a Master's degree in Theology and a Doctorate of Divinity. He currently serves as Dean of Education at Word of Faith Bible College.

Assisting Bishop Cade in "TEAM BUILDING" and making "MAJOR PLAYS" is the dynamic Dr. Betty Cade, his wife who is also a former coach and cheerleader. Dr. Betty, the motivation for ministry, believes in effectively supporting and encouraging the movement with divine teaching, profound impartation, and unconditional love for others. With TEAMWORK, Bishop and Dr. Betty have been able to empower the masses, build communities, bridge racial and denominational gaps, and transform followers into leaders and leaders into agents of change.

Bishop and Dr. Betty are the proud parents of an ALL-STAR TEAM of four loving children, Diedra (Charles) Robb, Shawn (Brandy) Davis, Minister Derrick (Grace) Davis, and Dr. Robbie (Dr. Maurice) Furdge. They are also the grandparents of nine talented grandchildren.

As the journey continues, Bishop Robert and Dr. Betty Cade preach the gospel of the Kingdom, empower the nations, and build communities as they train and equip the masses to infiltrate the marketplace with Kingdom strategies and dominate in their sphere of influence.

Dr. Maurice Furdge is an inspiring motivational speaker, community leader, and profound teacher, whose captivating messages have been known to challenge and provoke listeners to live life on Purpose by maximizing their potential. His thoughtful and passionate delivery captures the hearts of those who encounter his life-altering messages, reminding them that they are chosen to make a difference and destined to make an impact in society.

An advocate for education, Maurice graduated (class valedictorian) from Coahoma Agricultural High School and received a Bachelor of Science degree in Biology/Pre-Medicine *(Summa Cum Laude)* from Alcorn State University. Maurice continued his educational pursuit at Quillen College of Medicine in Johnson City, Tennessee, where he received his M.D. in Internal Medicine.

Dr. Furdge currently serves as a travel physician, offering services in multiple states, and as a ministry leader and teacher at Word of Faith Ambassadors Worship Center.

Dr. Furdge is married to Dr. Robbie Cade Furdge, and they are the proud parents of 5-year-old Michael Lawrence Robert Furdge. Dr. Furdge and his wife are serial entrepreneurs, owning seven (7) businesses, and are the founders and directors of a non-profit organization. Together, they serve as mentors to over 50 youth and young adults.

INTRODUCTION / PURPOSE

If you're looking for a manual or tips to get what you want from God in five minutes or less, I'm sorry: this is not that book. If you're looking to "pimp" God or manipulate Him into giving you a "big blessing," I'm going to apologize now: this is not that book. If you're looking to obtain the power and miracles of God to "wow" and impress people, I regret to inform you that this book may not be for you. If you're looking to get something without sacrificing anything of yourself (time, energy, attention, resources, etc.), let me just tell you before you get too far into this book…this ain't that.

However, if you're looking to learn more about God, this book may help. If you're desperate for a miracle and desire to know how God operates in the miraculous, this book may help. If you're interested in knowing how teaching and the miraculous are connected and intertwined, this may be the book for you. If doing things your way isn't working…If you're tired of a life devoid of relationship with little understanding of God…If you've tried everything you know how to do and are at your wits end…I prayerfully hope this book can be a bridge to connect you back to the Source - Our Father, the King of Kings, the Lord of Lords, and Master of Miracles - once again.

Perception of Teaching

It is often said that "where a person's treasure lies, there is where you'll find their heart." Or better yet, what a person values is where you'll find their money, their time, their affections, and their attention. We, as a society, place a premium on entertainment. We love to be entertained – whether it is watching a television show on Netflix, going to movies, browsing the internet or social media, watching YouTube videos, cheering on our favorite sports teams and athletes, or going to concerts and listening to our favorite artists / musicians.

Therefore, it's no wonder that some of the highest paid occupations are in the realm of entertainment: actors, actresses, athletes, internet personalities, musicians, etc. They have fame, fortune, and influence because society values their giftings and talents. Perhaps it is because people are looking for an escape from the issues, problems, and stressors they face on a daily basis. Sometimes the only way to escape is by being entertained and distracted from reality. I give credit to the majority of those in the entertainment industry; their discipline, development of their craft, and attention to detail are second to none. Many of them have sacrificed a great deal to climb into the upper echelon of their professions.

All the while, other equally (if not more) important giftings and occupations go unnoticed or dramatically unappreciated. Some examples are:

1. Paramedics/EMTs (rushing to save lives and get people to hospitals),
2. Farmworkers (growing the food we eat)
3. First Responders/Firefighters/Police officers (putting their lives in danger to keep law and order in society)

4. Social workers (working with people and families to inform them of benefits and programs to help their situations)
5. Nurses/Respiratory Therapists/Physicians (especially in light of the recent Coronavirus pandemic)
6. (Last, but certainly not least) Schoolteachers.

Just the very gift of Teaching itself is often overlooked. No other occupation or gifting is as interwoven into every fabric of our society. For about 12 to 15 years of a child's life, teachers are responsible for our children for about 8 hours a day! In colleges, teachers/professors are tasked with the obligation of being *de facto* parents and mentors to young adults while they navigate this thing called "life." If you're employed in any occupation in this world, it's likely you've had a teacher: Doctors have had teachers – Lawyers have had teachers – Politicians and Presidents have had teachers – Nurses, Construction workers, CEOs all have had teachers – Actresses and Actors have had teachers – Athletes have had teachers – Musicians have had teachers – Heck, even Teachers have had teachers. There is no aspect of life that doesn't involve some degree of teaching and instruction.

Therefore, I conclude that Teaching is one of the most important giftings and occupations that we have in this world. Yet, it is also one of the most undervalued. Teachers make far less income than the average entertainer. They are less famous than musicians, acknowledged as less influential than athletes, less respected than Presidents, less powerful than CEOs, less prominent than doctors or lawyers, less recognizable than actresses or actors. All the while, they are asked to do so much with little fanfare or appreciation.

Teaching is very powerful even though it's not very ostentatious or elaborate. Even in ministry, among the five-fold ministry giftings (Apostle, Pastor, Prophet, Evangelist, and Teacher), Teaching is often viewed as the least of the five. Many want to be an apostle like Peter, John, and Paul…or be able to "see the future and prophesy" like Elijah…or be a great pastor like TD Jakes, I.V. Hilliard, Joel Osteen, etc.…or be the next amazing evangelist like Billy Graham. No one wants to be a teacher in the body of Christ when discussing the five-fold ministry. The Teacher has been relegated to Sunday School and Vacation Bible School, in most ministries. This is a sad reality.

Teaching is Essential

Unfortunately, we (as a society) have a distorted and depreciated view of teaching. However, one of Jesus' most common titles was "Rabbi", which means "Master Teacher". Let's see what Jesus thought about teaching:

Luke 10:38-42
*[38] Now as they went on their way, Jesus entered a village. And a woman named Martha welcomed him into her house. [39]And she had a sister called **Mary, who sat at the Lord's feet and listened to his teaching.** [40]But Martha was distracted with much serving. And she went up to him and said, "Lord, do you not care that my sister has left me to serve alone? Tell her then to help me." [41]But the Lord answered her, "Martha, Martha, you are anxious and*

troubled about many things, **⁴²*but one thing is necessary. Mary has chosen the good portion, which will not be taken away from her.*"

Martha was hosting Jesus. The scripture says, "She was serving" – "<u>*entertaining*</u>" guests, if you will – serving food, cleaning, making sure guests were taken care of and had what they needed. She was operating and serving in her area of gifting. The scripture says that she was "distracted with much serving." All the while, Jesus was teaching.

Martha's sister, Mary, had a decision to make: 'Should I help my sister entertain?' or 'Should I listen to Jesus' teachings?' This may be the position that many of us find ourselves in: <u>Should I entertain? Should I focus on my gift? Should I throw myself completely into what I want to do? Or...Should I put everything on hold and listen to Jesus teach me?</u> Mary chose the latter.

Martha was upset at the decision Mary made not to help her serve. She was angry that Mary decided not to entertain with her. She was frustrated that Mary decided not to get distracted with her. When people are busy but not effective…they notice that other people aren't being busy with them. Martha was upset and requested that Jesus tell Mary to stop learning from HIS teachings and come help her entertain. Martha had the mindset that many of us have today; she felt like her entertaining was MORE important than Jesus' teachings.

Jesus' response to Mary was, "You're anxious and troubled." The new phrase of the day would be, "You're doing too much" or "doing the most." He told her that "one thing is necessary" – one thing is essential – and Mary had chosen it. **The one essential thing is true teaching…and it will never be taken away.** Even down to your children's children's children, teaching can be transferred and is generational. It doesn't matter if your home is taken away; no one can ever take away what you know. It doesn't matter if someone steals all of your possessions, puts you in jail, or accuses you unjustly; they can never take away what you've been taught.

So many of us chase jobs, but you can be fired. We chase fame, but the people that praised you today can turn against you tomorrow. We chase money, but the stock market could crash and your money would be deemed worthless. We chase big homes and extravagant things, but if we lose the ability to pay, the lender will take it all back. We often choose that which can be taken away. But teaching…true teaching, can never be taken away. And not only can teaching not be taken away, but it unlocks everything you've been chasing. You want friends? <u>LEARN to be friendly.</u> You want a better financial situation? <u>Get some teachings on financial management.</u> You want to know why your life is the way that it is? <u>Stop just plowing through life, take a step back, and learn from your past mistakes</u>. Get some teaching about who you want to be and where you want to see yourself in the next 5, 10, 20, even 50 years.

Through this book, I pray that the Holy Spirit teaches you. I pray that your thinking will be challenged. And I pray that your life will be changed for the better. I want you to see how the miraculous life that you've been searching for is intricately tied to teaching. **True Teaching is the one essential thing.**

What Do You Mean by "Teaching"?

In Jesus' time (and many years before), there were many philosophers who came up with different philosophies. Many different "schools of thought" were created; as a result, there are a variety of teachings produced from them. Many people may ascribe to various Greek philosophies (teachings from Plato, Aristotle, Socrates, etc.), Eastern holistic rituals, religious dogma, or teachings of other intellectual persons or "spiritual" gurus. When I talk about "teachings" in the coming pages, I'm referencing the teachings of God (unless otherwise expressly stated). "True Teachings" also refers to God's commandments and statutes, His doctrine and principles, His words, instructions, promises, inspired scriptures, and revelation thereof. I'm referring to the Kingdom teachings and concepts and the active voice of God that speaks to us if we're willing to listen and hear Him.

I readily admit that I (in and of myself) cannot teach you anything. I know nothing – I understand nothing except that which The Holy Spirit teaches me and The Father allows me to learn. There are things that I'm just instructed to do that I don't understand…it's in my best interest to just do them. There are commandments that I personally may not feel like doing…it's in my best interest to keep them. There are teachings that are not popular with mainstream society…it's in my best interest to live by them. That's my testimony. That's my life in a nutshell as a Kingdom Citizen… I do what the Father tells me to do – period!

I'm ignorant compared to the vast knowledge and wisdom that God holds. And yet, I am able to do the impossible because I'm connected to Him. All that I know is because He has allowed me to understand. There is so much that I don't know, and I am in the process of ever learning. So, when God talks, I listen.

If something in this book helps you...To God be the Glory. If something written unlocks the miraculous in your life...To God be the Glory. If you, your family, a loved one, or a friend is healed...To God be the Glory. If you get your breakthrough or your life is forever changed...To God be the Honor and Glory!!!

Let's allow God to permanently damage our ignorance and change our perspective so that we can see and experience life from the viewpoint of the Kingdom of Heaven.

Let's Be Honest – Self-evaluation:

1. What do you value? What consumes most of your time, money, and attention?
2. When is the last time you've invested in education (college, post graduate studies, buying books, messages, podcasts) to improve yourself?
3. How important is teaching in your life? Would you choose to spend your last 10 dollars on teaching or food? Teaching or going to the movies? Teaching or game tickets?
4. What are your goals in life? What kind of teaching could help you reach these goals?
5. What do you wish you knew or had learned when you were younger that you learned when you were older? How would this information have impacted your life?
6. What are you hoping to get out of this book? What are your motivations? What drew you to this book?

CHAPTER 1: MIRACLES

*"You have to **see** the miracles for there to **be** miracles."*
- Jandy Nelson

If you will, please allow me to pose this question: **"What is a miracle?"** It is important for each individual to accurately and adequately define this for themselves. I'm not asking what you've been told, nor am I asking about what television or the internet tells us. I'm not referring to illusions or cheap magic tricks. Seriously...What would you consider a miracle in your life? What do you consider worthy of being called a miracle in the lives of others?

This is an important concept to articulate and communicate because what one person may consider to be a miracle, another person may not. **What I may deem "miraculous" may not be a miracle in your eyes.** If someone pays my light bill, some may not consider that a miracle. If someone offers a kind word, there appears to be nothing miraculous in the act. If someone invites me to their home for a meal, I might not consider that to be a miracle. These may be viewed as some fortunate, nice events.

But...if I've lost my job and have no money that light bill being paid appears pretty miraculous. If I'm saddened, depressed, feeling worthless or even suicidal that "kind word" seems like a much needed "life-saver" to keep me from going over the edge. If I'm homeless and haven't had a decent meal for weeks or months, that invitation to a warm home and meal is viewed differently than if my food or shelter needs are met.

Some of us may think of a miracle as something on a grander scale: winning the lottery, obtaining a job you didn't think you qualified for, living beyond the time frame modern medicine may have estimated due to a serious illness, being the only person to survive a plane crash or natural disaster. Do you see a common pattern or theme here? A miracle is based on an individual's perspective, the need or desire present, and the circumstances surrounding the situation. Just because a miracle may not be one from your perspective doesn't make it any less miraculous to someone else. Because you may not have that particular need or understand the situation doesn't mean that a miracle hasn't transpired.

Merriam Webster defines "miracle" as:
1: an extraordinary event manifesting divine intervention in human affairs
2: an extremely outstanding or unusual event, thing, or accomplishment
3: a divinely natural phenomenon experienced humanly as the fulfillment of spiritual law

Some of our preconceived notions or initial understandings of miracles are centered around these definitions. Some people may define a miracle as something that is normally beyond human capabilities (i.e., a mother lifting the car after an accident to rescue her children). Others yet may define a miracle as an interruption of the laws of nature as we know them (i.e., walking on water). Miracle is derived from the Latin word "miraculum" derived from the root word "mirari" (to wonder at, to marvel). And miracles do just that...make us wonder, marvel, gasp to the point of taking our very breath away, at times, and give us hope and belief where the impossible once dominated. We are fascinated with miracles because they seem so rare in this day and age. It is this rarity that usually leaves us in awe and wondering, "What did I just see?" "What did I just hear?" or "How did that just happen?!!!!"

Blessings vs Miracles

Of note, let's not confuse <u>miracles</u> and <u>blessings</u>. The two are quite similar and related; they are on the same spectrum of God's goodness (with miracles being on the more extreme, extraordinary end of the spectrum). Miracles are often associated with dire situations, while we associate blessings with situations that are not as extreme. Like the definition says, miracles are "extraordinary" and "unusual"; whereas blessings may not necessarily be as remarkable.

To put it more accurately: **All miracles can be considered blessings, but not all blessings can be considered miracles.** So, using the example of the light bill — if I have the money to pay the bill and it's not a strain, yet someone decides to pay it for me, most people would consider that a blessing. Versus the situation where I'm preparing to open a pack of candles or kerosene lamps to see in the dark and someone decides to pay the light bill for me. Many people would consider the latter miraculous.

Likewise, if a person has a deadly disease that has been shown throughout history to have been the cause of death in individuals, then a miracle would be for the person to live or to be cured of the disease. If a person is blind, then the miracle would be for the individual to attain sight. If a person is deaf, the miraculous would be hearing. If a person's issue is in finances, the miracle would be money or the ability to attain money. If someone were dead, the miracle would be life. Natural law states that you can only stand on solid matter; therefore, the miracle would be walking on matter that is not solid…i.e. water or air. I think you see the pattern.

Without the situation of a deadly disease…living often gets overlooked. Without the precedent of blindness…sight is often taken for granted. If a person can already hear…there is no need for the miracle of hearing to occur. When people are financially secure…they don't need money to make ends meet – (Now we may want more money, but it's not a NEED). If I'm already standing on solid matter…you would not be impressed if I walked across the room. Our situation and perception are vital elements when discussing the miraculous.

Miracles are seen all throughout the Bible – Old Testament and New Testament: Moses and the parting of the Red Sea…the conquest of Jericho by simply walking around a walled fortress and shouting….Elijah's calling down fire from Heaven... the birth of Jesus Christ to a Virgin Mother…the feeding of thousands of individuals with three fish and five loaves of bread…the raising of people from the dead...Peter walking on water and even through prison walls…people healed from leprosy. The Bible is filled with the miraculous. We will look at some of these and others in greater detail to attain greater insight into the mind of God and thus our potential to experience the miraculous, but first let's deal with our own mindset and why the miraculous appears to be such a foreign concept.

Where are the Miracles?

Most of us have heard about all these amazing people in the Bible and the miracles performed for and/or through them. This is what contributes to the confusion and frustration of many believers. We believe in the same God as those individuals. We pray to the same God to whom David prayed. We worship the same God whom Daniel worshipped. We run into some of the same issues and circumstances that Job, Moses, Samuel, Elijah, and the "heroes" and "forerunners" in the Bible were confronted with on what seems like a routine basis. We have some of the same problems. We have some of the same needs or desires. We can sympathize or empathize with some of their plights so strongly because we have been there or are currently there right now!! It is frustrating because we wonder, "Where is MY miracle?" "Why doesn't God do the same thing for me?" "What was so special about 'those' people?" "Does God not hear my prayers?" "**AM I DOING SOMETHING WRONG?**"

You are not alone in these frustrations. I have been there. I feel your pain. Some of us either have yet to experience the miraculous, or we don't experience it on a consistent enough basis for it to seem like more than mere coincidence or luck. Because of this lack of results (or inconsistent results), we tend to give up in order to avoid the frustrated, confused, or neglected feelings.

We know God is great. God is Awesome. His Word is true. We readily confess that "God is good all the time…and all the time, God is good." Yet…why are YOU not seeing the miracles you need or have needed in your life that are consistent with what you profess to believe? "Why did my mother die – we prayed for her?" "Why did I lose my house – we begged God?" "Why was I molested as a child – I cried out to God for years – where was He? I could have used a miracle." These are real words from real people filled with real anguish and real pain. There are answers to all these questions: some may seem fair, while others may not. But I assure you, God is not looking down and enjoying your pain and suffering. His ultimate desire is for you to be the best, to have the best, to dominate, to be the winner He designed, and to have the impact on this earth that He intended and planned from the foundations of this World. It is in God's best interest for you to succeed.

Failure is NOT in God's Plan for YOU

I'm not here to offer you some deep, mystical, "name it, claim it, put a picture up and frame it," "your check is in the mail," "turn around 3 times," "5 steps to your…" answer to get a miracle. I'm simply going to offer you keys / principles to unlock the doors of the miraculous. Let's be honest, that is how we feel; We feel as if we are locked out of a place with God that others have been granted. We feel as if we are knocking on a door in desperation, only to be told that the wizard is not home. We give up! We may not allow ourselves to verbalize it, but most of us have given up. Some of us have stopped praying altogether to avoid the disappointment. We go to church and hope to check into heaven as soon as possible to escape from some of the more disappointing aspects of our reality.

I've been there. I know how it feels to cry out to God, only to feel shut out. **But you can't lose faith**. Remember these 3 truths when doubt begins to arise:

1. **Trust and believe that God is who He says He is**: The Great "I Am," Provider, Healer, Protector, Savior, Father, King, Lord, Righteous Judge, Creator, Strength in times of weakness, Ever-present Help, etc.

2. **He has your best interest in mind.** God wants you to win. He set up His system for you to win.

3. **He knows what we need in order for us to be who He created us to be**. He's given you everything you need to be successful.

I know what you're saying, "I do have faith…" or "I did believe, and nothing happened." Oftentimes, when we lack results, the first instinct is to place the blame on God: "Well, it must not have been His Will" or "God must have had another plan." At times, this may very well be possible; however, this approach removes us from being responsible for failed results. Many of us think, "God is all powerful. He does what He wants to do anyway." With this mindset we are alleviated from looking in the mirror and seeing if there is any error in our ways. This method of thinking allows us to remain ignorant and blameless if the desired results aren't achieved. Let us go further along this journey together to permanently damage our ignorance and obtain keys to experience the victory we read about in the scriptures.

Let's Be Honest - Self Evaluation:

1. Have you ever experienced the miraculous in your life? What was it? Did this impact your relationship with God?

2. What miracle have you prayed to God for and it didn't happen? Did this have an impact on your relationship with God? What was your response (i.e., hurt, disappointment, frustration, confusion, etc.)?

3. Is your current prayer life a result past failed prayer requests?

4. Do you think God is able to perform the miraculous in your life? Why/why not?

5. Do you think God WILL perform the miraculous in your life? Why/why not?

CHAPTER 2: THE FIRST MIRACLE OF JESUS: WATER INTO WINE

"Learning is the beginning of wealth. Learning is the beginning of health. Learning is the beginning of spirituality. Searching and learning is where the miracle process all begins." - Jim Rohn

"Gwen"

My daughter and grandson came into my room in a panic. "It's Gwen! They found her... dead!" they exclaimed.

I said, "Okay."

They blasted, "We need to get out there...the coroner is on their way!"

I got up, slipped on some clothes as fast as I could, and dashed out the house. One of the thoughts racing through my mind on the way to the house was, "Lord, what am I supposed to do?"

Gwen was one of our staff ministers, but more than that...she was like family. Everyone knew Gwen, and if you ever came to the church, you heard her. We'd often laugh because prior to every sermon that I preached she'd shout, "We Love You, Bishop!!" Now I was rushing to her house because she was found unconscious...Not Gwen, Not Now.

By the time I made it to the house, the coroner had arrived. Through tears and sobs, her daughter explained that her mom wasn't breathing and her heart had stopped beating. Everyone looked at me with eyes that pleaded, "Do Something, Bishop!" I knew the coroner, so I asked him for a few minutes with the body. I asked everyone to leave the house, and my daughter and I went inside. Lying on the bed was Gwen. With all the faith and belief that I had, I prayed for Gwen: "Come on Gwen, Get Up! We're not going out like THIS." This wasn't just a stranger. This wasn't some woman in my community. This wasn't just a member of the church. This was Family! This was Gwen! "God...please..."

I knew how God used Elijah to resurrect the widow of Zarephath's son. I knew how Elisha resurrected the Shunammite woman's son. I knew how Jesus resurrected Peter's mother-in-law, the widow of Nain's son, Jairus's Daughter, and Lazarus. I knew how Peter resurrected Tabitha. I knew that Jesus had healed countless numbers of people...and here I stood, praying for one – Laying hands on one – Crying out to God to resurrect Gwen. There was no movement of life – No breathing of lungs – No resurrection miracle this day: Gwen was gone.

Gwen needed a miracle; her family needed a miracle...I needed a miracle! I didn't know why this happened. I was hurt, disappointed, and crushed as I sat on the porch of Gwen's house. Tears began to roll down my eyes. I kept thinking about how helpless I felt in the face of an impossible situation. I wondered what else I could have done. I needed a higher power. I needed God.

This feeling of helplessness and sense of despair must be how the people felt before Jesus performed His first miracle. They too were in a situation that seemed impossible:

John 2: 1-11

*On the third day there was a **wedding** at Cana in Galilee, and the mother of Jesus was there. ²**Jesus also was invited to the wedding** with his disciples. ³When <u>the wine ran out</u>, the mother of Jesus said to him, "**They have no wine**." ⁴And Jesus said to her, "Woman, what does this have to do with me? My hour has not yet come." ⁵His mother said to the servants, "**Do whatever he tells you**." ⁶Now there were six stone water jars there for the Jewish rites of purification, each holding twenty or thirty gallons. ⁷Jesus said to the servants, "Fill the jars with water." And they filled them up to the brim. ⁸And he said to them, "Now draw some out and take it to the master of the feast." So they took it. ⁹When the <u>**master of the feast**</u> tasted the water now become wine, and did not know where it came from (though the servants who had drawn the water knew), the master of the feast called the bridegroom ¹⁰and said to him, "Everyone serves the good wine first, and when people have drunk freely, then the poor wine. But you have kept the good wine until now." ¹¹ **This, the first of his signs, Jesus did at Cana in Galilee, and manifested his glory. And his disciples believed in him.***

This is an account of the first miracle performed by Jesus according to John's recollection. There is so much that we can learn from John's account. We could start from many of the various points in the scriptures, but let's start by focusing on the environment in which this miracle took place: **a marriage ceremony**.

The Background - A Marriage Ceremony

When we observe the scene, this marriage ceremony is the perfect backdrop to understand more about the miraculous. Scripture tells us that this miracle occurred during a wedding ceremony at Cana in Galilee. Jesus was invited to the wedding with his disciples.

This is significant because a wedding is simply a ceremony; however, because Jesus/God was involved, it was transformed from just a wedding ceremony into the institution established by God known as **marriage** (a physical representation of the spiritual union between male and female) – Two different yet compatible entities that have the inherent potential ability to become one and reproduce. Many couples have the ceremony of a wedding, but unfortunately Jesus/God may not have been "invited," consulted, or incorporated in how to function in a relationship with a counterpart to the magnitude of becoming one.

To understand the miraculous, it would help to grasp some basic principles of marriage. God created marriage. Marriage is good. Let me say this for those who struggle to believe in God's formula for relationship: THERE IS NOTHING WRONG WITH MARRIAGE, PERIOD!!! Now, the people in the marriage…that's an entirely different story. Every invention or idea is a reflection of (or gives insight into) its creator. Since God created Marriage, understanding elements of marriage should give us some insight into Our Father – Let's go back to the beginning.

Origin of Marriage

When God first created man (Adam), He placed him in a garden eastward in Eden (Genesis 2:8,15). Eden is the place where the presence of God exists. It is more of a spiritual place than a physical place. So, we can deduce that because God placed Man in Eden (which means the Presence of God), this is where mankind was designed to function.

God is a God of order. Fish were placed in water because that's where they function best – the same for birds in the air and the animals on the ground. In any other environment, they couldn't function to their maximum potential. Humans don't make cars and place them in water, nor do we make boats and ships and try to operate them in the air. That would be idiotic: we put them where they function best. So, it is with God: when He created mankind, He placed us in the environment that would allow us to function and fulfill our intended purpose. That environment for you and I was, is, and forever will be Eden…in God's very presence.

Once outside of the intended (functional) environment, a creation malfunctions. Malfunction is a two-part word. The root word is '**Function**' which essentially means "to operate," and the prefix, '**Mal**,' means "badly or poorly." So, I'm not saying that you absolutely cannot function outside of the intended environment. I am saying that you will function poorly or beneath your intended capabilities. However, in the presence of God, Adam functioned perfectly. Once removed from the presence of God, man began to malfunction – the first murder occurred when Cain killed Abel; the people attempted to build the tower of Babel; man became exceedingly evil and wicked; etc.

But while in Eden, Mankind flourished. Adam was in direct communication with God, accomplishing Heaven's agenda on the Earth. However, God saw Adam's limitation: he was alone. He didn't have the ability to reproduce, multiply, and fill the earth. He could only be in one place at one time. Man was limited.

Therefore, in this same spiritual environment, God created a helpmate for man. God brought forth the woman He created from Adam's rib (Genesis 2:21-22). Adam chose her after recognizing that she came from him. It was here that the concept of marriage originated.

Marriage Relationship

Our union in marriage is a physical representation of what God desires in the spiritual realm. God wants us to be married to Him, united with Him. He calls the church His "bride" and Christ the bridegroom. God wants to be one with us. We learned and believe that God is Amazing, Mighty, Powerful and able to do Great and Wondrous works. If I'm one with God, then the same applies to me - *I can do all things through Christ who strengthens me* (Philippians 4:13). "All things" means **all things**, everything - <u>even the miraculous</u>. A benefit of being one (or in marriage covenant) is unadulterated access. Adam was one with God. He had access to God's mind: he knew what God wanted done. He had access to God's wisdom, knowledge, resources, power, and authority to accomplish ANYTHING.

Jesus had this mindset of unity with God. So much so that in 1 Corinthians 15:45, Jesus is referred to as "the last ADAM." He was in the same position in Eden that the "first Adam" was in. Jesus was in constant communication and relationship with the Father. So much so that He would say things like, (paraphrasing) "*If you've seen me, you've seen the Father - we are one.*" "*I only do what I see my Father do - I can't do anything different, we are one.*" And the miracles that were performed by Jesus are the ones that are forever etched in our minds to this very day.

We want the miracles to manifest, right? This backdrop of a marriage provides a key element: **Deep Relationship/Oneness**. Let's establish a true and deep relationship with the Source of the miracles. How would you feel if your spouse or the person you're dating, or a friend, only talked to you when asking for a favor? It would be hurtful if your friends only called you when they needed money to get them out of a bind. It would be very insulting if the only time your spouse acknowledged your presence was when they wanted you to have sex, cook, clean, or fix something that was broken.

This is not how loving relationships – let alone marriage relationships – are designed to function. Are you not more inclined to give your favor to those that check on you on a consistent basis? Would you not give more of your time to those that you talk to on a regular basis? Are you not more inclined to lend money or other resources to those that have proven themselves trustworthy?

These are all rhetorical questions: **Of course, the answer is "YES"**. Generally, we give more to those with whom we are in a deeper relationship. And so it is with God. However, we only acknowledge His existence once a week (that's if we go to a church service consistently). We think about what's important to Him once a month. We listen to His ideas and thoughts "every now and then." We obey His words when it is convenient for us. Yet the minute trouble arises, we pick up the phone and call Him "on the main line." How fair is that? Is that the type of relationship that you would want to be a part of?

To go a step further, when we do communicate, we are asking for extraordinary miracles – <u>Healing from a disease</u>, <u>Saving from a critical situation</u>, <u>Money to keep your home</u>, <u>or (in this case) wine for a wedding.</u> For me, the greater the request - the deeper the relationship has to be. I'll lend anyone 10-20 dollars. When we start talking about "THOUSANDS OF DOLLARS" …we need to have loaned each other that type of money before, be close family, or you once saved my life, took a bullet for me, or something.

Therefore, the deeper and more loving our relationship with God, the more miraculous the response. In Exodus 33:11, God is said to have "spoken to Moses face to face, as one speaks to a friend." When Moses needed a miracle of escape from the pursuit of the Pharaoh's army, God parted the Red Sea, and the people of Israel escaped on dry land; whereas their enemies were destroyed. The same impact can be seen in the lives of Elijah, Elisha, David, Samuel, Jesus, the Apostles, etc. They developed a deep loving relationship with God;

therefore, it's no coincidence that they experienced the miraculous.

Oneness/Deep Relationship is key; however, relationship alone won't bring the miraculous. Let's go further…

Wine

At this marriage celebration, the people ran out of wine. John 2:3 says that "they wanted wine." And this is where the bulk of our focus will be placed…*wine*. Usually, a Jewish wedding lasted about 7 days. If the wedding lasts 7 days, then (obviously) the wine should last 7 days. Simple math, right? So, one of two things happened: Either it was poor management of resources (an underestimation of the volume of wine needed) or poor management of people (more guests showed up to the wedding than expected).

At any rate, the amount of wine that they had was drunken. All gone. And this was going to be the height of embarrassment at the wedding. Instead of people celebrating the union and the couple's happiness, they would be laughing at them. Instead of admiring the holy union, the people in the community would be mocking them. Their families would be brought to open shame. "How could something like this happen?" "They knew the wedding celebration was going to be 7 days…" "If they didn't have the money, they should have asked someone or just saved up…" "She must be pregnant…that's why they got married in such a rush and didn't have enough". None of these things may be true, but the door to such scrutiny is opened when proper planning isn't instituted. And sometimes stuff just happens unexpectedly, no matter how intricate the planning.

Imagine hosting a Super Bowl party, but you forgot to pay the cable bill. Or promising to pick up an important client from the airport, but you run out of gas on the way. Yes, we're all human. And yes, these kinds of things happen…but it is embarrassing and puts a stain or mark on your reputation. This was the predicament that the bride and groom faced. They needed wine, but there was no other way to get more wine on such short notice. They needed a miracle.

They Wanted Wine

The scripture tells us that "they wanted wine." Who wanted wine? **They did**. Who was "**they**"? … Everyone. **The couple** wanted wine because it would allow the continuation of the ceremony. **The families** wanted wine because it would save them from the embarrassment of not being able to meet the traditions of the ceremony. **The people** wanted wine because it would allow them to continue the celebration and have a good time. **The servants** wanted wine because it would allow them to continue to have employment. **The governor (master of the feast)** wanted wine because he was presiding over the festivities. **Mary** wanted wine because she obviously had some connection with the couple and didn't want to see them embarrassed. Everyone involved had their own reason for wanting wine – everyone except Jesus. Jesus told his mother, (paraphrasing) "They ran out of wine? It's not my fault, nor is that any of our business. I am not the bridegroom…It is not my time yet. "

A common principle among humans is that **we don't want what we already have…and we desire that which we do not have**. If I have the latest iPhone (that works and is functioning), I don't have a desire for the latest iPhone. If I have 1 billion dollars, my desire isn't to have 1 billion dollars in my bank account, trust fund, or stocks and bonds. If I have a wife, my desire isn't to have a wife. If I have steak for dinner, my desire isn't to have steak for dinner. If I already have these things, they are not a desire or a want. I know you're thinking, "What are you trying to say?" … "Why are you telling me this?" **Jesus didn't want wine because He already had it**. Yes, Jesus already had wine. No, He didn't have some bottles of wine that He had stashed to the side for just such occasions. Jesus had what wine represents!!!

What is "Wine"?

The Bible is a prophetic and spiritual book. Reading a spiritual book and interpreting by logic or natural understanding unfortunately (and oftentimes) leads to much confusion. There are many types, signs, and symbols all throughout the Book.

Signs are those things which indicate when a significant event is about to occur. For instance, you know Fall is coming when the leaves begin to change color, the temperature begins to drop, or the birds fly south to a warmer climate. By correctly interpreting the signs, you're able to decipher what is likely to occur.

A **symbol** is an object that represents or stands for an idea, visual image, belief, action or another material entity. A dove is a symbol for peace. A crown is a symbol for royalty. Light is a symbol of knowledge. Darkness is a symbol for ignorance. The 'skull and crossbones' is a symbol for poison. The flag is a symbol for the country thereof. And wine is a symbol for teaching, joy, or blessings.

A question that I've asked God often is, **"Why?"** Why the need to communicate via symbols, signs, and obscure language? The answer is found in Deuteronomy 29:29 which says, *"The **secret things** <u>belong to God</u>, but **those things that are revealed** <u>belong to you and your children</u> that you might do all the law"* and further in Proverbs 25:2, *"It is the glory of God to **conceal a thing**, but it is the honor of kings to **search out a matter**."*

God conceals truths and secrets because He is Holy. He will not break His Word. He knows what we need, what we do not need, and where we are in life. God would love nothing more than to give us the answers to our prayers, problems, and predicaments. However, we have to understand the nature of God. **God will not give us something that we have not asked of Him or put effort to attain.** Doing so would violate your free will and dominion mantle found in Genesis 1:26 (*"Let MAN have Dominion over the earth... the fish of the sea, fowl of the air, ..."*). This is why God tells us to **ask** and **communicate** our needs and desires *(Matthew 7:7)*. God isn't going to violate His Word.

So, in order to keep His Word AND give you the help you need, He hides the truth and understanding you need in Scriptures. When you seek your answer, it is there waiting for you like buried treasure. When you begin to truly understand that you are a "king", it is your honor, pleasure, and duty to find these concealed truths. **When you truly want truth and secrets, then and only then, can they be revealed unto you.**

As a caveat, however — Be warned and very careful when seeking revelation via symbols and signs. Be mindful that you don't gravitate to an idea because it sounds good. Nor should we take scripture out of context or come up with something that doesn't even line up with the very Word of God. In theology, there is a principle known as hermeneutics: the principle of interpreting scripture. In Hermeneutics, there is what is known as the "Symbolic principle." This is a principle where a verse or passage of scripture containing symbolic elements can be determined only by a proper interpretation of the symbols involved.

The more we search the scriptures, listen to sermons, read books from God-inspired men, meditate and listen to the Holy Spirit, the more we (as "kings") uncover hidden gems and treasures from Our Father. One such gem that we will explore in great detail is what *"WINE"* represents. Wine is a representation of teaching, joy, blessings. I think one could easily grasp the symbolism of wine to joy and blessings given the celebratory nature often associated with wine and the feelings that such a drink can provide. However, wine and teaching? It isn't a correlation that comes as easily.

Wine and Teaching?

Upon first glance, there really is no correlation. The two appear to be very different: one is a drink, the other instructions – as different as apples and…apple computers. However, upon closer inspection, we will see that wine and teaching are quite similar. Follow me carefully…

Before we ever get to wine, we first start with the **vine**. From this vine comes the **fruit** known as *grapes*. The fruit is good for food and nutrition, but within every piece of fruit are **seeds** that contain the same genetic material and machinery to make another vine that produces grapes. The fruit is an extension of the vine because they share the same DNA and enable the reproduction of the vine via seeds. The ***grapes are then crushed, processed, transformed into wine***.

Teaching follows a similar pattern. We as **humans** are like trees or vines. The fruit that we, as humans, bring forth is not our jobs, our wealth, our cars, our possessions, our billion-dollar houses…but our *children*. (Obvious enough, right?) Children have the genetic material (DNA) and machinery to make more children and continue our bloodline.

But we also produce another kind of "fruit" that occurs every day but is less obvious. We produce thoughts and ideas – in design circles, this is commonly referred to as one's "brainchild." **These thoughts and ideas are the equivalent to "grapes," or our "fruit."** These thoughts and ideas give rise to businesses, wealth, inventions, houses, and… yes, it was a thought or idea that led to the production of children. The "fruit" (thoughts and ideas) are expressed and give rise to **seeds**: the words, pictures, vision, plans, blueprints, plays, inventions, artwork, music that is derived from our thoughts. ***The process and transferal of the original idea (expressed through words,***

pictures, explanations, revelations, etc.) from one individual to another is Teaching. Just as the seeds of the fruit possess the potential to reproduce the tree - our words, visions, plans, etc. (through teaching/instruction) are able to be implanted and reproduce certain aspects of the teacher in the student.

Wine:	Teaching:
1. Vine/trees produce grapes (Fruit).	1. Individuals produce Thoughts/Ideas (Fruit).
2. Grapes produce Seeds.	2. Thoughts/Ideas produce words, pictures, explanations, etc. (Seeds).
3. Seeds reproduce more Vines/Trees.	3. Words, pictures, explanations, etc. reproduce (certain aspects of) the original Individual.
4. Processed form of grapes is **Wine**.	4. Processed form of Thoughts/Ideas is **Teaching**.

It was the words and teachings of Dr. Martin Luther King, Jr. that led to people (black and white) adopting the mindset of the Civil Rights leader and the policy of nonviolence. Therefore, you didn't just have one Dr. Martin Luther King, Jr. who would preach, march, practice nonviolence, die for the belief of equality... you had hundreds of thousands who would do the same. The same can be said of the Founding Fathers of this nation. Believing in Freedom and Equality, they were willing to defy the King of England, thus emboldening their fellow countrymen to take similar action. The same can be said about Steven Jobs, Nelson Mandela, Dr. Myles Munroe, and even Jesus Christ. These individuals reproduced some of their characteristics and ideologies in other people.

It's no surprise that after Jesus left the earth, His disciples did the same kinds of miracles and taught people just like He did when He was here…Why? How? Because Jesus reproduced Himself in them through His teachings. So, of course, they were going to act, talk, and carry themselves just like He did. They were given "wine" (teaching) on a daily basis. Let's look at two examples:

Mark 5: 37-42 – **Jesus Resurrects Jarius's Daughter**

*³⁷And he **allowed no one to follow him except Peter and James and John** the brother of James. ³⁸They came to the house of the ruler of the synagogue, and Jesus saw a commotion, people weeping and wailing loudly. ³⁹And when he had entered, he said to them, "Why are you making a commotion and weeping? The child is not dead but sleeping." ⁴⁰And they laughed at him. **But he put them all outside** and took the child's father and mother and those who were with him and went in where the child was. ⁴¹**Taking her by the hand he said to her, "Talitha cumi," which means, "Little girl, I say to you, arise.**" ⁴²And immediately the girl got up and began walking (for she was twelve years of age), and they were immediately overcome with amazement.*

Acts 9:38-41— **Peter Resurrects Tabitha**

³⁸Since Lydda was near Joppa, the disciples, hearing that Peter was there, sent two men to him, urging him, "Please come to us without delay." ³⁹So Peter rose and went with them. And when he arrived, they took him to the upper room. All the widows stood beside him weeping and showing tunics and other garments that Dorcas made while she was with them. ⁴⁰***But Peter put them all outside, and knelt down and prayed; and turning to the body he said, "Tabitha, arise."*** *And she opened her eyes, and when she saw Peter she sat up.* ⁴¹*And he gave her his hand and raised her up. Then, calling the saints and widows, he presented her alive.*

In Mark's account, we see Peter was in the room when Jesus resurrected the daughter of Jarius. He was there when Jesus put everyone else out. Jesus was teaching Peter, molding Peter, reproducing aspects about Himself in Peter. By the time we reach the book of Acts, Jesus has returned to Heaven, but we see Peter heal in the same manner that Jesus had healed. He put everyone out of the room and resurrected Tabitha (Dorcas). The student became like the teacher. Peter had essentially become like Jesus in this instance.

"New Wine"

We also see the correlation between teaching and wine when the disciples received the Holy Spirit. Let's dissect the scripture:

Acts 2:1-13 - **The Return of the Holy Spirit**

When the day of Pentecost arrived, they were all together in one place. ²*And suddenly there came from heaven a sound like a mighty rushing wind, and it filled the entire house where they were sitting.* ³*And divided tongues as of fire appeared to them and rested on each one of them.* ⁴

And they were all filled with the Holy Spirit and began to speak in other tongues as the Spirit gave them utterance. *⁵Now there were dwelling in Jerusalem Jews, devout men from every nation under heaven. ⁶And at this sound the multitude came together, and they were bewildered,* ***because each one was hearing them speak in his own language.*** *⁷And they were amazed and astonished, saying, "Are not all these who are speaking Galileans? ⁸**And how is it that we hear, each of us in his own native language?*** *⁹Parthians and Medes and Elamites and residents of Mesopotamia, Judea and Cappadocia, Pontus and Asia, ¹⁰Phrygia and Pamphylia, Egypt and the parts of Libya belonging to Cyrene, and visitors from Rome, ¹¹both Jews and proselytes, Cretans and Arabians—**we hear them telling in our own tongues the mighty works of God.***" *¹²And all were amazed and perplexed, saying to one another, "What does this mean?" ¹³But others mocking said,* ***"They are filled with new wine.***"

This was when the disciples received the Holy Spirit on the "Day of Pentecost". Before ascending into Heaven, Jesus instructed them to wait in Jerusalem for the "Promise of the Father" (Acts 1:4). When the Holy Spirit arrived, the disciples began to speak in different tongues / languages. There were men from different parts of the world who were obviously there to take part in the Day of Pentecost rituals. These men heard the disciples teaching about God - "telling in our own tongues the mighty works of God". While they were astonished that they were being taught in their native languages, others made a notable assumption - they are filled with NEW WINE.

It wasn't "new wine" in the way they thought; but it was "wine" as it related to a new teaching...or should I say an original teaching. With these revelations we can see how wine is symbolic for teaching.

Fermentation

Matthew 9:14-17 — **New Wine, Old Wineskins**

[14]Then the disciples of John came to him, saying, "Why do we and the Pharisees fast, but your disciples do not fast?" [15]And Jesus said to them, "Can the wedding guests mourn as long as the bridegroom is with them? The days will come when the bridegroom is taken away from them, and then they will fast. *[16]**No one puts a piece of unshrunk cloth on an old garment, for the patch tears away from the garment, and a worse tear is made.*** *[17]Neither is **new wine** put into **old wineskins**. **If it is, the skins burst and the wine is spilled and the skins are destroyed. But new wine is put into fresh wineskins, and so both are preserved.**"*

If wine is symbolic for teaching, wineskins (or animal skins used as vessels for wine) are symbolic of the people who receive teaching. The reason that Jesus says that you can't, or shouldn't, put new wine into old wineskins is because of the nature of the process of making wine. Wine was made by pouring the juice from grapes (new wine) into a new wineskin. This juice would then undergo a fermentation process. While undergoing fermentation, the gases produced from the yeast would cause the wineskin to expand and stretch. Overtime, the wineskin would lose its ability to expand and stretch. Because an old wineskin had lost its elasticity, it was not prudent to put new wine in the vessel. The old wineskin would burst during the fermentation process of the new wine.

The same goes for teaching people. It is difficult to teach people who are set in their ways and thoughts about a topic. Jesus came and chose 12 unlearned men, individuals who gave up homes and businesses and sacrificed time with family and friends in pursuit of the Kingdom. They hadn't been hardened or lost their capacity to learn by being indoctrinated with the teaching and customs of mankind. This is why Jesus wanted His disciples to have characteristics of new wine skins or new cloth—possessing the elasticity and capacity to be stretched, adapt, expand, and learn something that they had never heard before. Therefore, when He introduced the new patch of cloth or the new wine (the new/original Kingdom teachings), they could adapt and adjust to the teaching. It wouldn't "tear" them, "burst" them, confuse them, or frustrate them because they would have been conditioned to handle the revelation.

If we're going to see the miracles of God, establishing a relationship with HIM will be key. We must go deeper than the "occasional check-in," "only-pray-when-I'm-in-need" type of relationship and form a stronger bond in which we know God and He knows us. Beyond relationship, we also have to be able to handle and be receptive to what God has said and is saying. We have to have Wine.

The Revelation on Gwen's Porch

As I sat crying on Gwen's porch, God revealed to me that I needed "wine." He told me that, if I didn't increase in knowledge, many more would die just like Gwen!! If I wasn't prepared, many people would die physically, spiritually, emotionally, financially, mentally, relationally, etc. It wasn't that I didn't have faith; rather, my power and authority weren't at the level to resurrect Gwen. Yes, I believed like Jesus, but did I consecrate and pray like Jesus did? I had faith like Elijah and Elisha, but did I fast like they fasted? I trusted God like Peter, but did I sacrifice like he did to qualify to operate in the miraculous? The answer was a resounding "No" ... I needed more wine.

Let's Be Honest – Self Evaluation:

1. How would you describe your relationship with God (i.e., Strangers, Associates, Friends, Family, Married)?

2. Have you ever or are you living life based on your own philosophy (i.e., What you think, How you feel, According to your limited understanding)?

3. In what aspects of your life do you depend on the teachings of God (i.e., finances, health, relationship with other people, etc.)? In what aspects of your life are you NOT depending on the teachings of God?

4. Are you teachable? What makes you teachable? What makes you unteachable?

5. Are there teachings, ideas, concepts, beliefs that you have had to relinquish?

6. Are there teachings that you find difficult to let go of because they're what you were taught as a child?

CHAPTER 3: THE MYSTERY OF TEACHING

"The Scarecrow needed that brain, but the brain needed the scarecrow. The Tin Man needed the heart, but what good was the heart without the Tin Man? The Lion needed courage, but courage without the Lion is useless." - Bishop Robert Cade

Teaching is not a "one-way street." This is why it is so telling and profound that the first miracle occurred in the setting of a marriage. Teaching involves (at least) two individuals being "joined together," "becoming one"... just like in a marriage. Teaching not only allows individuals to become one in thought or ideology, but they then gain the ability to reproduce themselves...just like in a marriage. As you can see, the marriage was the perfect background for this miracle.

Furthermore, within the concept of teaching is the understanding that it is a relationship. Relationships are a "two-way street": there is something being given by both parties, people, or entities involved. Teaching is a **symbiotic relationship**. Both have a need that they cannot fulfill on their own.

When we view teaching from a relationship perspective, we can see not one entity but two. We see not just one need being fulfilled, but two needs are being fulfilled. Teaching is usually thought of as someone **giving instructions** (teaching, explaining, or demonstrating) concerning a specific skill, subset of information, knowledge or ideology. But in order to teach, there has to be a present willingness to learn, a desire to understand, or someone to **receive instruction**. If both of these entities are not present, teaching does not take place.

I have been around some amazing instructors in my lifetime; some have been mentors, pastors, businessmen, doctors, judges, lawyers, coaches, etc. However, no matter how amazing or gifted they are at their craft, if the person or people that sit under them are unwilling to learn, teaching does not take place. Words are spoken and examples are given, but they are just talking. If the person (or group of people) does not grasp the concept being put forth, teaching has not taken place. Instructions are given to no avail. It's like trying to give someone 100 dollars, but they won't reach out his/her hand to receive it. Did you successfully give them the money? No.

Likewise (and more obviously), if a person desires knowledge and instruction yet there is no one to provide instruction, teaching does not take place.

Acts 8:27-31 — **Phillip and the Ethiopian Eunuch**

[27]And he rose and went. And there was an Ethiopian, a eunuch, a court official of Candace, queen of the Ethiopians, who was in charge of all her treasure. He had come to Jerusalem to worship [28]and was returning, seated in his chariot, and he was reading the prophet Isaiah. [29]And the Spirit said to Philip, "Go over and join this chariot." [30]So Philip ran to him and heard him reading Isaiah the prophet and asked, **"Do you understand what you are reading?"** *[31]And he said,* <u>"How can I, unless someone guides me?"</u> *And he invited Philip to come up and sit with him.*

At this time, Phillip was now an apostle, performing miracles and baptizing. He came across someone trying to understand the writings of Isaiah. Phillip's question is applicable beyond this Ethiopian: "Do you understand?" Do you understand how to live the life you're living? Do you understand your Purpose? Do you understand sickness and healing? Do you understand wealth and poverty? Do you understand Faith? Do you understand God's teachings? Do you understand God? Do you even understand yourself - why do you do what you do, think the way you think, act in the manner in which you act? Do you understand?

The Eunuch (like many of us) had no knowledge, no understanding about what he was reading. And his response was very insightful and transparent: **"How can I understand if no one guides me?"** Why do we expect our kids to grow up into God-fearing Kingdom citizens if no one teaches them? How can we expect the poor and homeless to improve their situations if no one guides them? How can we expect men and women to have successful marriages if no one teaches them? (This holds true especially when they WANT to know how to better themselves.) Without a guide, this Eunuch was in the same position as someone who WAS NOT reading the scriptures. He needed Phillip. He needed a guide. He needed a teacher.

Teaching is indeed a symbiotic relationship. The instructor NEEDS someone to import knowledge into, while the ignorant (not meant as a derogatory term, but rather simply defined as "a person who does not know a particular thing") NEEDS someone to export knowledge.

The instructor with knowledge needs the ignorant, and the ignorant needs the instructor with knowledge.

"Hello...Can You Hear Me?"

The key to this symbiotic relationship is understanding. For an example, let's use one of the most common devices that no one can seem to live without these days: the cellphone.

Have you ever been on your cell phone and gotten bad reception? Of course, you have; we've all been there. Whether it is a particular region that we're in ("dead-spots"), the weather, or sometimes for reasons unknown (i.e., you have four full bars and still can't get good reception), communication is difficult. During these times, you can't quite make out what the person on the other end is saying. Almost universally, the first words that come out of our mouths are *"I can't hear you."* However, this isn't totally true. You could perhaps hear them making sounds. You may even be able to make out a few choppy words here and there. Yet the first words that come to mind are "I can't hear you." Why is that? It is because what we really mean is, "I don't fully understand what you're saying."

Innate to and intricate in hearing is understanding. The Bible teaches us that "faith comes by hearing" (understanding/grasping the full measure of an idea being put forth) and hearing (understanding/grasping the full measure of an idea being put forth) is obtained by the Word of God (Kingdom teachings). Words are simply ideas / thoughts manifested into the physical realm, where others may hear and understand what is inside a person's mind. Once I learn what was inside a person's mind, I have been taught what they think.

Before you can truly "understand" (hear), you must first receive instruction / teaching. Once we receive teaching (from the Word of God, pastors, teachers, mentors, etc.) then our hearing / understanding about God, His plans, and even the miraculous is clarified and expanded. As our hearing / understanding grows, our faith is strengthened. But it all starts with teaching.

Thinking Like God

To take our Understanding to another level... your words are an extension of you. Your words and thoughts are a reflection of who you are in your heart. This is where we see such concepts:

Proverbs 23:7

"For as he thinketh in his heart, so is he...."

Luke 6:45

*"A good man out of the good treasure of his heart bringeth forth that which is good; and an evil man out of the evil treasure of his heart bringeth forth that which is evil: **for of the abundance of the heart his mouth speaketh.**"*

The more we obtain teaching from God, the more we are able to develop a heart after Him; a heart that mirrors who HE is and what HE stands for. God desires that we learn from Him so that He can reproduce Himself in us. This means that the more that we think like God thinks, we should act like God acts, talk like He talks, and do what

He does. We should develop His character and integrity. What's important to God becomes important to us. His priority becomes our priority.

Teaching should take what we've learned prior and "count it as dung" if it doesn't line up with God's teaching. Even if something seems like a good idea or seems right or acceptable and legal in society, if God says that it's wrong or bad, then we should view it as wrong or bad...and vice versa. Adopting this mentality is a very important step in entering into a Kingdom relationship with God and obtaining the miraculous.

We'll discuss this in greater detail later, but let's look at King Saul. In 1 Samuel 15, Saul was instructed by God to destroy the nation of Amalek: every person, every animal, everything. However, Saul had a "good" idea. He thought it would be a good idea to spare Agag (king of the Amalekites) and keep the animals to sacrifice them unto God. On the surface, it was a good idea, but because Saul's "good" idea was contrary to God's instructions, the throne was taken from Him!! God had made Saul the King of Israel; many would consider that a miracle. Yet, because he didn't follow the teaching/instructions of God, he forfeited his miracle.

In Genesis 3, the same thing occurred with the Woman in the Garden of Eden. Man was instructed to not eat of the tree of the knowledge of good and evil. The serpent presented a counter argument to the Woman. The scriptures indicate that she thought the "fruit was good for food." She thought eating the fruit would be a "good idea." However, when her male counterpart (Adam) partook of the fruit, their good idea cost them the garden of Eden and dominion over the physical realm.

In short: Just because something seems like a good idea doesn't make it God's idea.

Two Different Systems

I know you're asking, "What does this have to do with me getting my miracle?" The answer is, "EVERYTHING." It is not necessarily about what is good or what is evil, but more-so about the concept that our thinking should align with God's thinking. If we want the miracles of God, we are going to acquire them through God's Kingdom system. Therefore, we have to understand how God thinks in order to function in His Kingdom system. These two different systems are referenced many times in scriptures:

Acts 26:17b-18a

*I am sending you to them to open their eyes and turn them from **darkness to light**, and from the **power of Satan to God**.*

Ephesians 5:8

*You were once **darkness**, but now you are **light in the Lord**. Live as children of light.*

Ephesians 6:12

*For we do not wrestle against flesh and blood, but against the **rulers, against the authorities, against the cosmic***

powers over this present darkness, *against the spiritual forces of evil in the heavenly places.*

Colossians 1:13

*He has rescued us from the **dominion of darkness** and brought us into **the kingdom of the Son** he loves.*

1 Thessalonians 5:5

"You are all **sons of the light** and **sons of the day**. We do not belong to the **night or to the darkness**."

    Unfortunately, we didn't come into the world knowing how our Father thinks or how His system operates. We have been trying to obtain miracles according to how we "think" God's system operates – which is ultimately based on our experience in this world. So essentially, we attempt to understand God based upon our interaction with the world's system that we experience on a daily basis. In our experience, no one gives you something for free. In our experience, it's first-come, first-served. In our experience, power and seniority are given priority over the weak and inexperienced. In our experience, it's not about "what" you know but "who" you know. In our experience, "rich" people are given priority over "poor" people.

    Just like we learned how the world's system operates, we have to learn how God's Kingdom operates. Once we understand how God thinks, we can pray and communicate with Him effectively. Until we learn how God thinks, we will talk ***at Him***, but not ***with Him***…We will do good things, but not God-things…We will be busy, but not effective. We learn how God thinks through His written Word [therefore, we must read and study the Bible], through revelations from the Holy Spirit [therefore, we must pray and meditate], and through the revelations given and understood through others [therefore, we must consider resource books, listen to our pastors and brothers and sisters that have searched the scriptures].

Why Didn't the Miracle Happen?

Sometimes, we look back at our situations and evaluate the results. We assess whether or not we received a miracle, whether our prayers were answered, or even if it seemed like God heard us or not. When performing our evaluations, it is almost impossible not to look over our shoulders at our friends, neighbors, or other people that we know in similar situations. We then make the common mistake of comparing ourselves to them based on how we THINK God's system works, as opposed to how His system actually works...especially if they received a positive result and we didn't.

This is especially true of those of us who say we are believers: "How could God bless them and not me?" ... "I go to church and pay my tithes, and they don't; how could God bless them with a miracle and not me?" ... "They openly commit (insert sin here), and I do my best to uphold the laws of God. Why is God so unfair?" ... "I've been a Christian for 30 years, and God didn't answer my prayers, but He seems to answer the prayers of this person who doesn't even go to church." If we are honest with ourselves, many of us have had some of these thoughts.... Many of us continue to have these thoughts. We do good.

We try to be darn near perfect and faithful according to God's Word, yet other people "pass us in the line to be blessed." Other people that aren't making nearly the effort that we are making get to experience the miracles of God, while we experience "the cold-shoulder of God."

We feel this way because we don't understand God. There is no "line" that God has placed you in; nor is there a particular numerical order for when God hands out miracles. We think that God is unfair and unjust. We have come to a false conclusion that "God is going to do what He wants to do anyway, so what good is there in praying or asking or crying out to Him." These are misperceptions that we have of God because we don't understand Him or His system.

Different Levels

To help us cope with these misperceptions, we have to understand certain concepts about how God operates. We tend to think that "God deals with all of us the same…no matter what". This is perhaps one of the most misunderstood concepts about God and why many view Him as "being unfair" at times. However, to be more accurate, God is honest, just, and more than fair …**He just deals with us where we are.**

Think of it in terms of how parents deal with their children. I can remember when my daughter, Robbie, was a child. When she was newly born, she was so tiny and helpless. She couldn't walk; she couldn't talk; she couldn't fix herself a meal; she couldn't provide shelter for herself; she was unable to even protect herself. But she knew how to do one thing… and boy could she do it well: CRY!!!!

At every cry, my wife would drop everything. All Robbie had to do was cry, and she would run to see if she was hungry, if her diaper needed changing, if she wanted to be held and rocked to sleep, if she was too hot, if she was too cold, or just wanted one of us around.

Eventually as she got older, we held her less. She gradually began to crawl. As time continued, she fell down a lot in the process of learning to walk. As she got older, she learned to babble, which led to her learning certain words: "Ma Ma"—"Da Da"—"Mon-nee." We potty trained her, so she didn't soil herself so much. As she matured in these basic life processes, she would continue to cry sometimes; however, we encouraged her to "use her words" to tell us what she wanted, to use her developing mobility to crawl, or to walk to get a certain toy that was out of reach. We cheered her on when she successfully used the potty and avoided messing up her clothes and the bed sheets. She was rewarded with juice, milk, or snacks when she used her words. She could have whatever toy or object that wasn't harmful to her if she walked over to it.

As she continued to mature, more was expected of her. Crying was no longer an option; it didn't get her the results that it did when she was younger. Even though she used her words and asked for something, it wasn't an automatic guarantee that she would get it at this stage. She had to demonstrate that she was ready to handle the responsibility of driving the car. Sometimes, she had to convince us that it was a good idea to let her go to certain places or give us a reason to give her the money she asked for. There were even times that she had to remind us of our own words or promises that we, as parents, had previously made. Sometimes, we told her "No," just to see how she would respond.

When it comes to asking God for the miraculous, it is no different than children at different stages asking for something from their parents. We are all at different stages in our spiritual walk. I wouldn't treat my 40-year-old daughter like I would my 18-year-old nephew, nor would I treat my 18-year-old nephew like I would my 4-year-old grandchild. It is not equal, but it is fair. What I'm trying to articulate to you is a vital principle: **The reason it probably "feels" like God is treating you differently is because He's dealing with you where you are, all the while dealing with another person at their level.** God's ultimate goal is to mature you into the person He destined you to be.

For some people, all they have to do is cry out and they receive their miracle. This is often seen for those who are babes in Christ. I remember upon first getting saved, I could just say something as benign as, "Man, I'm hungry," and someone would knock on the door with food. I could lament about not having money, and I would have a check in the mail or someone would just give me $20 out of the blue. This seemed to be the case when Jesus saw a certain funeral procession in Nain *(Luke 7:11-17)*. The widow woman was simply grieving: she was burying her only son. She didn't ask Jesus to heal her son – she probably didn't believe that it was even possible. But Jesus had compassion on her: <u>He raised her son from the dead.</u> She didn't demonstrate great faith, or give some eloquent speech, nor did Luke give insight into how she served God, day and night. All that is noted is that she was grieving over the loss of her son: she was simply crying.

However, there comes a time when simply crying out no longer works. When you've gained a greater understanding of God, who He is and His capabilities, it is then that God requires us to "use our words." God wants us to pray, to communicate, to ask him in a more defined manner, or to put forth some effort toward our request. No more crying when you're hurt.... No more wishing things would get better when you or a family member are sick.... No more hoping that your financial situation will improve.... No more crying.... What do you want from Him? Say it! Articulate it! Write it down! Draw a Picture! Communicate with our Father!

Eventually, we will reach a point where simply asking no longer works. As we learn more about God and His Kingdom, we mature and reach new levels. Just as my daughter had to remind us of what we promised her, God eventually requires us to pray and ask according to Kingdom protocols and promises. God cannot and does not lie. Because of this attribute, God is only responsible for what He has spoken or promised. Jeremiah 1:12 (ESV) says that the Lord "watches over His word to perform it." God's goal is to grow us up to a level where we come before Him like the King that He is and behave like the kings that He created us to be! You can't just come before the King any kind of way. You don't just come before the King empty-handed. To motivate the King to act on your behalf, there are certain words and ideology to use. But you have to study and/or be taught to reach this point.

At one point, you may have gotten some results through prayer even though there were aspects of your life that were not in line with God's character. You had an attitude problem.... You had an issue with lying... You were fornicating.... You were watching pornography.... You weren't treating your spouse with love or respect according to the Word of God. You will reach a point where God requires your actions to line up according to His Word. You may pray eloquently; you can fast and pray all day and night; however, you won't experience blessings and miraculous results because you're mature enough (from God's perspective) to know better – mature enough to do better – mature enough to BE better.

A Mother's Wisdom

When I was young, a wise woman with four kids once explained to me how she treated every one of her children differently. I thought this was strange. I asked, "Why would you treat your kids differently?" She explained that she treated each one of her kids differently because they were different. One kid was very obedient, therefore, just the threat of punishment was enough to get him in line. Another child was more daring; therefore, she had to carry out the threat of punishment to keep him in line. One of her daughters was very insecure; therefore, she constantly showered her with words of affirmation (i.e., "I love you," "you're special," "you're going to be great," etc.). The other daughter acted independent and mature; therefore, she was intentional about not letting her grow up too fast so that she could enjoy being a kid (i.e., not wearing her hair like an adult, no dating until a certain age, no going to certain places or parties, etc.).

Her goal was to maximize every child's potential. She noted that it would have been easy to have one method of parenting and expect each child to fit into that style, but she, as a mother, knew her children. She studied each child's strengths, weaknesses, abilities, and tendencies so that she could produce a parenting style that would be suitable to that particular child. She wanted each child to be the best according to their potential. If she only threatened punishment, then only one child would reach his full potential. If she only gave words of affirmation but wasn't firm, every child wouldn't flourish. If she placed all her energy and focus on making sure they didn't grow up too fast, all of the children wouldn't benefit.

I didn't understand at the time, but this mother demonstrated a parental aspect that mirrored God. There are billions of people on the earth. Though there are similarities, each one of us is different and unique. God is OUR Father. God wants EVERY ONE of us to succeed; He wants all of us to develop into the best versions of ourselves. He wants us to experience the miraculous; however, like any parent, God wants us to be able to handle the responsibility that comes with the blessings / miracles that He bestows upon us.

If saying "no" or "not yet" to our requests contributes to the development of a better mature person whose potential is fully actualized, then God's answer is to our benefit, not our detriment. It wasn't to hurt us, but to help us. God deals with us where we are and responds accordingly to grow us into mature human beings.

Let's Be Honest - Self Evaluation:

1. In what area of your life could you use more teaching? More understanding? A guide? A mentor?

2. Are there times in your life when you have ignored or rejected sound teaching? Why was it ignored? Is there anything that you have done or could do to rectify these decisions?

3. Have you experienced God as a young, immature believer and gotten results? How did that impact your relationship with God?

4. Did you once experience results from God, but now it seems like He isn't even listening to you anymore? How has that impacted your relationship with God?

5. Have you prayed for miracles and felt jealous or betrayed that God didn't answer your prayers but answered the prayers of someone else?

6. Have you ever thought God was unfair or unjust? When? Why?

CHAPTER 4: A TALE OF TWO WINES

"There are basically two types of people. People who accomplish things and people who claim to have accomplished things. The first group is less crowded."
- Mark Twain

I pray that this concept saturates your understanding: **<u>Wine is symbolic for Teaching.</u>** As mentioned before, everyone at the wedding wanted wine except for Jesus. Or from a spiritual standpoint… everyone wanted teaching or desired to be taught except Jesus. He had the very thing they desired. He had wine — He had teaching. And even though it was "not His time to reveal Himself" – because they had the desire, the faith of His mother, and the obedience of the servants – the miraculous had to manifest.

"Where there is No Teaching, there can be No Miracles." Miracles rarely, if ever, occur in the absence of teaching or without some level of understanding. Of course, there are exceptions depending on the stage/level of an individual (as discussed as Chapter 3). I don't want us to be naive and believe that we fully understand God or foolishly place Him in the box of our small comprehension. However, I do wish to unlock and rediscover a pattern of teaching often associated with the miraculous. Let's dig deeper….

Rabbi - Master Teacher

Jesus had many titles – the Christ, Son of God, Son of Man, King of kings, Lord of lords, Master, The Way, Bread of Life, The Truth, The Word – but as I've mentioned before, the title that seemed to be utilized most when addressing Jesus (especially amongst His disciples) was "Rabbi," which means "Master Teacher."

Everywhere Jesus went, He taught. It seemed as if everything He did was a teaching moment for those He was preparing and training: **Fishing** wasn't just fishing, but it was a way to teach them about their destiny and purpose and life: *"fishers of men" (Luke 5)*. **Going to visit a friend** was an opportunity to give them a first-hand lesson on Resurrection Power: *the resurrection of Lazarus (John 11)*. **Washing the disciples feet** wasn't just about cleanliness, but a lesson and example of true *Leadership Service (John 13)*. **Dinner** wasn't just dinner, but it was an opportunity to teach about His future sacrifice: *The Last Supper (Matthew 26)*.

Searching the scriptures reveals that He did a lot of teaching, oftentimes, in association with the miraculous. Here are just a few examples:

Matthew 5:2 [The Beatitudes]

*And he opened his mouth and **taught** them, saying...*

Mark 1:22

*And they were astonished at his **teaching**, for he **taught** them as one who had authority, and not as the scribes.*

Matthew 11:1

*When Jesus had finished **instructing** his twelve disciples, he went on from there **to teach** and preach in their cities.*

Mark 10:1

*And he left there and went to the region of Judea and beyond the Jordan, and crowds gathered to him again. And again, as was his custom, **he taught them**.*

Luke 4:15

*And he **taught** in their synagogues, being glorified by all.*

Luke 5:3

*Getting into one of the boats, which was Simon's, he asked him to put out a little from the land. And **he sat down and taught** the people from the boat.*

John 8:2

*Early in the morning he came again to the temple. All the people came to him, and he sat down and **taught them**.*

    At His core, Jesus was a true Teacher. The disciples only asked Him to show them how to do one thing…pray. And even in this very important act, they didn't ask Jesus to pray FOR them. They asked Him, "TEACH us how to pray." He showed them how to speak to a storm – teaching through demonstration. He inspired Peter to walk on water – teaching through encouragement and motivation. He trusted them to feed the 5,000 – teaching through empowerment and delegation. He reassured them when they couldn't cast out a particular demon ("This kind only comes out by fasting and praying") – teaching through their failure and <u>frustration</u>.

True Teaching

I think it's safe to say, Jesus was a masterful Teacher. In order to be a master teacher, I would think one must be able to reach people of all backgrounds, nationalities, experiences, bias, preconceived notions, and most importantly learning styles. People from all backgrounds recognized the significance of Jesus. Even though He wanted to initially focus on "the lost sheep of Israel," we see that He had significant interactions with those from "outside" of the nation of Israel (i.e., the Centurion Soldier, the Syrophoenician Woman, the Samaritan Woman at the well, etc.). There were individuals from tax collectors and economic leaders to the common everyday working people who sought to hear the teachings of Jesus. Children ran to Him. Elderly people inquired of Him. "Vertically-challenged" individuals climbed trees just to get a glimpse. Prostitutes, thieves, "sinners" flocked to hear His gospel. Even some religious leaders - though most were reluctant - came to Jesus and admitted that His message/His teachings were like nothing they'd ever heard.

However, the true test of a great teacher is being able to teach Everyone, so that Everyone learns and acquires the same information to be effective. This was a constant task for me with coaching. On a basketball team, I had 12-15 young men; they were all different. Some were intellectual...Some were what many would consider "from the streets." Some were momma's boys...Some were from broken homes...Some were warriors...Some were soft...Some were skillful, while others had heart like you've never seen. And it was my job as a coach to teach ALL of them how to play the game of basketball...together.

I would learn first-hand what the wise old woman (mentioned at the end of Chapter 3) meant: children (and by default, all people) are different. What one person likes, desires, or needs – another person may not. In dealing with my teams and teaching them to play basketball, it would have been easy for me if they all could have **learned from just listening** to me talk. If they could have put everything into practice by just listening, my job would have been 1000 times easier. But that wasn't the case.

There were maybe one or two who could learn in that manner: I could draw up a play or tell them to do something, and they would do it the exact way that I saw it in my mind. But there were others who were more **visual learners**: they could learn what I was trying to teach them through seeing the plays/schemes/drills. So, in practice, after they saw it demonstrated a time or two, they were able to catch on. There were still others who didn't get it by listening to it being explained nor by seeing it demonstrated – these gentlemen were "**hands on learners**." They had to participate in the drills and plays in practice. Once they ran through it personally, they were able to understand what I had envisioned.

That's three different learning styles, and that was just on the surface. This didn't take into account how the young men would respond to other intricate matters. I would be able to be harder on some of them than others.... I would have to take some of them to the side and be more delicate.... I would have to tell one to keep shooting to build confidence, while another could miss 10 straight shots and believed he was going to make the next 10 baskets.... I would have to be a father-figure to some, a mother/nurturer to others.... Some had all the athletic gifts in the world, and I had to push them in the classroom.... Others had intellectual gifts, and I had to push them in the gym. I had to know their strengths, their weaknesses, their backgrounds, their mindsets, their goals, their pitfalls, negative influences, positive influences, etc. – All for the sake of teaching them the game of basketball. No one particular style of learning made a player smarter or better than the next. They were just different. And as a Coach/Teacher, it was up to me to put each player in a position to be ready when the game was played.

Jesus' situation with teaching was not much different than mine as a coach. Jesus taught in the synagogue when the situation called for it, but He also taught in boats. He taught using the law, and He was also able to get His point across using analogies to agriculture. He taught the disciples plainly, and He spoke to the people in parables... Whatever it took to get the message across about the Kingdom.

One of the reasons Jesus **needed** to perform miracles was because He was a Master Teacher. Everyone wasn't/isn't going to learn about the Kingdom of God through His words alone. So, for His visual learners, I believe God allowed miracles. The miracles (at times) were a visual demonstration of His teachings about the authority and power of the Kingdom of God. Some people believed and gave glory to God for the teachings; others did so because they got understanding through the miracles of healing, finances, food, etc.

Jesus also had some participatory learners (learning through participation). In Luke 10, Jesus sent out 70 of His disciples, two by two. They had to participate in teaching, healing, and casting out demons in order to grasp the weight of the message. They had listened to Jesus teach. They had witnessed Him performing miracles. But when they participated in the ministry, they returned excited and had a greater understanding of the Kingdom message.

The Bus Driver

As a coach, I was called "the Bus Driver." Because unlike most coaches, I just sat on the bench with a lollipop in my mouth. I didn't scream. I didn't yell. I wasn't standing up the entire game. I called out plays and defenses, made substitutions, and we won Championships. During the game, I didn't have to say or do very much. People assumed that I had naturally talented teams that could play well together. But if you came to practice, you'd see a much different scene – In practice, I was "talking passionately" (Some may say I was screaming and yelling), demonstrating by example, interrupting plays to show them how to break down offensive and defensive schemes. In practice, I was all over the court. In practice, I was in their faces and correcting every single mistake or flaw that arose. I was so invested in teaching during practice that by the time the game was to be played, I had nothing left to do or say. We'd gone through the drills. I taught the defense and offense. All my players had to do was implement what they had been taught, and we'd be successful. Game day was the test...and teachers rarely talk during the test.

I can remember when we faced the top ranked team in the State for the Championship...the Cecilia Bulldogs. Many thought that we didn't have a chance. We were a small school by comparison; we weren't known as a "basketball power." No one expected us to compete, let alone win the game. All the commentary from the media, basketball aficionados, and even our fans was about how good they were and that our luck would finally run out. However, I saw a different team than everyone else saw. What I was hearing from the people didn't reflect the attitude of my players. I could see the look on my players faces...they were not afraid. They were laughing and joking like they'd done the entire season. They had the attitude that this was just another game for them.

The Cecilia Bulldogs at that time were nicknamed "The Dream Team." They had excellent guards and two guys that were 6'9" – future professional basketball prospects. Our tallest athlete was 6'6". They had pretty much destroyed everyone that they faced. Everyone believed that Cecilia would win easily. Many thought it was impossible for us to win. Some even said that "it would take a miracle..."

What all of those people and Cecilia didn't take into account was that we had built a solid foundation of confidence. My team had heard that we weren't "good enough" all year long – We believed differently. We had beat some of the best basketball teams in the region at that time: Peabody, Natchez, Carroll, Wossman, etc. Those teams had athletes that were 6'8" and 6'9" just like Cecelia. We were used to playing against teams with height and size advantages. My boys weren't afraid because they knew that what they had learned through teaching had prepared them for this moment. Winning all those games gave them confidence in the teaching, coaching, and themselves. No one could make them believe that we weren't a championship team.

To make a long story short...we won the school's first ever Basketball State Championship. Years later, I asked one of the players that was on the team, "How did we win that championship?" He told me, "We believed in you, Coach, because you believed in us. You were one of the few that encouraged us, disciplined us, loved us, told us that we were important, made us feel 'like somebody'. That made the basketball game easy compared to most of our real-life circumstances. You drew up a play – it worked. You gave us a game plan – we won. It reached the point that if you said it, we believed it – on and off the court."

God is the same way! He's sent teachings and game plans in the scriptures. He's sent coaches and ministers to encourage and develop you. You've been in practice situations. You've been given the opportunity to perfect your responses and reactions in practice circumstances. If you've learned, studied, and listened, then all you have to do is implement what God taught when the test comes. However, most of us are lost when the moment arises. We don't know what to do when the crisis comes because we didn't listen when the Coach was trying to teach us...we didn't utilize the practice time effectively...we didn't learn the plays…or we don't believe in what we've been taught.

God wants you to win. Because when you win, He wins.

The Road to Failure is Paved with Good Intentions

I'm afraid that many of us are trying to play the game without being taught. I see many people attempting to perform spiritual acts with no training or teaching. Praying, preaching, exhorting/encouraging, sharing the Gospel, prophesying, spiritual warfare, etc. are all important tasks that we shouldn't just DO, without first being taught. Neither are they tasks that we should just bestow upon individuals without proper instruction. Action without prior instructions often leads to error because much is done in ignorance.

So, when we pray not knowing how or what we should be praying for, we're trying to do a good thing, yet it can be ineffective…unless the Holy Spirit intervenes. However, even then, it's the Holy Spirit's job to teach us and guide us. When we share the Gospel without first being taught what the gospel truly consists of, we have the potential to lead people astray – even though that is not our intention. To prophesy without first being taught how, when, or the purpose of prophesying can cause many to travel a path not meant for them. Therefore, operating in ignorance not only places that individual in danger, but so many other people can be harmed in the process. "Good things" and actions done with good intentions can lead to bad results if there is no teaching.

Two Types of Wine

I wanted to show you the importance of Teaching so that you can see the immense power that it contains. In the words of Stan Lee's *Spider-Man*, "With great power comes great responsibility..." – or for a more Scriptural reference, *"To whom much is given, much is required" (Luke 12:48)*. This is true and aptly applies to teaching. Teaching is a double-edged sword. On the one hand, it can be used to instruct individuals in truth, help them learn how to perform certain tasks, propel them into their purpose in life, and impact the earth realm with everything God has placed in them. But on the other hand, if I am taught incorrectly, I can not only hurt myself but lead a generation of people down a path of destruction.

This is why we have to pay special attention to the words of the governor at the feast in John 2. Let's look at the King James version....

When the ruler of the feast had tasted the water that was made wine, and knew not whence it was: (but the servants which drew the water knew;) the governor of the feast called the bridegroom, And saith unto him, **Every man <u>at the beginning</u> doth set forth good wine; and when men have <u>well drunk</u>, <u>then that which is worse</u>: but thou hast kept the good wine until now.**

The governor (or ruler) of the feast tasted both wines and deemed that the wine that Jesus made was the "**good**

wine." This good wine was compared to ANOTHER type of wine.... we'll call this **bad wine** – or **that (wine) which is worse**. There are two types of wine, or should I say there are **two types of teaching**: good teaching and teaching which is worse (bad teaching). The good wine was obviously of higher quality and more potent than the other. Even the timing of when and to whom the wine was given denotes a difference. Good wine was usually given first and to sober individuals. Why? Because sober people would be able to tell the difference in the quality. Bad wine (or wine which is worse) was usually given last and to individuals who were drunk (e.g., ignorant, not in control, under the influence of something or someone else). Why? Because in their drunken state, they would NOT be able to tell the difference in quality. How is this important to teaching?

This is significant because Jesus produced good wine for drunk individuals. To put it more plainly... He gave good teaching to ignorant people, people who didn't know any better, people who are often taken advantage of. This was not usually the custom then, and it is often not the custom in our society today. In the world of business, the true secrets of generational wealth are often given at luxury resorts, on yachts, and in seminars that cost a small fortune to even get into the room. True wealth tips are often exchanged on the golf course of exclusive country clubs to those that can afford such luxuries. Job promotions and advancements are given to family members of those already in high positions.

Even in many churches today, "the Word" often goes forth to the individuals that likely have had some understanding of God in some capacity. We form groups and have prayer meetings and Bible studies with individuals of the same ilk and mindset. Rarely do we reach out to those individuals who do not even know God.

Rarely do we give good teaching to those who are ignorant or not in control. Rather, we allow them to be consumed with "that which is worse." They are given teachings that say: "Do drugs" ... "Have Sex" ... "Feel Good" ... "YOLO (You Only Live Once)" ... "Nobody loves you" ... "You aren't worth anything" ... "Fight those who don't like you" ... "Look out for number one/Take care of yourself" ... "Make that money / Get the bag" ... "You can do bad all by yourself." All of these are examples of "bad wine" of which people are drinking on a daily basis – and the world is all too happy to keep their cups full. They need "good wine"/God's teaching. But alas... until they have a desire for it, until they want the good wine, they won't fully experience the miraculous works of God. Don't get me wrong... they may be successful for a while, and they may experience a benefit or two – for the Lord allows it to rain on the just and the unjust; however, they won't experience the sustained miraculous living that comes from following God's plan and His Kingdom system.

To go even further, in Matthew 7:6, we are instructed to not give that which is precious to people who don't have the desire. We are cautioned to "not cast your Pearls before dogs or swine." This isn't meant to be derogatory, but rather to highlight a perception. "Pearls" (teachings of God) are of great value; however, a "dog or swine" (individuals who don't want to learn God's ways) aren't able to appreciate the value. We may recognize the teachings that a person needs to be able to change their lives, and we may have a strong desire to help them; unfortunately, until they want "wine" (good teachings), there is very little we can do.

The Danger of Bad Wine

I have often wondered how people – not just people in the world but even those who claim Jesus as Lord and Savior – could support groups, movements, and causes that have principles that are downright hateful or contrary to God. When looking at the revelation from the governor, I can understand why. The governor's proclamation brings out an important point of how some people or groups use teaching to influence others. The governor reveals that most people give out the good wine first, and then when people have drunk that wine (believed in that teaching), they put out the bad wine or the wine which is worse.

There are those that will give you good wine (good teaching) first to get you to buy into their vision or cause. If I mentioned the name of Hitler, most would scoff and give some version of "I could never have followed someone like that evil man." However, Adolph Hitler gave the German people "good wine" first. At the time, Germany was facing economic instability after losing World War I. Their enemies blamed them for the war and placed harsh penalties and restrictions on the Germans. Hitler told the poor German people that the penalties placed on Germany were too harsh and that the cause of many of their problems was the result of their government failing them. He asserted value in their lives by proclaiming that German people were great. He promised solutions: jobs for the German unemployed, prosperity for failing businesses, closure of the gap between the wealthy and the poor, expansion of the German military, and restoration of German pride and prominence in the world. This was the kind of teachings that most Germans, if not all, would support and believe in.

However, once the German people drank this "good wine" from Hitler, they were given the "wine which was worse." Through propaganda and controlling the media, Hitler gradually mixed in teachings that the Jews and other minority groups were a major source of the Germans problems – that these groups of people were less than human – that the Germans were victims and did nothing wrong in WWI – and that they were being taken advantage of by other European countries. They eventually began to teach that the German/Aryan race was superior to all other races – that Hitler alone could solve their problems – that lies, fear, intimidation, and violence were suitable tactics as long as it was in support of the Nazi government. The means justified the end result: a unified, powerful German Empire with Hitler as its Supreme Leader (Führer)

This teaching led many well-intentioned Germans to support and take part in starting World War II, killing many millions of Jews and other minorities in the Holocaust, the mass murdering of civilians, persecuting anyone who spoke out against the Nazi party and Hitler, euthanizing the disabled, and many other atrocities. If these teachings and ideologies had been introduced first, most people would have thought Hitler and the Nazi party delusional and radical; however, because they believed in the promises and hope of a restored and powerful

Germany, most didn't realize what was happening until it was too late.

Hitler gave them the "good wine" first; then the "wine which was worse" was given later. And the people were too drunk, too influenced, and so enamored with what they heard first that they were unable to discern that they were being led astray or down a path of destruction.

Unfortunately, this isn't just a concept that applies to Nazi Germany. This has occurred throughout history and attracted people to groups like the Ku Klux Klan (KKK) and other white supremacist ideology, domestic terrorists, gangs that prey on their own communities, cults like those led by David Koresh, the Taliban, ISIS, etc. Even our major political parties (e.g., Republicans and Democrats) use the same tactics of giving you teachings that you can agree with and get behind, only to be followed by or infused with teachings that may not align with your values at all.

Promises of peace, unity, family, shared goals, a better future, financial security…all in all "a better life" – in general, this is what is promised. This is the "good wine" that draws most people in. Afterwards, they are given the "wine which is worse." Then they learn that you have to kill or hate black people and other minority groups to belong … or sell drugs and steal to get to this "better life" … or commit suicide to get to Heaven … or walk over your fellow man to get to the American Dream. It's all the same tactic.

Religion utilizes this age-old tactic as well. More people have been killed, more hatred has been spewed, more damage has been done in the name of religion through various wars and conflicts than any other entity in history. However, God's "wine"/teaching is always to improve you and your situation without compromising integrity or damaging and hindering others. Proverbs 10:22 teaches, *"The blessings of the Lord, it maketh rich and he addeth no sorrow with it."* When we are blessed with the teachings of God, it improves our situation, enhances our minds, strengthens our commitment, and adds unmerited favor. It brings no sorrow or regret. The "good wine" is always given *last* because His teachings are designed to take you higher and higher to the miraculous life that we are destined to live.

This concept of two types of teaching is not only seen at the declaration of the ruler of the feast. It is also seen in other aspects of scripture:

Matthew 5:19 (ESV)

Therefore, whoever <u>relaxes one of the least of these commandments and teaches others to do the same</u> will be called least in the kingdom of heaven, but whoever <u>does them and teaches them</u> will be called great in the kingdom of heaven.

"Good wine" here is denoted by doing the commandments and teaching others; while "bad wine" is characterized as not keeping commandments ("relaxing" them) and teaching others not to keep them as well. Here, it is clearly seen that putting <u>*God's teachings into action*</u> and <u>*teaching others to do the same*</u> contributes to whether you will be the "greatest" or "least," according to the way that the Kingdom of Heaven operates. God has no issue with you desiring to be great. He even TEACHES you one of the ways to achieve greatness: **"Keep my commandments and teach others to keep them."**

It is vital to be around those individuals who are teaching sound doctrine. We should surround ourselves with people who not only "drink good wine," but also give "good wine" to others. Jesus warns of "bad wine" in the scriptures...let's dissect further.

Erroneous Teaching

Matthew 15:9

In vain do they worship me, ***teaching as doctrines the commandments of men****.*

Matthew 16: 6-12

[6]Jesus said to them, ***"Watch and beware of the leaven of the Pharisees and Sadducees."*** *[7]And they began discussing it among themselves, saying, "We brought no bread." [8]But Jesus, aware of this, said, "O you of little faith, why are you discussing among yourselves the fact that you have no bread? [9]Do you not yet perceive? Do you not remember the five loaves for the five thousand, and how many baskets you gathered? [10]Or the seven loaves for the four thousand, and how many baskets you gathered? [11]How is it that you fail to understand that I did not speak about bread? Beware of the leaven of the Pharisees and Sadducees." [12]****Then they understood that he did not tell them to beware of the leaven of bread, but of the teaching of the Pharisees and Sadducees.***

Luke 12: 1

In the meantime, when there were gathered together an innumerable multitude of people, insomuch that they trode one upon another, he began to say unto his disciples first of all, **Beware ye of the leaven of the Pharisees, which is hypocrisy.**

Jesus taught His disciples many things; however, the ***only*** thing He told them to beware of was erroneous teaching and hypocrisy – the doctrine of the Pharisees and Sadducees. He didn't tell them to beware of demonic forces – He sent them out to cast out devils. He didn't tell them to beware of losing their lives – He taught them to not fear death. He didn't tell them to beware of powerful people, or jail, or anything of the sort. But He did tell them to beware of erroneous teaching. This is because erroneous teaching not only hinders you from enjoying the miracles of God, but it poisons everyone you encounter and the generations to come after you.

Jesus was adamant about the importance of not just hearing the Word of God but hearing and doing the teachings that He presented to the people. We can't be hypocrites. People are always watching. If you are teaching the right things but doing otherwise, you make the good teachings ineffective. People will want nothing to do with God or His teachings because some "Christians" are not living up to the standard that they preach about. People want nothing to do with God or His teachings because some "pastors" pick and choose which scriptures/sins/issues they want to place emphasis on while overlooking others. People want nothing to do with God or His teachings because some "believers" use it to beat others down instead of build others up. This was the same kind of hypocrisy demonstrated by the Pharisees and Sadducees.

The doctrine of the Pharisees and Sadducees kept them from recognizing the most significant event to ever impact the earth – the coming of the Christ. In the presence of Christ - healing, wisdom, forgiveness, and teaching was present. The manifestation of what they had spent years studying about was right before their very eyes; however, because they held onto their doctrine, they wouldn't receive what Jesus brought to the world. Are you holding on to a teaching, a belief, a doctrine that is keeping you from living in the miraculous?

Just because we've been taught something since we were children, or read it in a book, or found it on the internet doesn't make it true. We have to be diligent in studying and proving what is **original truth** (based on the standard set by God) vs *"my truth"* or *"what sounds good"* or *incomplete truths* or *man's opinion* based on what is _popular_ or _acceptable_.

Teaching is powerful and potent. However, it can also be unassuming. When talking about the most powerful things in this world, teaching is often not first on the list. Yet, in Hosea 4:6, God says, *"My people are destroyed for lack of knowledge...."* The old slogan is true: "Knowledge is Power." However, the only way to obtain knowledge is through teaching…whether it be through instructors, books, or via experiences from the school of life. Without teaching one cannot obtain knowledge; even worse… through erroneous teaching ("bad wine"), people continue to have a lack of knowledge. And God informs us that our lack of knowledge (due to rejection or lack of proper teaching) is the primary reason for the destruction of His people.

When Teaching Goes Wrong

Growing up in Alabama, I was taught that I wouldn't amount to much of anything. My environment wasn't the most encouraging and motivating place. There were few examples of people who got out and did something productive with their lives. People didn't go the extra mile for me because I was special. No one was telling me, "You can do it." My father was a gambler who had 27 children; I had siblings whose names I didn't know or even knew what they looked like. Everything around me was consciously and subconsciously teaching me to "be a gambler" ... "stay in the hood" ... "you're not special" ... "you'll never be successful." I didn't believe in anything positive, let alone know anything about God and who I was really called to be on this earth.

One day my dad sent me to the store with a large amount of money in an envelope. Nothing out of the ordinary happened on the way: I walked to the store, said hello to some people I knew, bumped into a person or two on the street, but otherwise just a normal day. When I got to the store to drop the money off, I couldn't find the envelope in my pockets! The money was gone!!! I panicked. I felt sick. I wanted to run, vomit, pass out, and scream—all at the same time. What was I going to tell my dad? I must have dropped it. I retraced my steps…Nothing. I asked people who were around if they had seen an envelope…Nothing. I had lost the money. My dad and mom were going to kill me.... I was done for.... This was going to be the day that I died.

When I finally went home hours later, my father was waiting for me. He asked if I had dropped the money off. When I told him I had lost the money, he just looked at me. He asked, "What happened? ... Where did you go? ... How could you lose such a large amount of money? ... Did you drop it? ... Did you check in all your pockets?" etc. I just sat there trying to answer his questions as best I could, nearly about to cry.

He then called for a man to come out of the back. He asked me, "Have you ever seen this man before?"

I replied, "I don't think so."

The man pulled an envelope out of his jacket pocket: Not just any envelope....MY ENVELOPE. My dad went on to explain that he paid this man to 'pick-pocket' me. He was one of the people that I had accidentally "bumped" into on my way to the store, I concluded. My dad said that he wanted me to learn an important lesson: "EVERYONE IS OUT TO GET YOU; TRUST NO ONE." From that moment on... it felt as if everyone was out to get me. I was suspicious that everyone had an ulterior motive. My dad may have had good intentions, but this "lesson" damaged my outlook on people and relationships.

This was "wine" that I grew up drinking. So, when it came to my friends — "I wonder what they want from me." When it came to my family — "Never Trust Anyone." When it came to my marriage - "Does she really love me like she says she does?" When it came to the ministry - "It's only a matter of time before they turn on me." It was even affecting my relationship with God because I was taught to "never trust anyone," so could I really trust God? ("Are these preachers just trying to take my money?") I had to realize that just because I had been taught this, didn't make it right. I had to re-evaluate the effect this was having on my life and undergo a re-education. I had to discard my old way of thinking and adopt a new mindset.

Just as I was taught incorrectly, we all have been – in some shape, form, or fashion. For some of us, we were taught that we wouldn't amount to the greatness that we were destined to achieve. For others of us, we were taught to settle for less than we were worth (concerning jobs, relationships, expectations of life, etc.). What's damaging is that we take these teachings throughout life, and they have a negative effect on how our lives turn out. Even more damaging is that we teach these wrong teachings to our children and the next generation, just as the previous generation taught them to us. It is a never-ending cycle…unless someone puts an end to it.

If you're not where you want to be in life, evaluate what you've been taught: What are your perceptions of your purpose, health, wealth, destiny, relationships, your worth, your community, your children, your impact on society, etc.? In whatever area of your life that you feel is lacking or that does not line up with the picture your Heavenly Father paints in the scriptures, you may have some teachings that need to be discarded and replaced with "good wine."

Incomplete Teaching

When swearing in a witness in a courtroom, the bailiff asks him/her, "Do you swear to tell **the truth, the whole truth,** and **nothing but the truth**?" This is important because telling partial truth could lead to someone being wrongfully jailed and convicted of crimes; as well as guilty individuals being set free. Not telling the entire truth can have the same effect as not telling the truth at all. In the same vein... probably more dangerous than a lack of teaching or wrong teaching is incomplete teaching. This type of teaching involves elements of truth mixed with elements of falsehoods – or some of the truth while other parts of the truth are missing. Therefore, an individual that makes decisions based on this type of information is unable to make the best decision and can cause unintentional damage and destruction.

This is one of the favorite tactics of the enemy: he gets us to focus on certain parts of the truth while ignoring others. This is dangerous and leads us into behavior and mindsets that are unbalanced. If I don't have the entire truth about what God says about healing, healing is stagnated or limited. If I only have partial truth about God and money, I'm limited financially. If I only have partial truth about God's love, I place a cap on what God wants to do in my life.

I can remember a time before the LGBTQ movement... Religious leaders and people affiliated with the Church would rail against homosexuality, as the sin of choice to be outraged about. It was an easy topic to choose because being gay wasn't as accepted in society and American culture as it is today. There was no media outrage, no protests, no calls for resignations. In fact, most of the culture and society agreed that homosexuality was wrong – and the "church" ran with it.

Why teach on something that may offend someone, as opposed to something that mostly everyone could agree with? The people that may not have agreed were shunned – in the minority – and couldn't give voice to their issues. Fornicating, drunkenness, lying, stealing, gluttony, hatred, etc. are sins that may have been "touched on" but weren't taught with the same fervor, urgency, and passion, nor given nearly the same attention as homosexuality.

I'm a Kingdom citizen. I'm an ambassador of Heaven. I believe in the scriptures. I have no personal opinion on the matter. I'm going to take the position that God took. So, in a technical manner, the "church" wasn't wrong. But they weren't completely "right" or blameless either. Homosexuality is a sin according to God's standard (an abomination as noted in Leviticus 18:22 and 20:13). These scriptures formed the basis for beating down homosexuals, "sending them to hell," and giving heterosexual Christians a feeling of superiority and the moral "high-ground."

However, the teaching was incomplete: what wasn't highlighted was that God didn't hate the person. He didn't call the person an abomination – He called the act (the sin/homosexuality) an abomination. God is OUR FATHER and He is Love; He loves all of His creations. Like any parent, you don't love it when your children disobey… or get pregnant before marriage… or do drugs… or sneak out the house… or mistreat others…but you do love your kids. Religion did/does an awful job of teaching in a manner that reflects an important aspect of God: **God is able to separate the sin from the sinner.** This is why God can hate what I may have done and yet still love me.

The scriptures say that He "chastises those whom he loves" and that "nothing can separate us from the love of God." Just because you love your children, doesn't mean that you consent and agree with everything that they may do or have done. Sometimes, it is because you love them that you have to give advice or counsel that is opposed to their behavior. If your child is hanging out with a crowd of friends that gets into trouble (i.e., smoking, drinking, doing drugs, terrorizing others), would you love them enough to tell them not to hang around those people? Would you love your child enough to tell them not to have sex before marriage, or at the very least to wear a condom to prevent pregnancy? Do you love your child enough to correct them if they are cheating on their spouse? Would you say something to your child out of love, or would you just sit idly by and encourage them in making bad decisions that could have dire consequences?

The Church taught God's law, but it did not teach God's love. Many thought it was "justice" when a homosexual person was discriminated against, beaten, or even killed. Hardly anyone in the church stood up and said that it wasn't right to treat a fellow HUMAN BEING this way because they were homosexual. Many thought it was "ok" to make fun of them, laugh at them, and make them feel less than human because they were gay. Though I disagree with the lifestyle, it wasn't and never should be ok to treat any human in that manner. When AIDS and diseases spread among the gay community, it DID NOT make God happy that people were dying. God loves everyone, even if He hates what they are doing. He loved Paul (a murderer), Moses (a murderer), David (a murderer and an adulterer), Judas (a traitor), Peter (a liar), etc. Even though He hates what they did, He still loved the person!!

Teaching about God's Love was largely ignored, and because **God's Love** wasn't taught and emphasized just as much as **God's Law**, a void was created. A space developed for the Truth to be abused or engrafted into a different message. And now, you see in the LGBTQ movement only the message of Love is highlighted when referencing God: "God is LOVE... God Loves everyone." This, too, is true...yet incomplete.

I'm not writing this to focus, highlight, or debate whether homosexuality is right or wrong. This is what God said – take your questions, debates, and theories to HIM. But how many miracles did not come to fruition because of this incomplete teaching? How many kind words or acts of Love were not shown that could have prevented a person from committing suicide? How many families were destroyed because of incomplete teaching? How much good was suppressed because a person was not treated with Love? How many people did things out of ignorance because they were never taught God's standard? How many times could we have come together and accomplished something great if people understood the entire truth?

Incomplete truths have caused a deep divide in our homes, churches, and country - and a house divided cannot stand. Our growth, understanding, and perception of God is limited by incomplete truths. We don't tap into the fullness of what God has for us and what He is capable of when we don't possess the complete truth.

In Genesis 20, King Abimelech was nearly killed because Abraham wasn't completely honest that Sarah was his wife. In Joshua 7, Joshua fought a war and lost because Achan wasn't completely honest that he had taken the spoils of war that were to be destroyed. In 2 Samuel 23, Uriah died in war because David wasn't completely honest that he had slept with his wife. In Acts 5, Ananias and Sapphira died because they did not tell the complete truth to the apostles about their profit from the land they had sold.

Incomplete truths are as deadly as outright lies and impair us from living a life of miracles.

Let's Be Honest – Self Evaluation:

1. Are you a good teacher? Are you able to identify the true teachers in your life? How do these individuals rank in being the most impactful in your life?

2. What type of teaching style best fits you? Do you learn better through listening, seeing demonstrations, or participating/being more hands on? Have you been mishandled because your learning style wasn't identified properly?

3. Looking back through your experiences, are you able to see the difference between good teaching and bad teaching?

4. Have you been a victim of being given "wine that was worse" (bad teaching) *after* being given "good wine" (teaching)? How did this impact you?

5. Have you been a victim of incomplete teaching? Have you known some truth, but the entire truth caused issues later in your life? …Incomplete truths about family? …Incomplete truths about people you're in relationships with? …Incomplete truths about life principles?

CHAPTER 5: THE ROLE OF THE GOVERNOR

REVELATION – PART I

"He who learns but does not think, is lost; he who thinks but does not learn, is in great danger." - Confucius

Before going any further into miracles, we need to take a step back and understand how we obtain knowledge and wisdom from God. Learning from God can be a slightly different process from how we are accustomed to learning or being taught. The same principles of teaching and learning still apply, but other factors have to be taken into account. The process of spiritual learning and insight can be found in the same scriptural account of the first miracle in John, Chapter 2:

*⁶Now there were **<u>six stone water jars</u>** there for the Jewish rites of **purification**, each holding twenty or thirty gallons. ⁷Jesus said to the servants, "**Fill the jars with <u>water</u>.**" And they filled them up to the brim. ⁸And he said to them, "**Now draw some out and take it to the master of the feast.**" So they took it. ⁹When the master of the feast **tasted the water now become wine**, and did not know where it came from (though the servants who had drawn the water knew), the master of the feast called the bridegroom ¹⁰and said to him, "<u>**Everyone serves the good wine first, and when people have drunk freely, then the poor wine. But you have kept the good wine until now.**</u>"*

Did you see the process? I know, I know...it's not expressly stated, but it's there. As I mentioned, God hides truth and mysteries, and it is our honor as kings to seek it out. How does this learning process occur? Let's look a little closer...

Six Stone Water Jars

Numbers hold great significance in scripture. The number one (1) generally symbolizes beginnings, wholeness, unity – One is the first number; it is only divisible by itself; and when many individual parts, elements, people come together they are often referred to as **one group** or **one entity**. The number two (2) means division or union – Man was divided into male and female; Marriage is the union two - male and female. Twelve (12) is the number of power/authority or government foundation – 12 tribes of the Nation of Israel; Jesus utilized a system of 12 personal disciples. There are many other examples...but you get the picture.

There were six stone water jars. Six (6) is usually associated with man, human weakness, manifestation of sin – Man was created on the 6th day; the mark of the beast in the Book of Revelations is three 6's (666), etc. The six stone water jars is a symbolic description of the condition that man or humanity was in without God: hearts of stone (we'll discuss the heart more in detail later) ... lifeless ... living life based on rules, traditions, and rituals (Note: the water jars were used for a purification ritual prior to entering the festivities). The six stone water jars represented mankind's hardened, empty condition during this time period. Humans, like the water jars, were created to be filled with "water." Let's continue shall we...

The Water

Next, we see Jesus tell the servants to fill the water pots with water. Now, "water" can have a few different meanings as well. It can symbolize troublesome times ... salvation ... life ... but here, "water" will be interpreted as the Word of God. Given that the scripture (John 2:6) mentions that the water in the waterpots were used for a Jewish purification or cleansing ritual, we can see the correlation with the Word of God referenced in the scriptures:

Ephesians 5: 25-27 instructs:

[25]Husbands, love your wives, just as Christ also loved the church and gave Himself up for her, [26]so that He might sanctify her, **having cleansed her by the washing of water with the word,** *[27]that He might present to Himself the church in all her glory, having no spot or wrinkle or any such thing; but that she would be holy and blameless....*

Jesus in his teaching of the true vine tells His disciples in John 15:3:

"Now you are **clean through the word** *which I have spoken to you."*

Ezekiel 36:25

*I will sprinkle **clean water** on you, and you shall be **clean from all your uncleannesses**, and from all your idols I will **cleanse you**.*

Hebrews 10:22

*Let us draw near with a true heart in full assurance of faith, with our **hearts sprinkled clean from an evil conscience and our bodies washed with pure water**.*

John 4:13-14

*Jesus said to her, 'Everyone who drinks of this water will be thirsty again, but those who drink of the water that I will give them will never be thirsty. **The water that I will give will become in them a spring of water gushing up to eternal life.**"*

It is the acceptance of the **Blood of Jesus Christ** that covers/takes away our sins and brings Salvation to our Soul; however, it is His **Word (Water)** that cleanses us from unrighteousness to align our thoughts and actions with our Father's Will. Therefore, when Jesus tells them to fill the six water pots with water, it's symbolism for filling man with the Word of God.

Being filled with the Word of God is a very important step in learning from God. However, complete teaching or learning hasn't taken place yet because translation has yet to occur. We as humans have been conditioned to be natural-minded. But when God speaks to us, He speaks to us from His perspective, which is from a spiritual mindset.

This is why the next step is very crucial, yet often overlooked.

The Governor

After filling the six water pots up to the brim with water, the servants were instructed to draw out of one of the water pots and take it to the master of the feast (aka "the governor"). (Six (6) is symbolic for man, while "water" can be interpreted as the Word of God.) The governor becomes the 7th "water pot" because he is the next "vessel / person" to be filled with water!! Seven (7) is the number of spiritual completion. (7 days of the week; God rested on the 7th Day; The book of Revelations speaks of 7 Churches, 7 Angels of the Churches, 7 Seals, 7 Trumpet Plagues; there are 7 Holy Days / Feasts of the Lord.)

So… who does this master of the feast (or governor) symbolize? The governor here is symbolic of the Holy Spirit.

To grasp this symbol and concept, you must first understand some kingdom concepts. The governor is important in any kingdom structure, especially when it concerns colonization and expansion. When a kingdom colonized other lands or territory, the king (or queen) would send select certain individuals to go the territory. These select individuals were led by the Governor. A governor would oversee the process of teaching the people already living in the territory how to mirror the new government regime.

For example, when the Kingdom of Great Britain conquered or discovered a new territory (i.e., Jamaica, the Caribbeans, the original American colonies), a Governor was sent to oversee the process of teaching the native people how to be British. They taught them how to dress like the British. They were instructed on how to speak the English language. They were trained in how to observe the British customs. They were directed how to prepare and eat the traditional foods of the British. They were expected to drink tea like the British. They were informed that they were required to pay taxes to Great Britain. They were ordered to observe British laws. They sang British songs, pledged allegiance to the King of Great Britain. Everything about them became British. This is why when Great Britain controlled a vast majority of the world, the popular phrase was, "Great Britain, the Empire on which the sun never sets" because Britain's territories and colonies were a mirror image of Great Britain. And so, it was with every other effective kingdom in history (i.e., Rome, France, Spain).

This was in a large part due to the effective job of the governors. The governor was the colony's direct connection with the king. If the king had anything he wanted to say to the colony, he would send word to the governor. If the colony had anything they wanted to address with the king, they would have to send word through the governor. The governor was of great significance. If there was something that the people didn't understand about an order or policy of the king, the governor would/could explain it. If the king had any question about how the colony was progressing or if there were any concerns, he would ask the governor.

God was the first to utilize the kingdom model; before there was Rome (or any other kingdom), there was the Kingdom of Heaven. God was the first to employ the colonization principle when He created earth and populated it with a species called "man." Of course, we know that man disobeyed God's commandment, fell – NOT from heaven, but – from his position of dominion and authority, and was banished from Eden (the presence of God).

What is often missed is that man lost his connection with God. Or to put it in royal, political terminology: **Man lost his connection with the King.** The connection isn't a **"What"** – rather the connection is a **"Who."** Who was this connection between God and mankind? The Governor – The Holy Spirit. We can extrapolate from scriptures the importance of the Holy Spirit and the role He plays in teaching us how to become true Kingdom citizens.

John 14:15-20

*15"If you love me, you will keep my commandments… 16And I will ask the Father, **and he will give you another Helper**, to be with you forever, 17even the Spirit of truth, whom the world cannot receive, because it neither sees him nor knows him. You know him, for he dwells with you and will be in you. 18I will not leave you as orphans; I will come to you."*

John 14: 25-26

*25"These things I have spoken to you while I am still with you. 26**But the Helper, the Holy Spirit, whom the Father will send in my name, he will <u>TEACH</u> you all things and***

***BRING TO YOUR REMEMBRANCE** all that I have said to you."*

When understood from this perspective, we can see the significance of the water being taken to the governor. It is the Governor who **teaches and gives us revelation and understanding concerning spiritual things**. After the fall of man, we became conditioned to depend upon our natural senses and understanding because we lost the spiritual connection. Our sinful nature kept us separated from God and would not allow the Holy Spirit to dwell and live in us. This is why, in the Old Testament scriptures, the Holy Spirit could only "come upon" certain individuals but never to stay...that is until Jesus was baptized. Luke 3:21-22 recounts:

*[21]Now when all the people were baptized, and when Jesus also had been baptized and was praying, the heavens were opened, [22]and **the Holy Spirit descended on him in bodily form**, like a dove; and a voice came from heaven, "You are my beloved Son; with you I am well pleased."*

There is no record of anyone having an encounter or experience with the Holy Spirit after this time. He even tells His disciples in John 14:17, *"...for he dwells with you and will be in you."* The "complete person" (the Holy Spirit) was within Jesus and dwelling with the disciples. Jesus had an intimate relationship with the Governor; and because of this relationship, He had spiritual insight. He had the connection to the Father (God) that Adam lost, but the rest of mankind did not. Jesus Christ was unlike any other human of that time. Because Jesus had this relationship with the Holy Spirit, He could know and understand what the Heavenly Father desired or was thinking. Now, you and I have this same potential.

This is why the servants were instructed to take the water to the governor – or to take the Word of God to the Holy Spirit – for it is the Holy Spirit that gives us revelation and understanding of the mind of God so that we can gain comprehension of what the word of God means.

Please understand that "the water" and "the governor" are both important. If you have no "Water," there will be nothing to bring to the Governor…or more plainly, **if you have no Word or no instruction, there is nothing for the Holy Spirit to translate into teaching, understanding, and revelation. And vice versa - if you don't have a connection to the Holy Spirit, there is no one to translate the word or instructions.**

You Are Vital in The Teaching Process

Also, allow me to highlight this point: Notice who it was that filled the water pots. It wasn't Jesus. It wasn't the governor. It was the servants. If we desire to understand the teaching and instructions from God that will open the doors to miracles, we have to do our part in the process.

1. **Recognize that we need teaching.** Some things that we learned have taken us as far as they are able. It was Mary who realized that the "wine was running out." The teaching and level of understanding had come to the end of its usefulness. It could take them no further. Some things we learned were just plain wrong or in

error, and we have to be willing to stop holding on to "what once was" and embrace "what shall be."

2. **Get filled with water.** Inundate yourself with God's teachings and principles. Fill yourself with the Word of God (through reading and studying the scriptures, meditation/prayer with God, sermons, conversations, etc.). The servants filled the stone water pots with water according to the instruction of Jesus.

3. **Go to the Governor.** Take that Word to the Governor. You may not even understand what you have been reading…that's fine, keep reading. Then meditate on the Word of God with the Holy Spirit inside you, so that He can reveal, teach, and guide you in this journey of life.

4. **Apply what you've learned.** As you begin to gain understanding from the scriptures, be intentional about applying them to your daily life. Live the word. Be a living demonstration of how God desires us to live so that you can experience the benefits.

5. **Teach and instruct others.** The next level of learning is teaching others. You can teach others through your words or through the example of your daily living. It is important to teach others because it shows that you have a heart for other people to be successful. We shouldn't want to be the only ones to experience the miraculous; We should want others to experience the benefits of God as well.

This process of learning is important when it comes to miracles because miracles are a manifestation of a spiritual event, from a spiritual source, and to meet a spiritual or natural need. Teaching is the key to getting your miracle every single time; Teaching will give you the tools to place yourself in an atmosphere to live miraculously.

Please understand that you can't just read a few scriptures and expect the miracle to happen. You can't just hear some facts about God and expect Him to do the miraculous. You can't just hear a sermon, watch *The Passion of the Christ*, get a bumper sticker, wear a t-shirt, and be spiritually inclined/equipped to take on the world. That Word (the "water") must be translated into Teaching ("wine"), so you can comprehend how to utilize it correctly and effectively to get the miraculous result.

Many people likely knew that the wine was running out – that they had a problem on their hands; however, it was Mary who recognized the problem and knew what to do. She had a relationship with the One who could solve the problem. Even though Jesus' answer to her request appeared to be in the negative, she responded in faith. She instructed the servants to do whatever Jesus told them to do. She didn't go back and forth with Jesus or continue to beg him to give her a positive answer. She responded in a manner that showed she had faith that the need was going to be met. She took what was in her possession (the service of the servants) and placed them under Jesus' control. As a result, the miracle manifested, and everyone benefitted.

Many people may recognize that a problem exists. However, because you are present, know what to do, and have a relationship with God, other people will be blessed. You won't fret because they say that it's never been done.

You won't panic because "the numbers don't add up." You won't fall to pieces because of the "doctor's report." When the bank tells you "No!" ... when people doubt you ... when your back is up against the wall...What is your response going to be?

Take whatever is in your possession and command it to line up with Jesus. This money – line up with the teachings of God (tithe, sow seeds, sound financial management, etc.). This marriage – line up with the Word of God (love her as Christ loved the Church, honor/respect him, communicate effectively, etc.). This vision – this business venture – this body under attack by disease – this mind under attack by depression – these children that have no direction – this attitude – line up with the Word. Do what He commands... And watch the miracles that follow, like changing water into wine.

Let's Be Honest – Self-Evaluation:

1. Are you holding on to old teachings? Is this holding you back from experiencing a greater life?

2. Is the Bible difficult to understand? Do you instantly get sleepy when you even attempt to study the Bible? Have you tried listening to the Bible, sermons, podcasts? What is the best method of filling yourself with the Word of God?

3. Have you had an experience with the Holy Spirit? Have you ever had Him reveal something to you and you knew that it could have only come from God? What was this experience?

REVELATION - PART II

Three (3) Styles of Teaching

All teaching/learning styles fall under three (3) basic categories: Experimentation, Information, and Revelation.

Experimentation

This type of learning involves learning from your experiences – learning from past successes and failures – obtaining teaching through lessons from the "school of life." This type of teaching is invaluable and could help to keep you from repeating mistakes and to learn what to do on a "first-hand" basis.

I can remember having a conversation with a close friend. He told me that when he was younger, he had started a business buying and selling timber; he acquired land with timber on it and would cut the timber for profit. He noted that he was becoming very successful. The problem was that he was becoming too successful, too quickly. He had acquired so much land and so much timber that his workers couldn't keep up with the demand. He recalled that he had to pay a lot of money for equipment, repairs, and other bills that he hadn't considered. He eventually had to sell the business, the land, and the equipment and file for bankruptcy.

He smiled as he relived the story. I hesitantly asked, "Why do you think you failed?"

He replied, "Oh, I didn't fail...I learned. You see, I learned that I should have just bought land and timber and hired someone else to do the cutting and everything else. I should have listened to my wife and grown the business gradually and slowly at a pace that we could handle. I went too big, too fast."

What I saw as failure, my friend saw as a teaching moment. There were things that he learned that he couldn't have known or understood unless he had the experiences that he did. He was grateful for the lessons. He noted that he passed these lessons on to his children, and they've started successful businesses. With a laugh he told me, "They credit me with learning from my mistakes…they say I taught them *what NOT to do*."

Where I'm from, we called learning from experience going to the "school of hard knocks." Experience is a very good teacher. It has its advantages, but it can be a costly education. Learning from experience can cost you great sums of money (as in my friend's case), time, relationships, resources, etc. And though you can acquire a great deal of wisdom from experiential learning, it is limited. If you don't have a certain experience, then you can't be taught certain lessons. Everyone's experience isn't the same; therefore, the lessons learned may not translate to others effectively. We should all value our experiences, but we can't allow them to limit our thinking, choices, assignment, and purpose.

Information

The second style of teaching is probably the most common: teaching through Information / Education. It is different from Experimentation because it goes beyond a person's experiences and can take into account the experiences, studies, and research of others.

This is the type of learning most often obtained in grade school, high school, college and beyond. We get an education in a certain major or training in a certain field of study. We even receive information and education on religion in Seminary School. On Sunday morning, we have Sunday School, and we listen to a sermon. All of this is teaching through information.

You don't have to jump from a 50-story building to know that gravity is real. You don't have to touch an active stove to know that it's hot. You don't have to live through a world war or the fight for civil rights to know that they were horrible and terrifying time periods for our country. You don't have to get popped by grease from cooking bacon to know that it hurts. Now granted - experiencing these things gives you a greater perspective and understanding, but I'd rather learn some things vicariously (through the experiences of others). Much pain and sacrifice can be avoided by learning from Information.

My friend with the timber business learned from experience, but he passed on the lessons to his children. His children learned through education and information and didn't have to fall victim to the same mistakes that their father did.

Learning from education is very valuable, yet it, too, is limited. If someone else hasn't learned a particular lesson or there is no one available to teach, then there can be little learned. Unfortunately, so many of us place too much value on education, information, and degrees that we miss out on the third type of teaching.

Revelation

The third style of teaching is teaching through Revelation. This is the type of teaching that God often utilizes. Revelation is making something known that was previously hidden, unknown, or secret. Revelation goes beyond experience or information. Experience can teach you lessons about the particular situation or circumstance that you've experienced – no experience, no teaching. Information can teach you lessons based on the extent of the known information – no information, no teaching. Revelation can teach you not only about what you or others have experienced, but it can also teach you about what NO ONE has EVER experienced. Revelation can teach you about not only the past or present but also about the future. Things that were hidden, secrets and mysteries that were not understood are revealed through revelation.

In the Old Testament times, prophets foretold of a Savior that would come. They passed this information down through the generations. Yet, when Jesus came, they didn't know who He was... as a matter of fact, they KILLED Him and released a murderer. The most educated men led this call for crucifixion. Why? <u>They had Education and Information, but no Revelation</u>.

We receive Revelation from God. There are many examples in the scriptures where people received teaching through revelation. When Jesus asked His disciples who did they think He was, only **Peter** responded, "You are the Christ, the Anointed One." Jesus told him, *"Flesh and blood did not **REVEAL** this to you, but my Father which is in Heaven."* When Nebuchadnezzar had a dream that he couldn't remember, it was **Daniel** who received revelation of the dream and the interpretation thereof. Daniel 2:19 tells us that "the mystery was **revealed** to Daniel in a vision of the night." In Genesis 41, **Joseph** revealed the meaning of the Pharaoh's dream concerning the 7 years of plenty and the 7 lean years.

My friend who had the timber business told me that – years later – he got a revelation about himself. He realized that he had been (and currently was) a poor manager: "Instead of staying on top of things, I just expected everything to work out. I didn't manage the resources effectively." It was 4-5 years after he had the experience that he got this revelation. Upon receiving this enlightenment about himself, he began to study books on management, talk to successful people about their management strategies, and study management in the scriptures. Without this revelation about himself, he would have continued to manage poorly.

Revelation is powerful because it can give answers beyond your experiences. Revelation can give insight beyond the information that is known and unlock the realm of the unknown - the secret mysteries of this world.

The Power of Revelation

Revelation is Truth that is revealed. It was there all along in darkness, but a light has been shone on it – a veil has been lifted so that you now understand what you were not able to understand before. How old were you when you finally got the revelation of what parents, or older people, often told you as a child: "You don't know how good you got it?" I remember scoffing and thinking that they were silly. I was a child; I couldn't do what I wanted to do. I couldn't go where I wanted to go. I couldn't wait to grow up. But when I entered college life and beyond, life began to hit me with those three and four-letter words (DUE, JOB, TAX, BILL, RENT, KIDS, WIFE, PAY, NOW). I had a REVELATION!!! I understood what those old people meant: *I had no idea how good I had it.*

When the governor tasted the water that was made wine, he called the bridegroom and told him, *(paraphrasing)* "WOW!!! What…is…This? I've been drinking all this time, and you had this in the back? You have saved the best for last…I mean, this is some good wine." The same occurs when man is filled with the Word of God (seeks after, reads, listens to sermons, meditates to hear, etc.), and that Word is taken to the Governor (the Holy Spirit who resides in us). The Holy Spirit opens up our understanding and gives us Revelation. The Word of God ("water") is translated into teaching ("wine") so that we can understand and apply it to our daily lives.

This occurred many times in scriptures Let's look in Luke 18:31-34 …

31And taking the twelve, he said to them, "See, we are going up to Jerusalem, and everything that is written about the Son of Man by the prophets will be accomplished. 32For he will be delivered over to the Gentiles and will be mocked and shamefully treated and spit upon. 33And after flogging him, they will kill him, and on the third day he will rise." 34But they understood none of these things. This saying was hidden from them, and they did not grasp what was said.

The disciples were told plainly by Jesus what was to occur, but the disciples couldn't understand it. **The**

meaning was hidden from them. They tried to understand spiritual things with their natural minds and senses. They tried to make His words fit their perspective and understanding of kings and kingdoms. They were trying to see it the way they were accustomed to seeing natural kingdoms operate. They were also damaged because they had <u>information</u> that had been passed down through history by the spiritual leaders with no <u>revelation</u>. I'm sure they thought, "A king's objective is to gain as much power for himself." ... "No one raised themselves from death." ... "A king never died for his people; the people are sacrificed for the king." ... "Jesus is our Leader; surely we would not abandon him when he needs us the most." ... "Is he really the one that the prophets said would deliver us from the Romans?" They just couldn't understand the spiritual implications.

John 13:21-30 — **The Betrayal**

[21]After saying these things, Jesus was troubled in his spirit, and testified, "Truly, truly, I say to you, one of you will betray me." [22]<u>The disciples looked at one another, uncertain of whom he spoke.</u> [23]One of his disciples, whom Jesus loved, was reclining at the table at Jesus' side, [24]so Simon Peter motioned to him to ask Jesus of whom he was speaking. [25]So that disciple, leaning back against Jesus, said to him, "Lord, who is it?" [26]Jesus answered, <u>"It is he to whom I will give this morsel of bread when I have dipped it."</u> **So when he had dipped the morsel, he gave it to Judas, the son of Simon Iscariot.** *[27]Then after he had taken the morsel, Satan entered into him. Jesus said to him, "What you are going to do, do quickly."[28]<u>Now no one at the table knew why he said this to him.</u> [29]<u>Some thought</u>*

that, because Judas had the moneybag, Jesus was telling him, "Buy what we need for the feast," or that he should give something to the poor. ³⁰*So, after receiving the morsel of bread, he immediately went out. And it was night.*

Jesus told them plainly that He would be betrayed. He even gave them a clue of what He would do to signify which one of them was the culprit. However, without the Holy Spirit to give insight and revelation, they just rationalized it away: "Oh, Jesus must be sending Judas on an errand...but I still want to know which one of us is going to betray Him." We can see it plain and clear as day in hindsight, but they could not. It was hidden from their understanding for their benefit. If they realized what Judas was going to do, they likely would have stopped him, which would have interrupted God's plan of Jesus' sacrifice.

2 Kings 6:15-17 — **The Eyes of the Young Man**

¹⁵*When the servant of the man of God rose early in the morning and went out, behold, an army with horses and chariots was all around the city. And the servant said, "Alas, my master! What shall we do?"* ¹⁶*He said, "Do not be afraid, for those who are with us are more than those who are with them."* ¹⁷*Then Elisha prayed and said,* **"O Lord, please open his eyes that he may see."** *So the Lord opened the eyes of the young man, and he saw, and behold, the mountain was full of horses and chariots of fire all around Elisha.*

Here we have a snapshot into the life of the prophet Elisha. Syria and Israel were at war; however, Israel always seemed to be one step ahead of the Syrians because God was revealing the enemies plans to Elisha. When the King of Syria was informed that Elisha was the one who was giving Israel their plans, he decided to seize Elisha. Syria marched toward Dothan with an army and surrounded the city. The servant of Elisha was afraid. He saw the army, the horses and the chariots, but he didn't see what Elisha saw! He didn't have the Revelation! Elisha prayed for God to open his eyes and give him the revelation. When the Lord opened the young man's eyes, he could see what Elisha saw: an army of fire surrounding them.

When you have Revelation, no matter what the situation looks like or what circumstances stand before you, you're not afraid or worried. Revelation allows you to see beyond the situation.

Matthew 16:13-17 — **Thou Art the Christ**

*[13]Now when Jesus came into the district of Caesarea Philippi, he asked his disciples, "Who do people say that the Son of Man is?" [14]And they said, "Some say John the Baptist, others say Elijah, and others Jeremiah or one of the prophets." [15]He said to them, "But who do you say that I am?" [16]***Simon Peter replied, "You are the Christ, the Son of the living God."*** *[17]And Jesus answered him, "Blessed are you, Simon Bar-Jonah!* **For flesh and blood has not revealed this to you, but my Father who is in heaven.***"*

Jesus asked His disciples who did they think that He was. It's one thing to say who other people thought Jesus was, but they had walked with Him – they had seen Him do the miracles; however, only Peter had an answer: "You are the Christ. You are the one prophesied about in scriptures. You're the Messiah – The Savior." Jesus noted that no man or studying or research (flesh and blood) REVEALED this to Peter. This REVELATION was given to Peter from God.

There are certain mysteries and secrets about which only God can illuminate our understanding; otherwise, we'll be like the other disciples, only able to answer what we've heard others say and no true revelation of our own.

Matthew 16:21-23 — **Get Thee Behind Me, Satan**

²¹From that time Jesus began to show his disciples that he must go to Jerusalem and suffer many things from the elders and chief priests and scribes, and be killed, and on the third day be raised. ²²And Peter took him aside and began to rebuke him, saying, "Far be it from you, Lord! This shall never happen to you." ²³<u>But he turned and said to Peter, "Get behind me, Satan! You are a hindrance to me. For you are not setting your mind on the things of God, but on the things of man."</u>

Jesus once again tells of His death and the things that are going to happen, leading up to and including His death and resurrection. Peter rebukes Him; he didn't understand nor could he comprehend what Jesus was telling him. Peter assumed that he was being a loyal and good friend to Jesus by saying that he wouldn't allow these horrible things to happen; however, this was contrary to Jesus' purpose. Peter had good intention, but because his good intentions were not in alignment with God, Jesus viewed them as a hindrance.

Joseph and the King's Dream

In Genesis 41, the King of Egypt had recurring dreams. He consulted his wise men and magicians; however, no one was able to discern what the dream meant. The Chief Cupbearer mentioned that Joseph could perhaps help the king. When brought before Pharaoh and inquired of his ability to interpret the dream, …

[16]Joseph answered, "I cannot, Your Majesty, but God will give a favorable interpretation." (Genesis 41:16 - GNT)

He responds that God will give the interpretation or revelation of what the dream means. When told the dream, Joseph gives the interpretation that the dream is God revealing to Pharaoh that there would be 7 years of plenty and 7 years of famine in the land. He also presented Pharaoh with a proposal / plan, taking into account the Revelation teaching….

*33 Now therefore let Pharaoh select a discerning and wise man and set him over the land of Egypt. 34 Let Pharaoh proceed to appoint overseers over the land and take one-fifth of the produce of the land of Egypt during the seven plentiful years. 35 And let them gather all the food of these good years that are coming and store up grain under the authority of Pharaoh for food in the cities and let them keep it. 36 **That food shall be a reserve for the land against the seven years of famine that are to occur in the land of Egypt, so that the land may not perish through the famine.**[37]<u>This proposal pleased Pharaoh and all his servants.</u> [38]And Pharaoh said to his servants, "Can we find a man like this, in whom is the*

Spirit of God?" ³⁹*Then Pharaoh said to Joseph,* **"Since God has shown you all this, there is none so discerning and wise as you are.**

Even the Egyptians were able to see that Joseph had insight that others didn't have. They recognized that the "Spirit of God" was with Joseph and that "God had shown Joseph all this." This Revelation not only saved Joseph and all the people of Egypt, but Joseph was also able to save his family as well.

John 2:18-22 — **Destroy This Temple**

¹⁸*So the Jews said to him, "What sign do you show us for doing these things?"* ¹⁹*Jesus answered them,* **"Destroy this temple, and in three days I will raise it up."** ²⁰*The Jews then said, "It has taken forty-six years to build this temple, and will you raise it up in three days?"* ²¹*But he was speaking about the temple of his body.* ²²<u>*When therefore he was raised from the dead, his disciples remembered that he had said this, and they believed the Scripture and the word that Jesus had spoken*</u>.

When Jesus told the Jews that He was going to destroy the temple and raise it again in three days, He was speaking in terms of His death and resurrection. They assumed that He was talking about the temple building in which they worshipped. Jesus spoke to them plainly, but they couldn't comprehend what He was telling them. They had no Revelation teaching that He Himself (His body/temple) would be raised after their attempted destruction. However, after He was resurrected, His disciples remembered His words and got the revelation.

Daniel 2: 17-23 — **Daniel and the King's Dream**

In this story from the Book of Daniel, the only information provided is that King Nebuchadnezzar had a dream that he couldn't remember. He was so distraught that he was going to put all the wise men to death because no one could tell him **what he dreamed AND the interpretation**. Daniel gathered his friends and began to pray....

*[17]Then Daniel went to his house and made the matter known to Hananiah, Mishael, and Azariah, his companions, [18]and told them to seek mercy from the God of heaven concerning this mystery, so that Daniel and his companions might not be destroyed with the rest of the wise men of Babylon. [19]**Then the mystery was revealed to Daniel in a vision of the night.** Then Daniel blessed the God of heaven. [20]Daniel answered and said: "Blessed be the name of God forever and ever, to whom belong wisdom and might. [21]He changes times and seasons; he removes kings and sets up kings; **he gives wisdom to the wise and knowledge to those who have understanding;** [22]**he reveals deep and hidden things; he knows what is in the darkness, and the light dwells with him.** [23]To you, O God of my fathers, I give thanks and praise, for you have given me wisdom and might, **and have now made known to me what we asked of you, for you have made known to us the king's matter."***

The mystery was **REVEALED** to Daniel: both the King's dream and the interpretation. Daniel notes that God "reveals deep and hidden things" and leaves no doubt that it was God who "made known to us the king's matter." By getting this revelation from God, ALL the wise were saved from execution and the King's vision about the future was revealed.

Luke 24:13-16, 28-32 — The Unaware Disciples

[13]That very day two of them were going to a village named Emmaus, about seven miles from Jerusalem, [14]and they were talking with each other about all these things that had happened. [15]While they were talking and discussing together, Jesus himself drew near and went with them. ***[16]But their eyes were kept from recognizing him.***

[28]So they drew near to the village to which they were going. He acted as if he were going farther, [29]but they urged him strongly, saying, "Stay with us, for it is toward evening and the day is now far spent." So he went in to stay with them. [30]When he was at table with them, he took the bread and blessed and broke it and gave it to them. ***[31]And their eyes were opened, and they recognized him.*** *And he vanished from their sight. [32]They said to each other, "Did not our hearts burn within us while he talked to us on the road, while he opened to us the Scriptures?"*

After His resurrection, Jesus appeared to two of disciples AND THEY DIDN'T RECOGNIZE HIM. They didn't have a Revelation of who Jesus was. They knew about Him, as evidenced in their conversation ("prophet mighty in deed and word before God" ... "condemned to death, and crucified" ... "we hoped he was the one to redeem Israel"), but they didn't even know who they were talking to. Jesus proceeded to give them Revelation of the scriptures - and He interpreted for them, from all the scriptures beginning with Moses and the prophets, the things concerning Himself. Their hearts – their subconscious mind – recognized Him: "Did our hearts not burn within us." But it was only when He broke the bread ("bread" is a symbol for Revelation teaching) that their eyes were opened.

Later in Luke 24, this account is given…

*[44]Then he said to them, "These are my words that I spoke to you while I was still with you, that everything written about me in the Law of Moses and the Prophets and the Psalms must be fulfilled." [45]***Then he opened their minds to understand the Scriptures,*** [46]and said to them, "Thus it is written, that the Christ should suffer and on the third day rise from the dead, [47]and that repentance and forgiveness of sins should be proclaimed in his name to all nations, beginning from Jerusalem. [48]You are witnesses of these things. [49]And behold, I am sending the promise of my Father upon you. But stay in the city until you are clothed with power from on high."*

You see… Jesus constantly gave His disciples the Word of God – filled them with it because they wanted to know (a desire by default of true discipleship). After being filled with the Word, the scripture says that He "opened their minds to understand the Scriptures." He shined a light on something they thought they understood. He gave them understanding of scriptures they probably had heard from their youth. They were finally being taught what the scriptures actually meant.

Before His ascension, He told them that He was "sending the promise of my Father". This promise is the Holy Spirit. The Holy Spirit would operate in the same capacity that Jesus had just done – "open their understanding of the scriptures and spiritual matters." The Holy Spirit accomplishes this feat by teaching us, bringing things to our remembrance and interceding on our behalf. Once this is done, we can then perform and function with the Holy Spirit, like Jesus Christ performed and functioned with Him.

The Deep Things of God

There are mysteries, secrets, and revelations that you will be able to grasp and understand from reading the Bible and other books, or hearing sermons, or going to bible study. However, there are certain mysteries, certain secrets, and certain revelations that God has hidden from your understanding. It is the Holy Spirit that uncovers these truths and allows us to understand what God is thinking. In 1 Corinthians, Paul teaches about how the Holy Spirit connects us to the very mind of God.

9But as it is written, Eye hath not seen, nor ear heard, neither have entered into the heart of man, the things which God hath prepared for them that love him. **10But God hath revealed them unto us by his Spirit: for the Spirit searcheth all things, yea, the deep things of God.** *11For what man knoweth the things of a man, save the spirit of man which is in him? even so the things of God knoweth no man, but the Spirit of God. 12Now we have received, not the spirit of the world, but the spirit which is of God; that* *we might know the things that are freely given to us of God.* ¹³***Which things also we speak, not in the words which man's wisdom teacheth, but which the Holy Ghost teacheth;*** *comparing spiritual things with spiritual.* ¹⁴*But the natural man receiveth not the things of the Spirit of God: for they are foolishness unto him: neither can he know them, because they are spiritually discerned.*

Paul makes the correlation that no one truly understands a man's thoughts ("the deep things") except the spirit of that man. Unfortunately, many of us aren't aware of ourselves because we've become so inundated with outside influences and stimuli. This is why we can be insightful about other people, but when it comes to ourselves, we can seem clueless. Because we aren't the most self-aware, psychiatrists probe and question diligently: "What do you think about this?" ... "How did that make you feel?" ... "When did you first remember thinking that?" – They are trying to get you to articulate YOURSELF to YOURSELF. No one is around you more than you. No one talks to you more than you. No one understands you better than you. No one knows you better than you...even though you may not realize it.

It's the same way with God. No one knows and understands God better than God. So, if I want to know His mind, His thoughts, I have to get it from Him...or better yet from His Holy Spirit, who can teach me all about our Father and reveal all things spiritual. The more teaching and revelation that I understand, the more accurately I can apply it to my life.

When there is revelation, the miraculous is possible. When people got the revelation of who Jesus really was, they received healing, salvation, etc. When Joseph got the revelation of Pharaoh's dream, he was able to formulate a plan to save all of Egypt and Israel from the famine. When Noah got the revelation that a flood was coming, he trusted God and built an ark.

When you get a revelation of what God has placed on the inside of you, you will experience the miraculous. No more depression because you will have come to the realization that you're awesome. No more despair about money problems because you realize that God has equipped you with the power to obtain wealth. No more worrying about sickness and disease because you have the revelation that "by HIS stripes we are healed." No more pity parties about where you started in life because with God all things are possible. No more caring what other people think about you because you realize that you are fearfully and wonderfully made.

You want a miracle? God is telling us, "First, get a revelation from Me…Learn of Me…Let Me Teach you what to do – and you will be equipped to manifest the miraculous!!"

Let's Be Honest - Self Evaluation:

1. Have you ever gotten a revelation about yourself? How did it impact your perception and plans?

2. Which has the greatest influence in your life: Experimentation, Information, Revelation? Rate each in percentage form.

3. Do you seek God for Revelation? Or do you seek the "things," "possessions," "riches" that you can get from Him?

4. Do you think like God? Or do you think that God is unfair, unloving, cold, cruel, etc.?

CHAPTER 6: TEACHING AND MIRACLES

"Take the first step, and your mind will mobilize all its forces to your aid. But the first essential is that you begin. Once the battle is started, all that is within and without you will come to your assistance." – Robert Collier

In nearly everything you can think of, there are essentials involved. In recipes, there are **essential ingredients**. In medicine, there are **vital signs**. In contracts, there are **essential details** that make it a binding agreement. In certain types of art, there are **characteristic markings and styles** that differentiate priceless works of art from cheap imitations. In science/physics, there are **essential elements, essential properties**, etc.

You can't make a very effective cake without eggs (or egg substitute). When building a home, it is folly not to pour a foundation first. Before a pilot flies a plane, it is essential that a course and destination are plotted and that there is enough fuel to get to the planned destination. I'm not saying that these are the only important or valuable elements in the various examples, but I do realize that they are **essential**. How do I know this? Because every single cake recipe I've seen involves eggs. Every blueprint for a stationary home involves digging and pouring a foundation before building. Before leaving the ground, every plane's protocol involves plotting a course and making sure there is enough fuel and certain maintenance protocols are performed.

The fact that an ingredient, entity, or component is consistently involved almost every time with something makes it essential. Some cakes involve certain spices/ingredients—vanilla flavoring, for example. However, not every cake requires vanilla flavoring...not every home requires brick...not every flight requires a plain-clothed Air Marshal on board for protection. They may be needed sometimes, but not as consistently as the essential ingredients.

(Of course, there are exceptions to the rule. Mobile homes or "tiny" homes don't require foundations being poured. For people that are allergic to eggs, egg substitutes are utilized. I'm sure that under emergency situations, planes have landed at different destinations than planned when they initially departed. But these are exceptions, not the norm.)

The same goes for teaching and the miraculous. While studying the scriptures, I've noticed a pattern that nearly every miracle is associated with some type of teaching, revelation, understanding, acquisition of knowledge or information. As a disclaimer, this chapter will be heavily inundated with scripture because I want to highlight the pattern and correlation between teaching and the miraculous. Let's begin our study...

PART I – NEW TESTAMENT MIRACLES AND TEACHINGS

*(***Moving forward in this chapter, the **Bolded** in the following scriptures is to highlight the teaching component, while the <u>Underlined</u> is to highlight the associated miracle component. ***)*

Matthew 4:23-24 — **Healing All Manner of Sickness and Disease**

*²³And Jesus went about all Galilee, **teaching in their synagogues**, and **preaching the gospel of the kingdom**, and <u>healing all manner of sickness and all manner of disease among the people</u>. ²⁴And his fame went throughout all Syria: and they brought unto him all sick people that were taken with divers diseases and torments, and those which were possessed with devils, and those which were lunatick, and those that had the palsy; and <u>he healed them</u>.*

Matthew 8:1-3 — **Healing Leprosy**

Chapters 5, 6, 7 of Matthew involved ***specific teachings** (**Beatitudes, Priority of the Kingdom, Adultery, Forgiveness, How to pray**, etc.).* Then in Matthew 8:1-3, we see…

When he was come down from the mountain, great multitudes followed him. ²And, behold, there came a leper and worshipped him, saying, Lord, if thou wilt, thou canst make me clean. ³And Jesus put forth his hand, and touched *him, saying, I will; be thou clean. And <u>immediately his leprosy was cleansed</u>.*

Matthew 9:35 — Healing Every Sickness and Disease

*And Jesus went about all the cities and villages, **teaching in their synagogues**, and **preaching the gospel of the kingdom**, and <u>healing every sickness and every disease among the people</u>.*

Matthew 14:35-36 — Touching the Hem of His Garment

*35 And when the men of that place had **knowledge of him**, they sent out into all that country round about, and brought unto him all that were diseased; 36 And **besought him that they might only touch the hem of his garment**: and <u>as many as touched were made perfectly whole</u>.*

These men obviously recognized who Jesus was along with His teachings and miraculous power (thus, the phrase they "had knowledge of him"). It also seems as if they had some knowledge of Malachi 4:2 - *"But for you who fear my name, the sun of righteousness **shall rise with healing in its <u>wings</u>.** You shall go out leaping like calves from the stall."* The Hebrew translation for *wings* in this scripture means <u>border, edge of garment,</u> **HEM**!!!

Perhaps, they learned or had heard this teaching found in Malachi that healing was in the wings or hem of His garment. They had faith that by touching the border of his garment, that they could be healed. Jesus didn't have to lay hands on them, say a word of prayer, or do anything that the customary rituals of healing warranted. They learned to tap into the miraculous in an entirely different way. And they were all made whole.

Matthew 19:1-2 — **Healing**

*And it came to pass, that when Jesus had **finished these sayings**, he departed from Galilee, and came into the coasts of Judaea beyond Jordan;* ²*And great multitudes followed him; and <u>he healed them there</u>.*

The "sayings" that Jesus finished were in reference to the teachings in Matthew 18 (***Who is the Greatest, Temptations to Sin, Parable of Lost Sheep, Brother Sins Against You, Parable of Unforgiving Servant***). After the teachings, he performed miracles.

Mark 1:39-42 — **Casting Out Demons / Healing Leprosy**

³⁹*And he **preached in their synagogues throughout all Galilee**, and <u>cast out devils</u>.* ⁴⁰*And <u>there came a leper to him</u>, beseeching him, and kneeling down to him, and saying unto him, If thou wilt, thou canst make me clean.* ⁴¹*And Jesus, moved with compassion, <u>put forth his hand, and touched him, and saith unto him, I will; be thou clean</u>.* ⁴²*And as soon as he had spoken, <u>immediately the leprosy departed from him, and he was cleansed</u>.*

Mark 6:12-13, 30 — **Disciples Sent Out Two by Two**

*₁₂And they went out, and **preached that men should repent**. ₁₃And <u>they cast out many devils, and anointed with oil many that were sick, and healed them.</u>*

*₃₀And the apostles gathered themselves together unto Jesus, and told him all things, <u>both what they had done</u>, and what **they had taught**.*

Allow me to provide some context for these scriptures. This was when Jesus sent His disciples out two by two and gave them "power over unclean spirits." The disciples utilized the same formula that Jesus employed: teaching the people that they encountered, followed by miracles, signs, and wonders. Notice, upon their return from their assignment in verse 30, they not only told Jesus the miracles that they performed, but they also told Him the principles they had taught.

Mark 6:4, 35-44 — **Feeding Five Thousand**

*₄And Jesus, when he came out, saw much people, and was moved with compassion toward them, because they were as sheep not having a shepherd: and **he began to teach them many things**.*

*₃₅And when the day was now far spent, his disciples came unto him, and said, This is a desert place, and now the time is far passed: ₃₆Send them away, that they may go into the country round about, and into the villages, and buy themselves bread: for they have nothing to eat. ₃₇He answered and said unto them, <u>**Give ye them to eat**</u>. And* *they say unto him, Shall we go and buy two hundred pennyworth of bread, and give them to eat?* [38]*He saith unto them, How many loaves have ye? go and see. And when they knew, they say, Five, and two fishes.* [39]**And he commanded them to make all sit down by companies upon the green grass.** [40]*And they sat down in ranks, by hundreds, and by fifties.* [41]*And when he had taken the five loaves and the two fishes, he looked up to heaven, and blessed, and brake the loaves, and gave them to his disciples to set before them; and <u>the two fishes divided he among them all.</u>* [42]<u>*And they did all eat, and were filled.*</u> [43]<u>*And they took up twelve baskets full of the fragments, and of the fishes.*</u> [44]<u>*And they that did eat of the loaves were about five thousand men.*</u>

Luke 4:31-36 (Mark 1:21-27) — Casting Out Unclean Spirit

[31]*And came down to Capernaum, a city of Galilee, and* **taught them on the sabbath days**. [32]*And they were astonished at his* **doctrine: for his word was with power.** [33]*And in the synagogue there was <u>a man, which had a spirit of an unclean devil</u>, and cried out with a loud voice,* [34]*Saying, Let us alone; what have we to do with thee, thou Jesus of Nazareth? art thou come to destroy us? I know thee who thou art; the Holy One of God.* [35]*And Jesus rebuked him, saying, Hold thy peace, and <u>come out of him. And when the devil had thrown him in the midst, he came out of him, and hurt him not.</u>* [36]*And they were all amazed, and spake among themselves, saying,* **What a word is this! for with authority and power he commandeth the unclean spirits, and they come out.**

Luke 6:7, 18-19 — Healing of Unclean Spirits

*⁷And he came down with them, and stood in the plain, and the company of his disciples, and a great multitude of people out of all Judaea and Jerusalem, and from the sea coast of Tyre and Sidon, which **came to hear him**, and <u>to be healed of their diseases</u>;*

¹⁸<u>And they that were vexed with unclean spirits: and they were healed.</u> ¹⁹And the whole multitude sought to touch him: for there went virtue out of him, <u>and healed them all</u>.

Luke records that the people came to hear him. Hear him do what? **Hear him teach.** Once again, we see the teachings are in conjunction with the miraculous - healing from diseases and unclean spirits; all that came were healed.

Luke 9:11 — Healing

*And the people, when they knew it, followed him: and he received them, and **spake unto them of the kingdom of God**, and <u>healed them that had need of healing</u>.*

Luke 13:10-13 — Spirit of Infirmity

*¹⁰And he was **teaching in one of the synagogues** on the sabbath. ¹¹And, behold, there was a woman which had <u>a spirit of infirmity eighteen years, and was bowed together, and could in no wise lift up herself.</u> ¹²And when Jesus saw her, he called her to him, and said unto her, Woman, thou art loosed from thine infirmity. ¹³And he laid his hands on* her: and <u>immediately she was made straight</u>, and glorified God.

Acts 2:42-44 — **Fellowship of the Believers**

*[42]And they devoted themselves to the **apostles' teaching** and the fellowship, to the breaking of bread and the prayers. [43]And awe came upon every soul, <u>and many wonders and signs were being done through the apostles</u>. [44]And all who believed were together and had all things in common.*

Acts 3:1-8 — **Lame Beggar Healed**

*Now Peter and John were going up to the temple at the hour of prayer, the ninth hour. [2]**And a man lame from birth was being carried, whom they laid daily at the gate of the temple that is called the Beautiful Gate to ask alms of those entering the temple.** [3]Seeing Peter and John about to go into the temple, he asked to receive alms. [4]And Peter directed his gaze at him, as did John, and said, "Look at us." [5]And he fixed his attention on them, expecting to receive something from them. [6]**But Peter said, "I have no silver and gold, but what I do have I give to you. In the name of Jesus Christ of Nazareth, rise up and walk!"** [7]<u>And he took him by the right hand and raised him up, and immediately his feet and ankles were made strong.</u> [8]And leaping up, he stood and began to walk, and entered the temple with them, walking and leaping and praising God.*

Of course, the miracle aspect is obvious: the man who was lame rose up and began to walk – that is amazing. The teaching aspect may not be as obvious. Peter and John were disciples of Jesus; they were with Jesus when he healed a man who was lame at the pool of Bethesda (*John 5:8-9*). It was even under similar circumstances: The man at the pool of Bethesda was in a place where an angel "stirred" the water for Healing – The man at the Beautiful Gate was at the Temple: the place of TEACHING! They were so close to places where miracles were known to occur, but their miracle and breakthrough seemed so far away. The healing of the lame beggar demonstrates a successful process of teaching: The disciples, who were once students, are putting into practice the lessons from their Master.

Acts 4:32-35 — **All Needs Were Met**

*[32]Now the full number of those who believed were of one heart and soul, and no one said that any of the things that belonged to him was his own, but they had everything in common. [33]And with **great power the apostles were giving their testimony to the resurrection of the Lord Jesus**, and great grace was upon them all. [34]There was not a needy person among them, for as many as were owners of lands or houses sold them and brought the proceeds of what was sold [35]and laid it at the apostles' feet, and it was distributed to each as any had need.*

Acts 5:12-16 — **Miracles, Signs, Wonders**

*[12]Now many signs and wonders were regularly done among the people by the hands of the apostles. And they were all together in **Solomon's Portico**. [13]None of the rest*

dared join them, but the people held them in high esteem. *[14]And <u>more than ever believers were added to the Lord, multitudes of both men and women</u>, [15]so that they even carried out the sick into the streets and laid them on cots and mats, that as Peter came by at least his shadow might fall on some of them. [16]The people also gathered from the towns around Jerusalem, bringing the sick and those afflicted with unclean spirits, <u>and they were all healed</u>.*

A portico is a porch with a roof and columns leading into the entrance of a building. This particular porch was named after King Solomon and was an entrance to the Temple. This area, a gathering place for the early church, was where teaching took place regularly and miracles were performed.

Acts 5:17-21 — **Freed from Jail**

[17]But the high priest rose up, and all who were with him (that is, the party of the Sadducees), and filled with jealousy [18]they arrested the apostles and put them in the public prison. [19]<u>But during the night an angel of the Lord opened the prison doors and brought them out</u>, and said, **[20]"Go and stand in the temple and speak to the people all the words of this Life."** *[21]And when they heard this,* **they entered the temple at daybreak and began to teach***.*

Here we see the correlation once again…The apostles were put in jail for Teaching the Word of God. The miracle came when an angel of the Lord opened the prison doors and freed them. The angel then instructed them to go out and continue doing what got them put in jail in the first place: TEACH.

Acts 8:12-13 — Simon the Magician Believes

¹²*But when they believed Philip **as he preached good news about the kingdom of God and the name of Jesus Christ**, they were baptized, both men and women.* ¹³*Even Simon himself believed, and after being baptized he continued with Philip.* <u>*And seeing signs and great miracles performed*</u>*, he was amazed.*

Acts 9:32-35 — Healing of Aeneas

³²*Now **as Peter went here and there among them all**, he came down also to the saints who lived at Lydda.* ³³*There he found a man named Aeneas, bedridden for eight years, who was paralyzed.* ³⁴*And Peter said to him, "**Aeneas, Jesus Christ heals you; rise and make your bed.**"* <u>*And immediately he rose*</u>*.* ³⁵*And all the residents of Lydda and Sharon saw him, and* <u>*they turned to the Lord*</u>*.*

Acts 9:36-41 — Resurrection of Tabitha

³⁶*Now there was in Joppa **a disciple named Tabitha**, which, translated, means Dorcas. She was full of good works and acts of charity.* ³⁷*In those days she became ill and died, and when they had washed her, they laid her in an upper room.* ³⁸*Since Lydda was near Joppa, **the disciples, hearing that Peter was there, sent two men to him, urging him, "Please come to us without delay."*** ³⁹*So Peter rose and went with them. And when he arrived, they took him to the upper room. All the widows stood beside him weeping and showing tunics and other garments that Dorcas made while she was with them.* ⁴⁰***But Peter put them all outside, and knelt down and prayed; and***

turning to the body he said, "Tabitha, arise." <u>*And she opened her eyes, and when she saw Peter she sat up.*</u> *⁴¹And he gave her his hand and raised her up. Then, calling the saints and widows,* <u>*he presented her alive*</u>*.*

I highlighted the portion of the text that noted that Tabitha was a <u>disciple</u> and that the <u>disciples</u> called on Peter because disciple means "student" denoting some level of teaching. But the direct element of teaching in association with the miracle is found in Peter's actions. Peter puts everyone out of the room, prays for and commands the healing and resurrection of Tabitha. This is a direct reflection of the method that Jesus used when healing Jarius's daughter in Matthew 9:24-25. Peter learned the lesson so well, that he was able to put it into practice. This is the culmination of teaching.

Acts 14:1-3 — **Signs and Wonders**

Now at Iconium **they entered together into the Jewish synagogue and spoke in such a way that a great number of both Jews and Greeks believed**. *²But the unbelieving Jews stirred up the Gentiles and poisoned their minds against the brothers.* ³**So they remained for a long time, speaking boldly for the Lord**, *who bore witness to the word of his grace,* <u>*granting signs and wonders to be done by their hands*</u>.

Acts 14:8-10 — **Healing of Crippled Man**

*⁸Now at Lystra there was a man sitting who could not use his feet. He was crippled from birth and had never walked. ⁹***He listened to Paul speaking.** *And Paul, looking intently* at him and <u>seeing that he had faith to be made well,</u> [10]*said in a loud voice, "Stand upright on your feet."* <u>And he sprang up and began walking.</u>

Acts 16:25-28, 35 — Paul and Silas Delivered from Prison

[25]**About midnight Paul and Silas were praying and singing hymns to God, and the prisoners were listening to them,** [26]and <u>suddenly there was a great earthquake, so that the foundations of the prison were shaken. And immediately all the doors were opened, and everyone's bonds were unfastened.</u> [27]*When the jailer woke and saw that the prison doors were open, he drew his sword and was about to kill himself, supposing that the prisoners had escaped.* [28]*But Paul cried with a loud voice, "Do not harm yourself, for we are all here."*

[35]<u>But when it was day, the magistrates sent the police, saying, "Let those men go."</u>

Acts 13:5-12 – Blindness of False Prophet

[5]*When they arrived at Salamis,* **they proclaimed the word of God in the synagogues of the Jews**. *And they had John to assist them.* [6]*When they had gone through the whole island as far as Paphos, they came upon a certain magician, a Jewish false prophet named Bar-Jesus.* [7]*He was with the proconsul, Sergius Paulus, a man of intelligence, who summoned Barnabas and Saul and* **sought to hear the word of God**. [8]*But Elymas the magician (for that is the meaning of his name) opposed them, seeking to turn the proconsul away from the faith.* [9]*But*

Saul, who was also called Paul, filled with the Holy Spirit, looked intently at him [10]*and said, "You son of the devil, you enemy of all righteousness, full of all deceit and villainy, will you not stop making crooked the straight paths of the Lord?* [11]***And now, behold, the hand of the Lord is upon you, and you will be blind and unable to see the sun for a time."** Immediately mist and darkness fell upon him, and he went about seeking people to lead him by the hand.* [12]*Then the proconsul believed, when he saw what had occurred, **for he was astonished at the teaching of the Lord.***

Here we see Paul and Barnabas teaching the Word of God. They had been going around the entire island, enlightening the people about the Kingdom of God. The proconsul (Serius Paulus) wanted to hear their teachings. This was a big deal. The proconsul was an official with great influence and authority in ancient Rome. This could have been Paul's chance to get the Kingdom teachings to one of the most influential places in the world: the Roman Empire. They were opposed by Elymas, "a magician...a false prophet." The false prophet didn't want the proconsul to believe the teachings of God. Paul calls him the "son of the devil". Elymas was implementing the same strategies and tactics of the Adversary: keeping people ignorant. (Either he doesn't want you to hear the teachings, or he attacks your faith in the teachings.)

Paul, however, wouldn't allow it to be so; he operated in the miraculous power and spiritual authority and bestowed blindness on this instigator. Usually the miracle was restoring sight; this time it was necessary to remove sight. Upon hearing the teachings and seeing this demonstration of power, the proconsul believed. The Bible says, "**for he was astonished at the teachings of the Lord**"!

PART II – OLD TESTAMENT MIRACLES AND TEACHINGS

I know what you're thinking: "Well, those were all New Testament examples…Maybe "teaching and miracles" was just a New Testament phenomenon or that was just the miracles associated with Jesus and the Apostles!" And you're right…those were only New Testament scriptures. However, even in the Old Testament, the same concept is present: Teaching was synonymous with the miraculous. Let's look at a few examples…

Noah and the Ark

In Genesis, God had decided that due to man's wickedness and evil heart that the earth should be cleansed. He was preparing to destroy mankind and found only one righteous man on the earth: Noah. When God spoke to Noah, He gave him some teachings to survive the coming destruction.

Genesis 6:14-16

[14]Make yourself an ark of gopher wood. Make rooms in the ark, and cover it inside and out with pitch. [15]This is

how you are to make it: the length of the ark 300 cubits, its breadth 50 cubits, and its height 30 cubits. ¹⁶Make a roof for the ark, and finish it to a cubit above, and set the door of the ark in its side. Make it with lower, second, and third decks.

Before Noah even built an Ark, he was given specific teachings, instructions, dimensions by God concerning the construction. He was given particular orders and intricate details on what to do with the animals. Because Noah followed these teachings, he and his family experienced the miracle of being saved from the destruction of the great flood.

Moses

We all know the great miracles God performed through His servant Moses – the Burning Bush, turning the staff into a snake, the leprous hand, the 10 plagues on the Egyptians, the parting of the Red Sea, manna from Heaven, providing water by striking a rock, etc. However, most people miss the element of Teaching that continually took place in the life of Moses. Moses was hesitant to even accept his calling and purpose due to his perceived issue with speaking. God then told Moses in Exodus 4…

*¹¹Then the Lord said to him, "Who has made man's mouth? Who makes him mute, or deaf, or seeing, or blind? Is it not I, the Lord? ¹²Now therefore go, and **I will be with your mouth and teach you what you shall speak.**" ¹³But he said, "Oh, my Lord, please send someone else."*

Before Moses performed even one miracle, God told Moses that He would TEACH him what to speak. Moses even went on to receive the first written TEACHINGS (The Ten Commandments) from God so that the people could live in a covenant relationship with Him. The end of the Book of Exodus and the entire books of Leviticus and Numbers are commandments, teachings, instructions on how the people of God were to live with one another and how to come before God, thus placing them in a position to experience the miraculous.

Entering the Promised Land

After Israel had spent years wandering around in the Wilderness, God was finally preparing Israel to enter into the Promised Land. In order to take possession of this land, they had to go to war with other nations. However, God would fight their battles for them. Before they set out to enter the Promised Land, God gave them teachings, commandments, instructions.

Deuteronomy 4: 1-2

*"And now, O Israel, **listen to the statutes and the rules that I am teaching you**, and do them, that you may live, and go in and take possession of the land that the Lord, the God of your fathers, is giving you. ²You shall not add to the word that I command you, nor take from it, that you may keep the commandments of the Lord your God that I command you."*

Deuteronomy 11:8-9

*8"You shall therefore **keep the whole commandment that I command you today**, that you may be strong, and go in and take possession of the land that you are going over to possess, 9and that you may live long in the land that the Lord swore to your fathers to give to them and to their offspring, a land flowing with milk and honey.*

Joshua 1:6-8

*6Be strong and courageous, for you shall cause this people to inherit the land that I swore to their fathers to give them. 7Only be strong and very courageous, **being careful to do according to all the law that Moses my servant commanded you. Do not turn from it to the right hand or to the left**, that you may have good success wherever you go. 8This Book of the Law shall not depart from your mouth, but you shall meditate on it day and night, so that you may be careful to do according to all that is written in it. For then you will make your way prosperous, and then you will have good success.*

    Before they took one foot to experience the miraculous wonders that God was going to do, they received teachings / laws / commandments that they were to keep first and foremost. Even in battles with Jericho and Ai, God gave them specific instructions to follow. He tells them directly that if they kept the teachings... success, prosperity, and good things would follow.

Naomi & Ruth

In the book of Ruth, Naomi's two sons and her husband all died in Moab. Ruth returns with her mother-in-law, Naomi, back to Israel. Things had become so bad that in order to get food, Ruth had to glean the fields (collect leftover crops after the fields had been harvested). They needed a miracle. Boaz, a wealthy ruler, had favor on Ruth. **Ruth received teaching/instructions about her relationship with Boaz from Naomi.** In Ruth 2:22, Naomi encourages Ruth to go out with Boaz's young women and to continue gleaning from his field. In Ruth 3:1-4, Naomi instructs Ruth to "wash and anoint herself...observe where he lies...uncover his feet and lie beside him...and he will tell you what to do". These relationship teachings eventually led not only to their marriage, but the redeeming of Naomi's land, wealth, and the birth of a son (Obed)...who was the grandfather of the future king of Israel, David.

David & Goliath

In the book of 1 Samuel, David was a shepherd boy who was anointed King of Israel. Israel was at war with the Philistines and their champion: a giant named Goliath. David just happened to be at Israel's camp when he overheard the insults and challenges that were being hurled at the people of God. David told Saul that he would take the challenge and kill the "uncircumcised Philistine" – a Shepherd Boy vs a Giant Warrior: David needed a miracle.

Saul gave David every logical reason not to challenge Goliath: he was too small ... he wasn't a warrior ... this was a mismatch ... Goliath had been a warrior his entire life. Let's study David's response in 1 Samuel 17: 34-37...

*³⁴But David said to Saul, "Your servant used to keep sheep for his father. And when there came a lion, or a bear, and took a lamb from the flock, ³⁵I went after him and struck him and delivered it out of his mouth. And if he arose against me, I caught him by his beard and struck him and killed him. ³⁶Your servant has struck down both lions and bears, and this uncircumcised Philistine shall be like one of them, for he has defied the armies of the living God." ³⁷And David said, "**The Lord who delivered me from the paw of the lion and from the paw of the bear will deliver me from the hand of this Philistine.**" And Saul said to David, "Go, and the Lord be with you!"*

David responded to the doubt and naysayers with his experience as a shepherd. He essentially told them of the teachings and lessons he had learned ABOUT GOD from fighting the lion and the bear while protecting his father's sheep. David was confident in what he had learned in those experiences, and he had no doubt that the same lessons would apply to his battle with Goliath. We all know the story.... David used a sling and a smooth stone and defeated Goliath. He cut off the giant's head and was well on his way to becoming King.

What giants are you facing in your life? What situation or circumstance are you facing that everyone is telling you that you can't win – that you can't be successful? What lessons, teachings, experiences can you use to overcome these obstacles?]

The Three Hebrew Boys and the Fiery Furnace

In the Book of Daniel Chapter 3, we see the Three Hebrew Boys facing a dire challenge. A statue was set up by King Nebuchadnezzar, and a decree was made. The decree stated that when certain music was played, everyone was to bow and worship the golden statue. Whoever did not worship the statue was to be sentenced to death in the fiery furnace. Shadrach, Meshach, and Abednego did not bow to the golden image when the music began. The King was informed of their reluctance to comply with the decree - and they were sentenced to death. This was their reply to the king:

[16]*Shadrach, Meshach, and Abednego answered and said to the king, "O Nebuchadnezzar, we have no need to answer you in this matter.* [17]***If this be so, our God whom we serve is able to deliver us from the burning fiery furnace, and he will deliver us out of your hand, O king.*** [18]*But if not, be it known to you, O king, that we will not serve your gods or worship the golden image that you have set up."*

These 3 young men believed in the teaching that "God is able to deliver" ...even from a burning fiery furnace. They believed it with such conviction - even in the face of certain death. These men would not serve any gods other than the One True God, even if it would have saved their lives. They wouldn't compromise. Of course, most know how the story goes. The king demanded that the fire be 7 times hotter than usual. The Hebrew boys were bound and placed in the fiery furnace. The furnace was so hot that even the men who tied them up and placed them in the furnace died. After a time, the king looked in the furnace to see the Hebrew boys unbound and walking with another person — "one who looked like the Son of God." They were delivered from the furnace without burns or the smell of smoke.

[Do you trust God to deliver you in pressure situations? Or will you succumb to the pressure and compromise what you profess to believe?]

Healing of Miriam

Aaron and Miriam began to talk about Moses behind his back. They were upset, jealous, frustrated that Moses married a Cushite woman; however, their gossip manifested in the form of calling into question Moses's role as God's anointed vessel: *(paraphrasing)* "Is Moses the only one God speaks to? He spoke to me just last week. Moses ain't that special." This infuriated God. He called Miriam, Aaron, and Moses down for a conference meeting.

Numbers 12: 8-15
[8]Why then were you not afraid to speak against my servant Moses?" [9]And the anger of the Lord was kindled against them, and he departed. [10]When the cloud removed from over the tent, behold, Miriam was leprous, like snow. And Aaron turned toward Miriam, and behold, she was leprous. [11]And Aaron said to Moses, "Oh, my lord, do not punish us because we have done foolishly and have sinned. [12]Let her not be as one dead, whose flesh is half eaten away

*when he comes out of his mother's womb." ¹³And Moses cried to the Lord, "**O God, please heal her—please**." ¹⁴But the Lord said to Moses, "If her father had but spit in her face, should she not be shamed seven days? <u>Let her be shut outside the camp seven days, and after that she may be brought in again</u>." ¹⁵So Miriam was shut outside the camp seven days, and the people did not set out on the march till Miriam was brought in again.*

Moses prayed for Miriam's healing. "O God, please heal her." God didn't respond with an immediate miracle but rather with instructions/teachings: "Put her out of the camp for seven days." They put her out of the camp and Miriam received healing. If Miriam wasn't put out of the camp or if she refused to leave, I believe she would have died of leprosy.

[Perhaps, this is how God responds to us. We ask for a miracle and get instructions/teachings/information. If we don't act on the information, the miracle lies dormant.]

Teaching is correlated with the miraculous. However, it is in the disobedience to teaching and instructions that we often forfeit our miracles.

Lot's Wife

In this example, the angels had to make Lot leave Sodom and Gomorrah before the destruction. Upon leaving, Lot and his family were given specific instructions: "DO NOT LOOK BACK…Don't stop anywhere in the valley…""

Genesis 19:15-17; 23-26

*15As morning dawned, the angels urged Lot, saying, "Up! Take your wife and your two daughters who are here, lest you be swept away in the punishment of the city." 16But he lingered. So the men seized him and his wife and his two daughters by the hand, the Lord being merciful to him, and they brought him out and set him outside the city. 17And as they brought them out, one said, "**Escape for your life. Do not look back or stop anywhere in the valley. Escape to the hills, lest you be swept away.**"*

*23The sun had risen on the earth when Lot came to Zoar. 24Then <u>the Lord rained on Sodom and Gomorrah sulfur and fire from the Lord out of heaven.</u> 25And he overthrew those cities, and all the valley, and all the inhabitants of the cities, and what grew on the ground. 26<u>**But Lot's wife, behind him, looked back, and she became a pillar of salt.**</u>*

Because Lot's wife didn't follow the instructions of the Angels on how to leave Sodom and Gomorrah, she forfeited the miracle of escape. She became a pillar of salt. Perhaps, she saw the Lord Himself bringing destruction, and like He told Moses, "No one can see my face and live." Whatever the reason…her disobedience to the instructions was her downfall.

Samson

Most know about the exploits of Samson. How in Judges 14, he tore a lion with his bare hands or how he struck down 30 men and took their spoils. In Judges 15, Samson caught 300 foxes and with torches set fire to the

Philistines grain and olive orchards. He also killed 1000 Philistines with just the jawbone of a donkey. But before any of these miraculous deeds were performed, an angel came and gave his parents specific teachings concerning the child...

Judges 13:2-5 – Samson's Birth Foretold
*²There was a certain man of Zorah, of the tribe of the Danites, whose name was Manoah. And his wife was barren and had no children. ³And the angel of the Lord appeared to the woman and said to her, "Behold, you are barren and have not borne children, but you shall conceive and bear a son. ⁴**Therefore be careful and drink no wine or strong drink, and eat nothing unclean,** ⁵**for behold, you shall conceive and bear a son. No razor shall come upon his head, for the child shall be a Nazirite to God from the womb**, and he shall begin to save Israel from the hand of the Philistines."*

Obviously, Samson's parents passed along this knowledge to their son. As long as Samson kept the teachings and didn't shave his head, he had supernatural strength and was used mightily by God. However, upon revealing his secret to Delilah, Samson's head was shaved. He lost his strength, and he was blinded and bound by the Philistines.

When we don't follow the teachings of God, we prohibit the miraculous in our lives.

PART III - FAITH IN THE TEACHINGS

Faith is essential to the miraculous, but it is intricately interwoven into teaching, information, and knowledge. As we've highlighted earlier, "faith cometh by hearing and hearing by the word of God." Your faith comes and is built from hearing/understanding the Revelation from God's Word/Teachings.

Faith doesn't exist unless you have something (some revelation, information, knowledge, teaching, some person, some object) to have faith in. You can have heard and studied the Teachings and the Word of God, but if there is no faith, you'll share the same fate as the person who doesn't have the information. We'll discuss faith in more detail later, but let's look at a few examples that reveal the effects of faith (and/or lack thereof) in the teachings of God...

Matthew 8:5-13 (also found in Luke 7:1-10) – **Faith of the Centurion Soldier**

⁵And when Jesus was entered into Capernaum, there came unto him a centurion, beseeching him, ⁶And saying, Lord, my servant lieth at home sick of the palsy, grievously tormented. ⁷And Jesus saith unto him, I will come and heal him. ⁸The centurion answered and said, Lord, I am not worthy that thou shouldest come under my roof: **but speak the word only, and my servant shall be healed.** *⁹For I am a man under authority, having soldiers under me: and I say to this man, Go, and he goeth; and to another, Come, and he cometh; and to my servant, Do this, and he doeth* *it.* *¹⁰When Jesus heard it, he marveled, and said to them that followed, Verily I say unto you, **I have not found so great faith, no, not in Israel.** ¹¹And I say unto you, That many shall come from the east and west, and shall sit down with Abraham, and Isaac, and Jacob, in the kingdom of heaven. ¹²But the children of the kingdom shall be cast out into outer darkness: there shall be weeping and gnashing of teeth. ¹³And Jesus said unto the centurion, Go thy way; and as thou hast believed, so be it done unto thee. And <u>his servant was healed in the selfsame hour.</u>*

Jesus marveled at **the centurion's faith**. But it wasn't just blind faith; it was faith in the teaching of authority. Most people thought healing was obtained by going to the sick (or possessed, or lame) and laying hands on the person. The centurion soldier understood authority at a level most people couldn't begin to grasp. If the centurion had authority over an area or soldiers when he was physically present, he had the same authority even though he was absent or miles away. His faith and understanding in authority led him to believe that Jesus had authority and power to heal by giving the command, just as he would give a command to any soldier or servant.

Matthew 8:23-26 – **Jesus Calms the Storm**

*²³And when he was entered into a ship, his disciples followed him. ²⁴And, behold, there arose a great tempest in the sea, insomuch that the ship was covered with the waves: but he was asleep. ²⁵And his disciples came to him, and awoke him, saying, **Lord, save us: we perish**. ²⁶And he saith unto them, Why are ye fearful, O ye of little faith?*

Then he arose, and rebuked the winds and the sea; and there was a great calm.

In this instance, it was the disciples that experienced the miraculous: their lives were saved from a great storm at sea. The fact that they were disciples means that they had been receiving and were continuing to receive teaching from Jesus Christ. They had left all to follow Him and to be baptized under His school of thought and teachings. Jesus gives them Teaching about what was holding them back (paraphrasing): "You are fearful...and it's impacting your faith." Their fear and lack of faith prevented them from operating in the miraculous. He then commences to perform the miraculous act of calming the wind and sea by speaking to the elements.

Mark 10:46-52 – **Blind Bartimaeus**

[46]*And they came to Jericho. And as he was leaving Jericho with his disciples and a great crowd, Bartimaeus, a blind beggar, the son of Timaeus, was sitting by the roadside.* [47]*And when he heard that it was Jesus of Nazareth, he began to cry out and say,* **"Jesus, Son of David, have mercy on me!"** [48]*And many rebuked him, telling him to be silent. But he cried out all the more,* **"Son of David, have mercy on me!"** [49]*And Jesus stopped and said, "Call him." And they called the blind man, saying to him, "Take heart. Get up; he is calling you."* [50]*And throwing off his cloak, he sprang up and came to Jesus.* [51]*And Jesus said to him, "What do you want me to do for you?" And the blind man said to him,* **"Rabbi, let me recover my sight."** [52]*And Jesus said to him, "Go your way; **your faith** has made you well."*

And immediately he recovered his sight and followed him on the way.

In this account, there was a blind man, named Bartimaeus who got wind that Jesus was passing by. He cried out, "Jesus, Son of David..." This phrasing denotes that Bartimaeus had some level of teaching. By calling him Son of David, he was recognizing that Jesus was a King (who was prophesied to come through the lineage of David's throne) and the Christ. He even further called Jesus, "Rabbi" (Master Teacher). This blind man had faith in the teachings about Jesus. Jesus announced to him that it was his faith (in Jesus) that made him well!

Luke 5:17-25 – **Take Up Thy Bed and Walk**

*[17]And it came to pass on a certain day, **as he was teaching**, that there were Pharisees and doctors of the law sitting by, which were come out of every town of Galilee, and Judaea, and Jerusalem: and **the power of the Lord was present to heal them**. [18]And, behold, men brought in a bed a man which was taken with a palsy: and they sought means to bring him in, and to lay him before him. [19]And when they could not find by what way they might bring him in because of the multitude, they went upon the housetop, and let him down through the tiling with his couch into the midst before Jesus. [20]**And when he saw their faith**, he said unto him, Man, thy sins are forgiven thee. [21]And the scribes and the Pharisees began to reason, saying, Who is this which speaketh blasphemies? Who can forgive sins, but God alone? [22]**But when Jesus perceived their thoughts**, he answering said unto them, What reason ye in your hearts? [23]Whether is easier, to say, Thy sins be forgiven thee; or to*

say, Rise up and walk? ²⁴*But that ye may know that the Son of man hath power upon earth to forgive sins, (he said unto the sick of the palsy,) I say unto thee, Arise, and take up thy couch, and go into thine house.* ²⁵<u>*And immediately he rose up before them, and took up that whereon he lay, and departed to his own house, glorifying God.*</u>

Jesus was teaching in a house where there were other people who were "knowledgeable" of God's Word. The Pharisees and scribes were doctors (teachers) of the Law/God's Teachings. The power of the Lord was present to heal as Jesus was giving the people teaching. The lame man's friends believed in the teachings and God's ability to heal so much that Jesus saw their FAITH. (You can't usually see faith, but He saw their faith based on their actions.) <u>These men tore a hole in the roof of someone else's house to get their friend to Jesus.</u> Now I can understand going to extremes to get something for yourself… but you must truly love someone – be utterly desperate – or believe that this man (Jesus) is able to heal – to go to such extremes for someone else. These friends lowered him down, and Jesus forgave the man's sins. THEIR FAITH got HIS SINS forgiven. Their faith placed him in right standing with God.

It is good to have friends, but sometimes it is even better to have enemies. The friends got him righteousness (forgiveness of sins); however, it was his enemies that got him healing. Notice: Jesus only began to bring up the issue of healing when the scribes and Pharisees began to have an issue…in their thoughts. They didn't even say anything. They didn't do anything or make a scene. But that was enough for Jesus.

I thank God for the thoughts or actions of an enemy. When people or enemies or haters have an issue with what God has done for you, Rejoice – because God looks at that as if they are questioning HIS credentials, His character, His power, His ability. When we confess our sins and are forgiven, we are like this man: We are in good standing with God.

Jesus may have had intentions to heal this man anyway – and maybe the faith of the friends was enough to put him in position to be healed. (Perhaps, but I truly don't know.) But because the Pharisees and scribes took issue with what God had done for him, Jesus made it a point to perform this miracle expeditiously and publicly.

[So, God may have blessed you with one (1) house...but because of your enemies THOUGHTS, He has four (4) more for you. God may have blessed you with a good job...because your enemy rolled their eyes, He's blessing you with a million-dollar-business idea. God may have blessed you with a spouse...because an enemy breathed hard in disgust, He added children who will call you blessed. Imagine if they actually SAY something... or DO something...]

Mark 6:1-6 – **Prophet Without Honor**

And he went out from thence, and came into his own country; and his disciples follow him. ²And when the sabbath day was come, **he began to teach in the synagogue:** *and many hearing him were astonished, saying, From whence hath this man these things? and what wisdom is this which is given unto him, that even* *such mighty works are wrought by his hands?* ³*Is not this the carpenter, the son of Mary, the brother of James, and Joses, and of Juda, and Simon? and are not his sisters here with us? And* **they were offended at him**. ⁴*But Jesus, said unto them, A prophet is not without honour, but in his own country, and among his own kin, and in his own house.* ⁵*And* <u>he could there do no mighty work, save that he laid his hands upon a few sick folk, and healed them</u>. *6 And* **he marvelled because of their unbelief**. *And he went round about the villages,* **teaching**.

Once again, we see Jesus teaching then attempting to perform miracles. However, this time He went back to His home country. He taught in the synagogues, and the people recognized the teaching as significant and wisdom to be put into practice. However, when they thought about who His parents were, who His siblings were, they refused to believe Him.

[You know how it is when people discount you because your parents had to work 3 jobs to keep food on the table, overlooked because somebody in your family was on drugs; your help isn't valued because they think, "Who are you to give me good advice?"]

With teaching alone, He did some miracles. But He was unable to perform miracles like He did in other places because the people didn't have faith in what they had been taught and Who was teaching them.

Matthew 15:22-28 – **Healing of a Woman's Daughter**

²²And, behold, a woman of Canaan came out of the same coasts, and cried unto him, saying, Have mercy on me, O Lord, thou son of David; **my daughter is grievously vexed with a devil.** *²³But he answered her not a word. And his disciples came and besought him, saying, Send her away; for she crieth after us. ²⁴But he answered and said, I am not sent but unto the lost sheep of the house of Israel. ²⁵Then came she and worshipped him, saying, Lord, help me. ²⁶But he answered and said, It is not meet to take the children's bread, and to cast it to dogs. ²⁷And she said, Truth, Lord: yet the dogs eat of the crumbs which fall from their masters' table. ²⁸Then Jesus answered and said unto her,* ***O woman, great is thy faith: be it unto thee even as thou wilt.*** *And* <u>*her daughter was made whole from that very hour.*</u>

Again, this was a person who wasn't from the nation of Israel. She was an outsider, from Canaan. She obviously had heard information, received knowledge or teachings, about Jesus and healing; otherwise, why even bring this issue to Him? Also, she called Him "Son of David," acknowledging Him as a King according to the Jewish teachings. Jesus responded in a manner that many would consider harsh, saying, *(paraphrasing)* "It isn't right to give the miraculous healing you're asking for to a dog. It's not right to give something of great value to a creature who is undeserving and to whom it doesn't belong."

She persisted. She believed what she had heard about this Man. She wasn't leaving without a miracle. Her response showed her determination: *(paraphrasing)* "They can keep the bread. I believe you have the power to heal my daughter; just the crumbs will be more than enough." Jesus noted that it was her faith in the teachings about His Kingdom authority over demonic forces that healed her daughter.

Matthew 12: 9-15 – **Healing on Sabbath Day**

*⁹He went on from there and **entered their synagogue**. ¹⁰And **a man was there with a withered hand**. And they asked him, "Is it lawful to heal on the Sabbath?"— so that they might accuse him. ¹¹He said to them, "Which one of you who has a sheep, if it falls into a pit on the Sabbath, will not take hold of it and lift it out? ¹²Of how much more value is a man than a sheep! So it is lawful to do good on the Sabbath." ¹³Then he said to the man, "**Stretch out your hand**." And <u>the man stretched it out, and it was restored, healthy like the other</u>. ¹⁴But the Pharisees went out and conspired against him, how to destroy him. ¹⁵Jesus, aware of this, withdrew from there. And **many followed him**, and <u>he healed them all</u>.*

Here, we see Jesus in the synagogue: a Jewish place of assembly and instruction/teaching. He was faced with the issue of whether it was "legal" or not to heal on the Sabbath Day. In this instance, as was often the case when met with religious opposition, Jesus taught through the asking of rhetorical questions: *(paraphrasing)* "If your sheep was in a hole on the sabbath day, who wouldn't get the sheep out? I know every one of you here would get your sheep out that day because the sheep impacts your finances and livelihood. Well, if you would do that for a sheep, would you not do the same for a human? If a sheep is that valuable, is a human not MORE valuable?" They understood the lesson He was teaching them, but they couldn't answer because He exposed the hypocrisy and error in their thinking and teachings.

After teaching them, He proceeded to heal the man. He gave the man instructions: "Stretch out your hand." The man believed in the teachings and instructions given and he "stretched it out". This faith and obedience led to his healing. After healing the man, Jesus was followed and then He healed all those in the multitudes.

Luke 5:3-9 – **Cast Your Nets**

*³And he entered into one of the ships, which was Simon's, and prayed him that he would thrust out a little from the land. And he sat down, and **taught the people out of the ship**. ⁴Now when he had left speaking, he said unto Simon, Launch out into the deep, and let down your nets for a draught. ⁵And Simon answering said unto him, Master, we have toiled all the night, and have taken nothing: nevertheless at thy word **I will let down the net**. ⁶And when they had this done, they inclosed a great multitude of fishes: and their net brake. ⁷And they beckoned unto their partners, which were in the other ship, that they should come and help them. And they came, and filled both the ships, so that they began to sink. ⁸When Simon Peter saw it, he fell down at Jesus' knees, saying, Depart from me; for I am a sinful man, O Lord. ⁹For he was astonished, and all that were with him, at the draught of the fishes which they had taken:*

This is Jesus' first encounter with Peter/Simon. We see the overarching theme of Jesus: Teaching the people – this time out of a ship that wasn't His own. After teaching, we see the miraculous being attempted. He gave Peter/Simon instructions for catching fish. Now... I want you to understand that this wasn't just about catching fish to eat. This was a business, and more fish meant more money. It had the potential to have a financial impact.

Peter / Simon was reluctant. He was an expert at fishing. However, he put faith in the teachings and instructions, and let down THE net (even though he was instructed to let down "nets" - plural). He caught more fish following the fishing teachings of Jesus than they had using the fishing methods they had used their entire lives.

Once again, Faith in the Teachings are tied to the miraculous.

PART IV - TEACHING THROUGH PARABLES

God is not forceful - He does not attempt to control you. It is against His nature to force you to do ANYTHING. If God forced you to do anything, He would be violating your free will to choose; as well as violating your dominion on the earth. In Genesis 1:26, God said, *"Let man have dominion over the fish of the sea, fowl of the air, over all the earth, and over every creeping thing that creepeth upon the earth."* Psalm 115:16 notes, *"The highest heavens belong to the Lord, but the earth he has given to man."*

So, if you've ever wondered why God didn't come and slap the apple out of the hands of Eve and Adam, this is the reason. If you've ever wondered why God doesn't answer your prayers of "God, make me do right...make me stop having sex before marriage...make me not use drugs... make me not be homosexual...make me not cheat on my wife.... Take it all away, Lord!!" If these are the type of prayers that you're praying, they are pointless. He will HELP YOU. The Holy Spirit will remind you and convict you, but He will not MAKE you do anything.

Neither will God teach you when you didn't ask to be taught. However, teaching was a very important aspect of Jesus' ministry. Therefore, to get past this dilemma, He used parables. Parables are short stories about common aspects of life that have a deeper, hidden truth beyond the surface topic. So, even though Jesus may have been talking about farming, or sheep, or a man building a house, He was really referring to the Kingdom of God or some deeper truth. When the people wanted to know the Truth or be taught, all they had to do was unwrap the parable and the hidden truth would be revealed. Essentially, the person would have received teaching without even knowing they had been taught.

In Matthew 13:10-11, the disciples didn't understand why Jesus would speak to the people in parables but speak to them plainly. He essentially explained to them, *(paraphrasing)* "You wanted to know the truth...You wanted to be taught; therefore, I speak to you plainly. But to everyone else, I'll give them the same teaching that I gave you...just in parabolic form."

Let's look at a few examples of Jesus teaching in parables...

Matthew 13: 2-3

*And great multitudes were gathered together unto him, so that he went into a ship, and sat; and the whole multitude stood on the shore. ³And he spake many things unto them in **parables**, saying, Behold, a sower went forth to sow;*

Matthew 13:31

*Another **parable** put he forth unto them, saying, **The kingdom of heaven is like to a grain of mustard seed**, which a man took, and sowed in his field:*

Matthew 13:33

*Another **parable** spake he unto them; **The kingdom of heaven is like unto leaven**, which a woman took, and hid in three measures of meal, till the whole was leavened.*

Matthew 13:44-53

*⁴⁴Again, **the kingdom of heaven is like unto treasure hid in a field**; the which when a man hath found, he hideth, and for joy thereof goeth and selleth all that he hath, and buyeth that field. ⁴⁵Again, **the kingdom of heaven is like unto a merchant man, seeking goodly pearls**: ⁴⁶Who, when he had found one pearl of great price, went and sold* *all that he had, and bought it.* ⁴⁷*Again,* **the kingdom of heaven is like unto a net, that was cast into the sea, and gathered of every kind**: ⁴⁸*Which, when it was full, they drew to shore, and sat down, and gathered the good into vessels, but cast the bad away.* ⁴⁹*So shall it be at the end of the world: the angels shall come forth, and sever the wicked from among the just,* ⁵⁰*And shall cast them into the furnace of fire: there shall be wailing and gnashing of teeth.* ⁵¹*Jesus saith unto them, Have ye understood all these things? They say unto him, Yea, Lord.* ⁵²*Then said he unto them, Therefore* **every scribe which is instructed unto the kingdom of heaven is like unto a man that is an householder, which bringeth forth out of his treasure things new and old**. ⁵³*And it came to pass, that when Jesus had finished these* **parables**, *he departed thence.*

Matthew 22:1-2

And Jesus answered and spake unto them again by **parables**, *and said,* ²**The kingdom of heaven is like unto a certain king**, *which made a marriage for his son,*

Matthew 25:1

Then shall **the kingdom of heaven be likened unto ten virgins**, *which took their lamps, and went forth to meet the bridegroom.*

Matthew 25:14

*For the **kingdom of heaven is as a man travelling into a far country**, who called his own servants, and delivered unto them his goods.*

Luke 5:36-38

*³⁶And he spake also a **parable** unto them; No man putteth a piece of a new garment upon an old; if otherwise, then both the new maketh a rent, and the piece that was taken out of the new agreeth not with the old. ³⁷And no man putteth **new wine** into **old bottles**; else **the new wine will burst the bottles**, and be spilled, and the bottles shall perish.*

Matthew 13:34-35

*³⁴All these things spake Jesus unto the multitude in **parables; and without a parable spake he not unto them**: ³⁵That it might be fulfilled which was spoken by the prophet, saying, I will open my mouth in parables; I will utter things which have been kept secret from the foundation of the world.*

God desires us all to know what He is thinking and to teach us His ways, methods, and mysteries. He wants us to know the secret mysteries that will propel us into miraculous living. However, if we don't want to know the truth – if we don't seek out the mysteries, then we only get parables, stories, Truth wrapped up in common anecdotes. Jesus teaches that inside the parables lie dormant "things kept secret from the foundation of the world." We should be diligent in studying and obtaining the revelation from these parables because they hold the keys that could unlock the miraculous in our lives.

Level of Relationship and the Miraculous

When viewing the miraculous in the scriptures, take note of the varying degrees in the levels of relationship with God:

Often servants, believers, people who demonstrate faith have miracles performed FOR THEM (i.e., the Centurion Soldier, the Woman with the sick daughter, the Woman with the issue of blood, etc.).

When you reach the level of the disciples and friends – they have miracles performed FOR THEM…. BUT they are LEARNING or in training to be the one PERFORMING the miraculous for others and themselves. This is a level of transition. We need miracles to be done on our behalf, but there are times in which we can tap into the miraculous authority for ourselves and others.

The next level is becoming a son and the image of Him (Jesus, Apostles, Paul, etc.). At this level, you **live a life of the miraculous** and are able to perform it in the lives of others. These individuals have information and teachings that allow them to be like Jesus: Teach others, develop their faith, and operate in the miraculous power of God.

Last Instructions of Jesus

Matthew 28:19-20 - The Great Commission

*[19]Go ye therefore, and **teach all nations, baptizing them** in the name of the Father, and of the Son, and of the Holy Ghost: [20]**Teaching them to observe all things whatsoever I have commanded you:** and, lo, I am with you always, even unto the end of the world. Amen.*

Jesus' ministry with His disciples was filled with the miraculous. Many people were healed, loved ones were healed, people were delivered from demonic influences, the disciples were delivered from storms at sea, fish and bread were multiplied, etc. The disciples were being taught and instructed so that they could duplicate what they had learned. They were expected to be just like their Teacher. And with a ministry filled with the miraculous, one of the last things that He told His disciples to do was **Teach**.

That word "baptize" means that they were submerged/immersed under a certain teaching, or school of thought. Sure, baptizing is associated with submerging one in water, but this is an act to demonstrate that the person is being submerged/immersed into the teachings and philosophical beliefs of whom they were submitting. Here, Jesus tells His disciples to baptize or immerse (teach) them in the name of the Father, and of the Son, and of the Holy Spirit.

Let's Be Honest — Self Evaluation:

1. When you evaluate your life, can you see how teaching is essential to the miraculous?

2. When examining Old and New Testament Miracles, what catches your attention? Why don't we seem to experience miracles more commonly like they did then?

3. Has a lack of faith inhibited the miraculous in your life?

4. Has God ever taught you through parables or through some real-life examplse to explain a spiritual concept, teaching, or principle?

CHAPTER 7: THE RESPONSIBILITY OF THE STUDENT

"Take the attitude of a student; never too big to ask questions, never know too much to learn something new." - Og Mandino

The Pandemic

In early 2020, a force impacted the world, unlike anything most people had ever seen. It was called the "Coronavirus" (aka COVID-19 or "the 'Rona"). The world has experienced viruses before. The "common cold" is caused by a virus. I mean…we have an entire season in which we are on guard for a virus ("influenza" aka "the flu"). But for some reason, this was different.

This coronavirus caused people to panic. It caused stores to go out of business. It caused hospitals to be overwhelmed. It caused a shortage of food, sanitizers, toilet paper, masks, etc. It caused cities and states to issue "stay-at-home orders." It shut down travel – airports that were once bustling industries of activity, expeditions and voyages became deserted. It disrupted economies – billions of dollars were lost. Restaurants closed their doors, only allowing take-out or drive-thru services. The media discussed the virus 24/7. We were in a global pandemic. It created a new term that won't soon be forgotten – "social distancing." This virus caused experts to advise people to stand at least 6 feet apart from one another, wash hands constantly, wear masks… and fear if life would ever go back to normal. Millions were affected; hundreds of thousands died.

However, it was also a time of self-reflection, bonding with family, and seeking God like never before. More people turned to God for answers in their panic. The "church" evolved (as a whole) and embraced social media to spread messages of hope, faith, power, and authority.

Many people wondered, "How could one simple virus cause such a drastic change in our lives?" The reason was simple: It was a virus/viral strain that the human body had never seen or experienced before.

In short, this is how our body's immune system works: Once we experience an infection (in this case, a virus) our body fights against it. As our body fights against the virus, our immune system learns, studies, and remembers how to effectively kill the infection. This learning is stored and manifested in the form of defense agents known as "antibodies." Each set of antibodies is specifically designed to kill a specific infection if it ever shows up in our bodies again. Over the years, our bodies have been exposed to many viruses, bacteria, and diseases; therefore, our immune systems have stored up a great number of antibodies for many infections. This is why you only get symptoms of the Chicken Pox virus once (the sores, the fever, the body aches, etc.). You may very well be exposed to this virus again throughout your life, but because you have antibodies, your body has learned how to handle it.

Similarly, we can gain immunity through vaccines or receiving antibodies from other people. Vaccines work by presenting the infection to your body in a weakened (or dead) form and allowing your body to defeat it - thus developing its own antibodies. Alternatively, an antibody transfusion allows one to utilize the antibodies from other people to fight the infection for you. Both strengthen the immune system with antibodies to fight off infection / diseases.

The immune system is very effective; however, the body can only respond to what has been presented to it or to what it has been previously exposed to. The body only develops "teachings" (antibodies) based on what is demanded of it. If there is no exposure, then learning doesn't take place to produce specific antibodies. So, as you can conclude, the reason this virus was so problematic, infectious, and deadly is because **no one in the ENTIRE world had antibodies to this Coronavirus**.

As I mentioned, millions were infected. Some people produced antibodies; however, for some people, they didn't produce the antibodies quickly enough to fight off the disease before they succumbed to the respiratory issues or other complications and died. There was no vaccine when this virus first spread throughout the world; no antibodies to be transferred to other people. The viral pandemic was caused because our immune system didn't have the "teachings" to effectively respond to the infection.

The Student's Responsibility

This understanding about the Coronavirus and our immune system highlights one of the most important elements in teaching: **The student dictates the response of the teacher.**

In teaching, a lot of weight and responsibility is placed on the shoulders of the teacher. Via experience, study, or revelation, the teacher has amassed a great wealth of knowledge. The teacher knows more than the student (in the particular area of knowledge being taught). The teacher understands more than the student. The teacher is in a position of authority. The teacher knows what the student needs to learn in order to be successful. However, it isn't the teacher that dictates what the student learns. It is the questions, interests, desires, and actions of the student that dictate what the teacher entrusts to the student. Even if the teacher knows that the student would benefit from learning certain things, he/she can only give it to students when they desire it or demonstrate that they are prepared to handle it. Even if the teacher introduces a topic and information to the student, it is the student that determines the level and depth of the lessons.

It is the same way with God. God will only give you Teaching (answers, strategies, plans, understanding, knowledge) to the degree of your hunger. If you don't want to know it, God withholds it. If you don't want to know how to be successful, God withholds this information from you...even if He has prepared great successes in your future. If you don't want to know how to make your marriage work, God withholds this information from you...even though He knows it could change your life. If you don't want to know God's plans and destiny for your life, He will withhold it from you...even though He knows you need it. If you don't want to know how to obtain the miraculous, God – unfortunately – withholds it from you...even though it is well within your Kingdom rights. We as children, students, disciples, and Kingdom citizens dictate the lessons and secrets that God reveals.

Just like our immune system only produces antibodies (teaching about how to defeat a certain infection) against what it has been exposed to, Master Teachers only give certain teachings when exposed to certain desires and cues from the students. When the student wants to know or demonstrates that hunger, the teacher gives freely and eagerly.

ASK...SEEK...KNOCK

Matthew 7:7-8
[7] *"**Ask**, and it will be given to you; **seek**, and you will find; **knock**, and it will be opened to you.* [8] *For everyone who **asks receives**, and the one who **seeks finds**, and to the one who **knocks it will be opened**."*

Here, Jesus is basically explaining to His students a valuable concept of teaching and the miraculous. He was teaching the disciples secrets of how to obtain what they wanted to receive from the Father. He tells us plainly to ask, to seek, and to knock. These are varying levels to which the student can have a desire to "pull on" or "make a withdrawal from" the Teacher... or children from their Father. A good Teacher knows at which level to release the information.

<u>Ask Level</u> - This is a level of verbalization. The student can place a demand on everything the Teacher has

at His disposal: knowledge, ability, resources, connections, teachings, etc. Whether the Teacher answers the request depends on the relationship. "Ask" is a level often reserved for intimate relationships (and in some cases immaturity). When the student has earned the respect of the teacher, simply verbalizing the request is enough to be entrusted with one's desires.

John 11: 41-43 – The Resurrection of Lazarus

⁴¹So they took away the stone. And Jesus lifted up his eyes and said, "Father, I thank you that you have heard me. ⁴²I knew that you always hear me, but I said this on account of the people standing around, that they may believe that you sent me." ⁴³When he had said these things, he cried out with a loud voice, "Lazarus, come out."

Of course, this is the account of when Jesus raised Lazarus from the dead; notice that Jesus makes an interesting statement: "Father, I thank you that you have heard me.... I knew that you always hear me." Jesus obviously had asked the Father for the miracle of resurrection power to raise Lazarus from the dead – Jesus simply asked, and the Father granted Him the request. Because their "Father/Son" relationship is one born of intimacy, respect, and trust, Jesus' requests of the Father were answered by simply asking.

Luke 11:1 – Teach Us to Pray

Now Jesus was praying in a certain place, and when he finished, one of his disciples said to him, "Lord, teach us to pray, as John taught his disciples."

The disciples recognized that Jesus prayed often. They recognized that John taught his students how to pray. So, they made a request to receive instructions on how to pray. Take note of this truth: No matter how critical prayer is, Jesus never taught them until they desired to know. No matter how life-changing prayer would be for their lives, Jesus withheld the teaching until they demonstrated a hunger to know. Once they verbalized their request, Jesus gave them a master lesson on how to pray and pray effectively.

1 Kings 3: 5, 9-12 – **Request for Wisdom**

*⁵At Gibeon the Lord appeared to Solomon in a dream by night, and God said, "**Ask what I shall give you.**"*

*⁹Give your servant therefore an understanding mind to govern your people, that I may discern between good and evil, for who is able to govern this your great people?" ¹⁰It pleased the Lord that Solomon had asked this. ¹¹And God said to him, "**Because you have asked this**, and have not asked for yourself long life or riches or the life of your enemies, but have asked for yourself understanding to discern what is right, ¹²behold, I now do according to your word. Behold, I give you a wise and discerning mind, so that none like you has been before you and none like you shall arise after you*

God tells Solomon to ASK for what he wanted. He didn't tell Solomon to "seek" for what he wanted. He didn't tell him to "work hard" for what he wanted. He simply told him to ask. The intimate relationship wasn't between God and Solomon, but rather between God and Solomon's father, David. God and David were so intimate that God entrusted David's son (Solomon) at the Ask Level. Could God trust you and I with, "Ask for whatever you want"? (Some of us would be asking for money, fame, influence, relationships, wealth, destruction of our haters, etc.)

Solomon's request pleased God. Not only because of "what" he asked for but "why" he asked for it. Yes, Solomon asked for wisdom, but he requested wisdom because he wanted to do an excellent job of leading God's people. Solomon could have asked for anything for himself, yet he valued God. God was a priority in his request. The scripture goes on to say that God not only made Solomon wise but that He also gave him wealth and peace from his enemies. Solomon's request showed God that He could trust Solomon at the Ask Level, just as He did his father, David.

Seek Level - At the seek level, you are searching for answers and teachings to issues you may be facing. You may not know exactly what you want or need; however, just because you're trying to find it and putting forth the effort (energy, interest, labor), the Teacher leads and points you in the right direction. To everyone that seeks, he will find it because at this level the Teacher will release what you need or guide you in the right direction.

I'm sure most of us can identify with the Seek Level. Most of us don't mind helping people if we can; but if we're going to help anyone, it is likely going to be someone that is at least trying to help themselves. You want to borrow money? ... At least show me that you're trying to be financially responsible. You want me to mentor you? ... At least show me that you're trying to work toward your goals and that you won't waste my time. You want me to help you find a job? ... At least show me that you've been filling out applications and going on interviews already.

This must be how Jesus felt about a certain Pharisee who came seeking knowledge in the middle of the night:

John 3:1-5 – **Nicodemus, the Night Student**

*Now there was a man of the Pharisees named **Nicodemus, a ruler of the Jews**. ²This man **came to Jesus by night** and said to him, "**Rabbi, we know that you are a teacher come from God, for no one can do these signs that you do unless God is with him.**" ³Jesus answered him, "Truly, truly, I say to you, unless one is born again he cannot see the kingdom of God." ⁴Nicodemus said to him, "How can a man be born when he is old? Can he enter a second time into his mother's womb and be born?" ⁵Jesus answered, "Truly, truly, I say to you, unless one is born of water and the Spirit, he cannot enter the kingdom of God.*

In this except of scripture, we see Nicodemus having a secret conversation with Jesus. Nicodemus met with Jesus in private because of the Pharisee's public denouncement of Jesus. Nicodemus risked position, status, and perhaps even his life to have this meeting. He readily acknowledged that the Pharisees knew that Jesus is a master teacher ("Rabbi") and that God is with Him. He didn't even ask Jesus a question. His actions and statement revealed that Nicodemus was seeking for something. He didn't seem to know exactly what it was, but he recognized that there is something about Jesus that could unlock his understanding of God. Now, Jesus only talked about the Kingdom of God in parables to anyone outside of His circle; however, because the student dictates the teachings, Nicodemus' thirst caused Jesus to reveal the concept of being born again. Nowhere else does Jesus mention this concept. Why? ... Because no one else asked the right question or demonstrated the desire to know.

Acts 8:29-31; 35-39 Philip and the Ethiopian Eunuch

*[29]And the Spirit said to Philip, "Go over and join this chariot." [30]So Philip ran to him and heard him reading Isaiah the prophet and asked, "**Do you understand what you are reading?**" [31]And he said, "**How can I, unless someone guides me?**" And he invited Philip to come up and sit with him.*
*[35]**Then Philip opened his mouth, and beginning with this Scripture he told him the good news about Jesus.** [36]And as they were going along the road they came to some water, and the eunuch said, "See, here is water! What prevents me from being baptized?" [38]And he commanded the chariot to stop, and they both went down into the water, Philip and the eunuch, and he baptized him. [39]And when they came up out of the water, the Spirit of the Lord carried Philip away, and the eunuch saw him no more, and went on his way rejoicing.*

Here, we see the concept of seeking very clearly. An Ethiopian eunuch was trying to gain some understanding by reading the scriptures. He was seeking knowledge and wisdom, but he didn't understand what he was reading.

When Phillip was sent to him by the Holy Spirit, the Ethiopian made one of the simplest yet profound statements when it comes to teaching: "How can I understand, unless someone teaches me." The man had a desire – he was putting forth the effort. God recognized this seeking behavior of the Ethiopian and sent Phillip to open his understanding. He was even baptized into the Kingdom doctrine. All of this started because he was seeking and putting forth the effort… even when he didn't know exactly what he was reading or what he needed.

2 Kings 20:1-6 – **Hezekiah's Plea**

*In those days Hezekiah became sick and was at the point of death. And Isaiah the prophet the son of Amoz came to him and said to him, "Thus says the Lord, **'Set your house in order, for you shall die; you shall not recover.'**" ²Then Hezekiah **turned his face to the wall and prayed** to the Lord, saying, ³**"Now, O Lord, please remember how I have walked before you in faithfulness and with a whole heart, and have done what is good in your sight." And Hezekiah wept bitterly.** ⁴And before Isaiah had gone out of the middle court, the word of the Lord came to him: ⁵"Turn back, and say to Hezekiah the leader of my people, Thus says the Lord, the God of David your father: I have heard your prayer; I have seen your tears. Behold, I will heal you. On the third day you shall go up to the house of the Lord, ⁶and **I will add fifteen years to your life**.*

King Hezekiah was sick. God sent the prophet Isaiah to tell him it was over. He would die from this disease. He was told to prepare for his death – that has to be hard to hear. This king knows God can perform miracles; he knows that God is Great; he knows God can heal him. Yet, the very Source that he's pleading to for healing tells him, "You shall die...and not recover." (What do you do? ... Who else is there to call on?)

Hezekiah began to operate at the Seek Level. I'm sure he didn't know what to do, but he put his face to the wall and began to communicate with God. He didn't ask God for healing. He didn't ask God to change His mind. He didn't ask God if He was mistaken. He didn't get angry and curse God. **He asked God to remember!!** Hezekiah was seeking a different outcome. He was searching for a different response – "Take into consideration my obedience, my faithfulness" – he wanted God to remember their relationship.

God wasn't moved by Hezekiah's tears but by his effort.... "I'm God; I told you that you're going to die, yet you come to MY throne and make an appeal?" Most people would have just given up. Hezekiah went to the Source "seeking." For his effort, God blessed Hezekiah with healing and 15 more years of life. This wasn't what Hezekiah even asked for, but this is what he found because he was seeking a different answer from God.

Knock Level - At this level, the Teacher requires the student to know exactly what it is they are asking for or to have actions that coincide with clear understanding of what they are desiring. "Knocking" goes beyond asking.... Sometimes you may verbally ask for something, but your actions differ (i.e., you pray for success but demonstrate characteristics and habits that breed failure). Sometimes you can ask for something but not understand the weight of what you're asking (i.e., in Matthew 20:21, the mother of James and John asked for positions of authority - to sit at Jesus' right and left hand). "Knocking" goes beyond seeking because you can be close to what the Teacher desires, but the Teacher will not release what you're desiring. The student can put forth effort to get results at the Seek Level; however, this isn't good enough at the Knock Level.

Matthew 20:29-34 – **Jesus Heals Two Blind Men**

*²⁹And as they went out of Jericho, a great crowd followed him. ³⁰And behold, there were **two blind men** sitting by the roadside, and when they heard that Jesus was passing by, they cried out, "**Lord, have mercy on us, Son of David!**" ³¹The crowd rebuked them, telling them to be silent, but they cried out all the more, "Lord, have mercy on us, Son of David!" ³²And stopping, Jesus called them and said, "What do you want me to do for you?" ³³They said to him, "Lord, let our eyes be opened." ³⁴And Jesus in pity touched their eyes, and immediately they recovered their sight and followed him.*

This is a perfect example of "Knocking" at the door of Healing. Jesus was leaving Jericho and crowds of people were following Him. Two blind men got word that Jesus was in the town and began to shout and beg Jesus for "mercy." When the crowd tried to silence them, they continued to yell for "mercy." Yelling for mercy didn't get them the miracle. Jesus recognized their actions and persistence (Seek Level), but to get what they wanted, Jesus required them to be specific. He wanted them to "knock on the door of sight." Jesus was basically telling them, "I know what you want. I know what you need. But I can't give it to you until you truly want it. Tell me what you want me to do." When they specifically articulated their desire for sight, Jesus healed their eyes.

I'm here to tell you...most of us are "begging for mercy" and God is instructing us to be specific. Most of us are so focused on getting God to "feel sorry" for us that we miss that He's commanding us to knock on the door of what we desire with clarity and conviction. We're so focused on wanting to appear humble and pious that we miss that the Teacher wants to open the door to finances, relationships, ideas, wisdom, strategies, resources, favor, authority, knowledge, power over circumstances...The Teacher is waiting to open the door to the miraculous, but only when we come correctly and knock.

Luke 8:42-48 – **Woman with the Issue of Blood**

25And there was a woman who had had a discharge of blood for twelve years, 26and who had suffered much under many physicians, and had spent all that she had, and was no better but rather grew worse. 27She had heard the reports about Jesus and came up behind him in the crowd and touched his garment. 28For she said, **"If I touch even his garments, I will be made well."** *29And immediately the flow of blood dried up, and she felt in her body that she was healed of her disease.* *30And Jesus, perceiving in himself that power had gone out from him, immediately turned about in the crowd and said, "Who touched my garments?" 31And his disciples said to him, "You see the crowd pressing around you, and yet you say, 'Who touched me?'" 32And he looked around to see who had* *done it. ³³But the woman, knowing what had happened to her, came in fear and trembling and fell down before him and told him the whole truth. ³⁴And he said to her, "Daughter, your faith has made you well; go in peace, and be healed of your disease."*

In this passage of scripture, we see an example of the "Knock" principle being highlighted. This woman had an issue of bleeding for 12 years. She had tried everything she knew for 12 years. She had spent 12 years' worth of wages on physicians that couldn't help her. Over 12 years, her condition had only gotten worse. I can imagine that she became desperate. However, she had faith that merely touching Jesus' garment would bring healing. She knocked on the door of Healing. She knew what she wanted. She fought the crowds. She fought the weakness. She fought the doubt of "this might not work." She didn't come begging, nor did she come asking. She wasn't "seeking" because she knew exactly what she wanted, who she wanted it from, and how she was going to get it. She came to get what she needed. She knocked so hard that Jesus perceived that the door of healing was knocked wide-open. She pulled so hard that Jesus felt it. (*"Who touched me?"*) She dictated the healing power that Jesus released.

Sometimes this is the faith, confidence, and tenacity that God desires to see from us when we make our supplications to Him. When you knock on a door, expect a response! When we pray, expect an answer! When we've done everything that we know how to do, have confidence that God is all powerful to take care of the rest!

Matthew 15:22-28 – **The Crumbs**

*₂₂And behold, a **Canaanite woman from that region came out and was crying, "Have mercy on me, O Lord, Son of David; my daughter is severely oppressed by a demon.*** *₂₃<u>But he did not answer her a word.</u> And his disciples came and begged him, saying, "<u>Send her away, for she is crying out after us.</u>" ₂₄He answered, "<u>I was sent only to the lost sheep of the house of Israel.</u>" ₂₅But she came and knelt before him, saying, "**Lord, help me.**" ₂₆And he answered, "<u>It is not right to take the children's bread and throw it to the dogs.</u>" ₂₇She said, "**Yes, Lord, yet even the dogs eat the crumbs that fall from their masters' table**." ₂₈Then Jesus answered her, "<u>O woman, great is your faith! Be it done for you as you desire.</u>" And her daughter was healed instantly.*

In this example, we see a Canaanite requesting that Jesus heal her daughter. She came to Jesus at the ASK LEVEL: "Have mercy...my daughter is severely oppressed by a demon." She ASKED that Jesus heal her daughter. But there was one problem: She was a Canaanite and Jesus was a Jew – They had no relationship and were historically viewed as enemies. Jesus ignored her. [Does this seem familiar? You ask God for what you want, need, or desire. You pray sincerely only to feel as if God is ignoring you!! No response!!]

Next, she continued at the SEEK LEVEL. Even after Jesus ignored her and the disciples wanted to send her away, she persisted. She continued to SEEK healing for her daughter even though He explained that His mission and purpose was to help the Jews...she was a Canaanite. Again, I remind you, the Canaanites and Jews despised one another. Yet this Canaanite woman humbled herself, knelt before Jesus seeking his help...only to be insulted like many Jews had probably insulted her before. ("the dogs don't have a right to what's reserved for the children"). Essentially, Jesus explained that He couldn't give her what she wanted because she didn't have a right to what she was asking for. Once again, it seemed like the door was slammed in her face. The Teacher wasn't giving her what she requested.

Her next statement articulates an understanding of what it will take to get her daughter healed: *(paraphrasing)* "If You want to operate according to Purpose and Rights... then true (Yes, Lord) ... the dogs do NOT deserve the children's bread. But the dogs do have a right to the crumbs that fall from the table. They can keep the bread, just allow me the crumbs. A crumb of Your power is more than enough for what I need." Once she knocked on the door of having her daughter freed from demonic oppression, her daughter was healed instantly! Even Jesus' demeanor changed as he praised her faith!!!

Importance of the Immune System

Immunity means to have protection from, exemption from, the ability to fight off, or defense against something. We see this in government — when someone from another country is important enough, they may have something called "diplomatic immunity." Usually, this is a diplomat, someone from his family, or someone in close association with a diplomat. This "immunity" means that they are not subject to certain laws and taxes of the country in which they are living. They have a certain level of protection that other people living in the same country don't have. God gave us an entire immune system predicated on this concept of protection.

I don't think we realize the importance of our immune systems. They are our "institutions" for learning how to fight against and providing a response to anything not designed to be in our bodies. This is why Human Immunodeficiency Virus (HIV) and Acquired Immunodeficiency Syndrome (AIDS) are two of the most deadly diseases known to man. HIV and AIDS are diseases that attack and destroy the immune system. Once your "learning institution to fight against diseases" is destroyed, you can't produce antibodies efficiently. Therefore, it's not the AIDS infection that kills people, but rather it's the "opportunistic infections" (the common cold, pneumonia, tuberculosis) that the body would normally destroy with ease that kill people infected with AIDS.

This is the revelation of the Enemy's tactics. He wants to destroy your ability to learn from God. He wants to keep you in the system of darkness. He wants you to remain ignorant. He is attacking your spiritual immune system. If you're ignorant, the devil doesn't have to destroy – you can be easily led astray. If you're not knowledgeable of the Truth, you'll be destroyed by something you should easily have been able to handle if you had just known. If you're not educated or taught correctly…You may even destroy yourself.

Let's Be Honest – Self Evaluation:

1. Do you remember the time at the beginning of "the pandemic"? How did life change for you and your family?

2. Are those changes still in place today? Did life ever go back to normal for you or did a "new normal" develop?

3. When you evaluate your life, has God ever required you to ask, seek, or knock? Do you go into depth with God concerning the lessons from your challenges? Have you taken advantage of the benefit that God is OUR Father and Teacher?

4. Have you operated at the wrong level (i.e., asking when you should have knocked – seeking when you should have been asking)?

5. Is your spiritual immune system weakened due to ignorance? Are opportunistic, trivial matters tripping you up and causing you to forfeit God's plans for your life?

CHAPTER 8: OBSTACLES

"Many times we are our worst enemy. If we could learn to conquer ourselves, then we will have a much easier time overcoming the obstacles that are in front of us."
  - Stephan Labossiere

"Cut the Trees..."

I remember when we were in our first church location at Word of Faith Ambassadors' Worship Center. It was a relatively small building on a lot that was about a little over two acres with an adjacent parsonage building. But we were full of hunger and thirst for the things of God, the Holy Spirit, and Kingdom Teaching. We had a packed house every Sunday and grew in every aspect. Cars would be parked on the gravel, grass, and even lined the road.

There were many pine trees that surrounded the buildings on the lot – I mean these were huge trees that had been there for years and years. I remember one day as I was walking around the building while praying, I received a spiritual impression from God: "Cut the trees and you'll see the church." I thought to God, "Yeah, I suppose people could see the building better if the trees were cut." But there were a few problems. **One:** I didn't know the first thing about cutting a tree down – let alone 20-30 huge trees. **Two:** These trees had been here longer than I'd probably been alive; some of the people had become accustomed to and loved the trees, so surely, they wouldn't want to see them go. **Three:** Such a project would take a financial toll on our bank accounts. **Four:**

Did I mention that I knew *NOTHING* about cutting down a tree?

We've learned that when God speaks, it is in our best interest to not only listen but to move into action. There were people (inside the church and outside the church) who had opinions that we were "making a mistake," "not doing the right thing," or that we "missed God." However, we gathered some of the men of the church and people from the community, and we proceeded to do as God instructed. We not only cut down the trees but uprooted them as well. Just as I had thought... people were able to see the church building more clearly from the highway and surrounding areas.

Personally, I thought that was the end of it. I had cut down the trees, and the church building was more visible: "High-five, God...job well done." It was at this point that God gave me another spiritual inclination. As I was looking at the open and cleared lot that was created, this time He said, "Do you see the Church?"

I was confused: "Yes, I see the church; EVERYONE can see the church now."

He responded, "Do you see the New Sanctuary? ... Build!!!"

Really? Really?! Now, here I was thinking that this was all about removing the trees so that eyes may see the existing building; however, God was interested in opening my vision to see His purpose and plans. I couldn't see the future building because it would be in the space that the trees had occupied.

Expansion was not on my mind, nor on the church's agenda. We were doing well, content with our growth and spiritual development. We were not saving up for a church building. We were not fasting and praying for a new sanctuary. It was unexpected. So, the main questions were: How were we going to fund this building project? Would the city even allow such a project? Would the people be on board with this "unexpected" expansion? And…did I mention that I was concerned about how we were going to pay for this building?

I'm not going to go into the minute details, but we ran into issue after issue. Some people who had been with the ministry were against the expansion, while others decided to no longer be a part of the ministry because of the vision – YES, people left because they said I was making a huge mistake. There were people (ministers) who were gathering and praying that the expansion vision would fail!!! These people were having meetings and praying that we would not grow because they "liked the small atmosphere and access to the leaders!!!" These were not the people in the community — These were THE PEOPLE IN THE CHURCH!!!

We ran into problems with the City Development, which seemed to throw hurdle after hurdle in our path. They said that we didn't have enough parking, so we had to tear down our adjacent parsonage building to make room for more parking. They claimed that the project would violate zoning laws. There were complaints from surrounding residents. And many, many more issues arose.

But at every turn, the favor of God was present. We found favor with the bank to finance the project. People were led to donate graciously. There were individuals who knew the laws in the City Council and spoke on our behalf. Everything just always "seemed to work out" in our favor. It wasn't in our own strength, our own intelligence, our own careful planning and funding...This project was truly a God-production.

We are now in a building that has more space and functionality than our previous location ever had. The end result is AMAZING... and in my estimation, nothing short of a miracle. But I told this story, not to focus on the church building (I don't want you to take this as confirmation and start building a new church), but to show you the obstacles that were in the way – Before we could get to the new building, we had to overcome the obstacles. The trees, lack of vision, people leaving the ministry, issues of funding, hurdles and demands of the city, murmurings of the people, etc. were all entities that attempted to prevent the vision from becoming a reality.

Likewise, there are obstacles that we must overcome in order to bring our miracle into fruition. We will further explore and examine teachings into some of the major things that are standing between you and your miracle. It is important to realize and be able to pinpoint obstacles that have the potential to arise and to understand how to face them. If you're unable to pinpoint, identify, and breakdown obstacles, you risk being unable to reach your goals.

Each obstacle is different and unique. The **trees** were a different obstacle than the issue of **people leaving**

our congregation. The issue of **funding** was a different obstacle than **the lack of vision**. The **complaints from the city** were a different obstacle than any other obstacle. It is important to identify these obstacles because the solution to overcoming each obstacle is different. We could cut down the trees, but we couldn't cut down the people on the City Council. We could raise the funds for the project, but no amount of money raised would stop the people from trying to come against the project. It was an obedience to the Word of God that initiated the vision; however, when it came to the City Council, the solution was people with information and knowledge of the system. Every obstacle isn't a matter of "waiting on God," nor does the answer to every issue involve the physical force of removal of trees. If the obstacles aren't identified and understood, many times we (unknowingly and by default) attempt to apply the same solution to every obstacle that arises.

What is the obstacle (or obstacles) to your miracle? What are you doing (or not doing) that is keeping you from the miraculous experience? What is keeping you from experiencing the benefits that God has promised in His Word? Let's cut down and uproot these "trees" that block our vision to the miraculous living in our lives.

OBSTACLE I: Sin/Lack of Repentance

"Let him who is without sin, cast the first stone…"
- Jesus

One of the first things that we as believers have to understand is that our mindset has to change. John's – and even Jesus' – message was, "Repent, for the Kingdom of Heaven is here." That word *"Repent"* doesn't mean to feel sorry for yourself, to feel bad or guilty about what you've done. "Repent" actually means to change your mind – change the way you think; do a complete 180-degree turn in your thinking.

Think about it using your friends as an example. Let's say that a few of your friends wronged you by stealing money. When you find out and confront them, they apologize profusely. They may feel really guilty about it, cry, and beg for your forgiveness. However, if their mindset hasn't changed about stealing, they will steal from you again if given the right opportunity. This is how we treat God. We feel guilty about our sin (lying, cheating, drugs, homosexuality, sexual promiscuity, etc.). We cry; we beg for forgiveness. But because our thinking hasn't changed, we find ourselves committing the same actions over and over again…even when we know it is wrong. We're not truly sorry for disappointing God: we're more so sorry that we got caught.

Clashing Systems: God's System vs The World's System

Why does Jesus tell us to change the way that we think? It is because He came to return a government system here on the earth: the Kingdom that Adam lost. In this Kingdom government, things are done differently than the World's system (or the way the World operates). This is often where the confusion comes into our lives. We want the blessings and the miracles that come with God's system, but we use principles and operate according to the World's system.

Think of it like this...China is a **communist government**, while the United States is a **democracy**. In a communist government, the government dictates how much money you receive, the amount of resources allocated to you – it was designed with the intentions of "making everyone equal," preventing poverty, and creating a more idealistic society. On the other hand, the U.S. employs a democratic system where the majority rules and you are allowed to make as much money as you want as long as you follow the laws – No one can take your wealth and give it to someone of lesser means. Well, you can conclude that it would be problematic and unproductive to utilize the methods and laws of the U.S. government in China and vice versa.

However, this is essentially what has been taking place in many Christians' lives: they try to use the World's principles in God's Kingdom government. Kingdom government is not a democracy. It is not a dictatorship. It is not a communist regime. It is not a republic. Nor is it a parliamentary monarchy. Here are just a few differences between a Kingdom government and the democracy form of government you may have been accustomed to experiencing:

- In a Kingdom, you don't vote for the King. The King chooses the citizens.

- In a Kingdom system, the Word of the King becomes law (even to the King Himself).

- You can't overrule the King with a vote or change the law because you "feel" that it is unfair or "not right."

- A King is only responsible for keeping His Words/Laws.

- Treason against the King/Kingdom results in death.

- The wealth in a Kingdom is commonwealth—Everything belongs to and is owned by the King. Thus, the King is responsible for providing the necessary resources to the citizens of His domain/country.

Have you ever been in a courtroom or watched the "law shows" on television? I love it. I seem to get roped into trying to figure out who did it, what tactics the lawyers will use to present their case, and how the jury will decide. While all of that is going on, the judge is who you have to keep your eyes on. The judge is the one that decides whether to allow certain testimony or certain pieces of evidence to come before the jury. The judge can sustain motions put forth by a lawyer or overrule them. Sometimes, he/she can decide whether a case even goes to trial or not. The judge is a powerful figure in the courtroom.

One day I was talking to a judge that I knew about how cases are presented and the nature of the Law. She told me something that blew my mind: she taught me that the judge knows (or should know) the Law through and through. However, if you don't present the law that could protect your rights, you could lose the case and possibly go to jail. EVEN IF THE JUDGE KNOWS THAT THERE IS A LAW THAT COULD PROTECT YOUR RIGHTS, if you (or your lawyer) do not present it before the judge, YOU LOSE the case. THE JUDGE CANNOT PRESENT THE LAW ON YOUR BEHALF. You can lose your freedom and citizenship rights, even though there is a law to set you free. NOW... if you appeal and present that particular law, the judge will rule on your behalf, and you can enact your citizenship rights and freedom.

There are Laws that God has in place. But because we don't know HIS Law or the Word of the King (Teaching), we can't get a ruling that grants us our Citizenship Rights. If we don't know that there is a law to grant us healing, we can't enact our right to be healed. If we don't know that there is a law that guarantees us protection, we can't enact our right to be protected. If we don't know that there is a law that promises wealth, wisdom, peace, etc., we can't enact those miraculous rights on our behalf.

Sin Separates Us from God

The question you're asking yourself of course is, "How is this relevant to getting my miracle?" As mentioned earlier, "Repent" means to change the way that you think. If you don't think like God thinks, you will miss much of what God has for you. Before you can even obey God, there must first be a change in mindset. If God says that something is wrong, we have to be in agreement with Him. As I've mentioned, "repentance" is changing the way we think - agreeing with God that what we did was wrong and what He said is right – period...end of discussion!!

Our sin can hinder the miraculous because it disconnects us from God.

Isaiah 59:2

*But your **iniquities** have made a **separation** between you and your God, and your **sins** have **hidden his face from you** so that he does not hear.*

The word *sin* is translated as "rebellion." It is not something deep or mystical: "sin" is simply whatever does not agree with God. God cannot co-exist with sin because it goes against His Teachings. When we sin, we are (consciously or unconsciously) choosing to disconnect from God and the Kingdom of Heaven. We disrupt our relationship with the Governor, the Holy Spirit; He is our Connection with God to teach and guide us. Our sin hides God's face from us and prevents Him from hearing our prayers and petitions, thus preventing us from experiencing the miraculous.

What sin does more than anything else is erode our confidence in God. Most of us (foolishly) think God is like most of the people we know. We inherently believe that when we sin (mess up, make mistakes, do wrong), God is mad at us. We believe, "God hates me because I've sinned, and He is punishing me." With this mindset, we don't go to God confidently. We don't pray because we think our prayers will not be heard. We don't attend church services. We don't even ask God for anything because we "already know that the answer is NO!" Therefore, we believe that God won't perform the miraculous in our lives because of our sin.

The Enemy attempts to use shame and guilt to keep us separated from God: this is deception. God does not hate us. He loves us. **Now, I will not misrepresent our Father—He does hate the sin**: He detests the act, the thoughts, the not living up to His Standard. He made us. He knows what He placed on the inside of us. He knows, more than anyone else, what we're capable of doing. He hates when we miss the mark; **however, He never stops loving us.**

Miracles in Spite of Sin

Depending upon your spiritual level and maturity, God performs the miraculous in spite of your sin. Let's look in the scriptures....

John 8:3-11 – **Woman Caught in Adultery**

[3]*The scribes and the Pharisees brought **a woman who had been caught in adultery**, and placing her in the midst* [4]*they*

said to him, *"Teacher, this woman has been caught in the act of adultery. ⁵Now in the Law, Moses commanded us to stone such women. So what do you say?" ⁶This they said to test him, that they might have some charge to bring against him. Jesus bent down and wrote with his finger on the ground. ⁷And as they continued to ask him, he stood up and said to them, "Let him who is without sin among you be the first to throw a stone at her." ⁸And once more he bent down and wrote on the ground. ⁹But when they heard it, they went away one by one, beginning with the older ones, and Jesus was left alone with the woman standing before him. ¹⁰Jesus stood up and said to her,* **"Woman, where are they? Has no one condemned you?"** *¹¹She said, "No one, Lord." And Jesus said,* **"Neither do I condemn you; <u>go, and from now on sin no more</u>."**

This is often an overlooked miracle; however, if you were the one saved from death row by stoning, I think you would put that in the miracle category. It's one thing when you're accused of something, and you're innocent – surely you don't think death is appropriate. However, what if what the people are saying is true? You did cheat on your spouse … you did abuse drugs … you did kill that person … you did what they say you did – You're guilty. Your inner fight for justice isn't with such passion; your protest against their words won't be very strong and convincing.

That's how this woman must have felt. They caught her. She knew she was wrong…and they were going to kill her for it. She had no fight: this Sinner … this Adulterer…this woman whom they had <u>caught in the very act</u>. She didn't even try to defend herself. She didn't cry out, "It wasn't me" or "It was an accident" or "I was set up." She was guilty by the Law. She was about to die. Nothing short of a miracle could save her.... But she probably felt that she didn't deserve a miracle. [Does this sound familiar?]

However, even in her "caught in the act" status, she experienced the miraculous. She didn't have to fight them. She didn't get the laws changed. She was simply in the presence of Jesus. **AFTER** she received her miracle, Jesus DEALT with her sin: "Go and, from now on, sin no more." Just because she received the miracle, God did not excuse or justify the sin. (**The sin must be addressed and corrected.**) Jesus essentially **taught** her how to not end up in this situation again – *go and sin no more*. If the sin issue wasn't addressed or dealt with, she has the potential to find herself in the same situation... facing death again...needing to be saved again...needing a miracle again. [Sound familiar?]

We see this concept of the miraculous again in John 5...

John 5: 2-3, 5-15 – **Healing at the Pool of Bethesda**

[2]Now there is in Jerusalem by the Sheep Gate a pool, in Aramaic called Bethesda, which has five roofed colonnades. [3]In these lay a multitude of invalids—blind, lame, and paralyzed.
*[5]One man was there who had been an invalid for thirty-eight years. [6]When Jesus saw him lying there and knew that he had already been there a long time, he said to him, "Do you want to be healed?" [7]The sick man answered him, "Sir, I have no one to put me into the pool when the water is stirred up, and while I am going another steps down before me." [8]***Jesus said to him, "Get up, take up your bed,***

and walk." ⁹*And at once the man was healed, and he took up his bed and walked.* Now that day was the Sabbath. ¹⁰*So the Jews said to the man who had been healed, "It is the Sabbath, and it is not lawful for you to take up your bed."* ¹¹*But he answered them, "The man who healed me, that man said to me, 'Take up your bed, and walk.'"* ¹²*They asked him, "Who is the man who said to you, 'Take up your bed and walk'?"* ¹³*Now the man who had been healed did not know who it was, for Jesus had withdrawn, as there was a crowd in the place.* ¹⁴*Afterward Jesus found him in the temple and said to him,* **"See, you are well! Sin no more, that nothing worse may happen to you."** ¹⁵*The man went away and told the Jews that it was Jesus who had healed him.*

This man at the pool of Bethesda needed a miracle. He was at the pool of Bethesda trying to get healed by getting into the pool when "the water was stirred." He had been in this condition for 38 years. I imagine that he had tried everything in 38 years. He needed the miracle of Healing. However, when Jesus asked him, "Do you want to be healed?", he didn't answer the question – he gave the excuse: "It's other people preventing me from getting my miracle." [Sometimes when we don't get our miracle, it's everyone else's fault but our own.] This man said, "No one helps me get in the pool" ... "People jump in before me" ... If allowed to keep going, he probably would have blamed the Angel for stirring the water at the wrong time.

He apparently had been in a "sin-state" because we see Jesus deal with the sin **AFTER** the healing in verse 14: "__See you are well!!! Sin no more...__" But notice: the sin didn't keep him from receiving the miracle of Healing.

Miracles Inhibited by Sin

It's not God's Will that we remain in a "sin-state." As we grow and become spiritually mature, God requires us to be in right-alignment prior to releasing the miraculous. As I mentioned earlier, everyone is not on the same level. Individuals may range from Unbelievers to Children to Servants to Disciples to Friends to Apostles, all the way to Sons of God. God may deal with the sin issue **after** the miracle (as noted in the examples above), but the standard and the level of maturity that He wants us to reach will eventually require us to deal with sin **BEFORE** the miracle is allowed.

Let's study some situations where sin prohibited the miraculous or where the sin had to be corrected prior to the miraculous.....

Sodom/Gomorrah

Genesis 18:20-21

[20] Then the Lord said, "Because the outcry against Sodom and Gomorrah is great and their sin is very grave, [21] I will go down to see whether they have done altogether according to the outcry that has come to me. And if not, I will know."

Genesis 18:32-32

*Then he said, "Oh let not the Lord be angry, and I will speak again but this once. **Suppose ten are found there.** " He answered, "For the sake of ten I will not destroy it."*

We know the story of Sodom and Gomorrah…. Sodom and Gomorrah were visited by God / Angels and were about to be destroyed because of Sin. Abraham pleaded and negotiated on the city's behalf. He begged God for a miracle – to save a city set for destruction. However, because there were not even 10 righteous people in the land, they couldn't receive the miracle. Because there were not 10 people in 2 cities who were righteous, God did not spare them. There was no miracle because their sin nature wasn't addressed appropriately.

As an aside, many Christians think that Sodom and Gomorrah were destroyed because of homosexuality. Ezekiel 16:48-50 notes that

[48] As I live, declares the Lord God, your sister Sodom and her daughters have not done as you and your daughters have done. [49] Behold, this was the guilt of your sister Sodom: she and her daughters had pride, excess of food, and prosperous ease, but did not aid the poor and needy. [50] They were haughty and did an abomination before me. So I removed them, when I saw it.

The Sin of David

In 2 Samuel, we see the account of David and how he slept with Bathsheba and impregnated her. To cover up this sin, he plotted and eventually had her husband, Uriah, killed during the war. He then married Bathsheba and thought that he had gotten away with what he had done. However, he was paid a visit by the prophet Nathan, who revealed that God saw what David had done and was very angry with David. Let's pick up in 2 Samuel 12:13…

*¹³David said to Nathan, "**I have sinned against the Lord.**" And Nathan said to David, "The Lord also has put away your sin; you shall not die. ¹⁴**Nevertheless, because by this deed you have utterly scorned the Lord, the child who is born to you shall die.**" ¹⁵Then Nathan went to his house. And the Lord afflicted the child that Uriah's wife bore to David, and he became sick. ¹⁶<u>David therefore sought God on behalf of the child.</u> And <u>David fasted</u> and <u>went in and lay all night on the ground.</u> ¹⁷And the elders of his house stood beside him, to raise him from the ground, but he would not, nor did he eat food with them. ¹⁸**On the seventh day the child died.** And the servants of David were afraid to tell him that the child was dead, for they said, "Behold, while the child was yet alive, we spoke to him, and he did not listen to us. How then can we say to him the child is dead? He may do himself some harm." ¹⁹But when David saw that his servants were whispering together, David understood that the child was dead. And David said to his servants, "Is the child dead?" They said, "He is dead."*

Because of David's sin, the child died. David prayed....he fasted....he cried...I'm sure he did everything he thought would grant the miracle of healing for his child. Even though the death was pronounced by the prophet Nathan, David still asked God for Healing. If you keep reading, David was questioned by his servants as to why he mourned when the child was alive. David responded, "The Lord may have been gracious, and the child may have lived." Ultimately, the child died because of David's sins.

Sin of Achan

Moses led the people out of Egypt and into the Wilderness. The people of Israel experienced the miraculous: they were fed manna from Heaven.... none got sick among them.... their clothes never wore out.... all of their needs were met. However, in spite of having a front row seat to the miraculous power of God, the people of Israel murmured, complained, and rebelled against God. They even built a Golden Calf when Moses went to get the Teachings of God for them to live by.

As time passed, Moses died, and the children of Israel eventually crossed into the Promised Land. It was time to grow up: the manna stopped, the clothes wore out, people started coughing and got sick, etc. They had a greater responsibility than before. They had to fight battles and subdue enemies in this Promised Land. This next account is a part of the instructions they were given as the blueprints to conquer the great-walled city of Jericho....

Joshua 6:18-19

18But you, **keep yourselves from the things devoted to destruction, lest when you have devoted them you take any of the devoted things and make the camp of Israel a thing for destruction and bring trouble upon it.** *19But all silver and gold, and every vessel of bronze and iron, are holy to the Lord; they shall go into the treasury of the Lord."*

So, the people were basically told not to take any spoils of war from the battle of Jericho. Everything was to be destroyed, and the silver, gold, precious stones, etc.

were to be placed in the treasury. Of course (most know the story), the great wall of Jericho fell, and Israel was victorious. Let's look ahead to what happened next in Joshua 7...

Joshua 7:2-5

*²Joshua sent men from Jericho to Ai, which is near Beth-aven, east of Bethel, and said to them, "Go up and spy out the land." And the men went up and spied out Ai. ³And they returned to Joshua and said to him, "Do not have all the people go up, but let about two or three thousand men go up and attack Ai. Do not make the whole people toil up there, for they are few." ⁴**So about three thousand men went up there from the people. And they fled before the men of Ai, ⁵and the men of Ai killed about thirty-six of their men and chased them before the gate as far as Shebarim and struck them at the descent. And the hearts of the people melted and became as water.***

God had been with them all this time. They were defeating their enemies and being victorious against some of the most powerful cities and nations. However, when they came up against a smaller nation (Ai), they were defeated: Men were killed, and the people were disheartened... none more so than Joshua. He cried out to God, frustrated that they were defeated. Let's look at God's response...

Joshua 7:10-12

*¹⁰The Lord said to Joshua, "Get up! Why have you fallen on your face? ¹¹**Israel has sinned; they have transgressed*** *my covenant that I commanded them; they have taken some of the devoted things; they have stolen and lied and put them among their own belongings. ¹²Therefore the people of Israel cannot stand before their enemies. They turn their backs before their enemies, because they have become devoted for destruction.* **I will be with you no more, unless you destroy the devoted things from among you.**

God revealed to Joshua that Israel did not experience the miraculous victory that they were used to experiencing because of sin. Sin was the obstacle to the miraculous. Essentially, God informed Joshua, "Before you can have victory, the sin issue must be resolved."

It was the sin of Achan that caused their defeat against Ai: the sin of one man caused the death of so many others...The sin of one man caused a nation to lose a battle...The sin of one man blocked the miracles of God. God would not allow them to be victorious until the sin-issue was dealt with.

Joshua 7:24-26

²⁴*And Joshua and all Israel with him took Achan the son of Zerah, and the silver and the cloak and the bar of gold, and his sons and daughters and his oxen and donkeys and sheep and his tent and all that he had. And they brought them up to the Valley of Achor.* ²⁵*And Joshua said, "Why did you bring trouble on us? The Lord brings trouble on you today."* **And all Israel stoned him with stones. They burned them with fire and stoned them with stones.** ²⁶*And they raised over him a great heap of stones that remains to this day.* **Then the Lord turned from his burning**

anger. Therefore, to this day the name of that place is called the Valley of Achor.

Achan admitted what he had done. But his actions were so detrimental, and the sin had made God so angry that Israel not only had to get rid of the stolen items, but they also stoned Achan, his family, his animals and all his possessions. Any trace or association with Achan was destroyed. After the sin was dealt with, God was no longer angry and in Joshua 8, they received the miracle of conquering Ai.

[Is there something you're doing or that you've done that is blocking the miraculous victory in your life?]

Nineveh Repents

Jonah 3:4-10

*⁴Jonah began to go into the city, going a day's journey. And he called out, "Yet forty days, and Nineveh shall be overthrown!" ⁵**And the people of Nineveh believed God.** They **called for a fast** and **put on sackcloth**, from the greatest of them to the least of them. ⁶The word reached the king of Nineveh, and he arose from his throne, removed his robe, covered himself with sackcloth, and sat in ashes. ⁷And he issued a proclamation and published through Nineveh, "By the decree of the king and his nobles: Let neither man nor beast, herd nor flock, taste anything. Let them not feed or drink water, ⁸but let man and beast be covered with sackcloth, and let them call out mightily to God. **Let everyone turn from his evil way and*** *from the violence that is in his hands.* ⁹*Who knows? God may turn and relent and turn from his fierce anger, so that we may not perish."* ¹⁰*When God saw what they did, how they turned from their evil way,* **God relented of the disaster that he had said he would do to them, and he did not do it.**

These events occurred after Jonah was vomited out of the great fish and went to Nineveh like he was instructed to do in the first place. Nineveh, like Sodom and Gomorrah, was set for destruction. They had 40 days, and then they would be overthrown. Nineveh needed saving: they needed a miracle. However, their miracle was being held up due to their sin.

Nineveh responded to the proclamation of Jonah with a fast. They consecrated themselves, and the King issued a decree: "Everyone turn from his evil way and from violence that is in his hands." They repented of their sin in hopes of a miracle.

Once their sin was dealt with, "God relented of the disaster that he said he would do to them, and He did not do it" – They were saved. **If Nineveh did not repent of their sin and evil ways, I have no doubt they would have been destroyed just like Sodom and Gomorrah.**

Solution to Sin

God has provided the solution to our Sin; we just have to receive the Law, the Teaching. The scripture says that "the lamb was slain from the foundation of the world" (*Revelations 13:8*). The decision for Christ to die for our sin was made before God even created the world. He knew we wouldn't be perfect, yet He loved us anyway. We need not "stay away" from our Father. He provided the solution to sin....

1 John 1:9

*If we **confess our sins**, he is **faithful and just to forgive us our sins** and to **cleanse** us from all **unrighteousness**.*

All we have to do to overcome the obstacle of Sin is believe in the sacrifice of our Big Brother, Jesus the Christ, and confess to Our Father that we are wrong and that He is right. Lying is wrong. Racism is wrong. Stealing is wrong. Cheating is wrong. Abusing our bodies (with drugs, gluttony, sexual immorality, etc.) is wrong. Manipulating people is wrong. God, your Ways are Right.

The issue we run into is that we attempt to justify our sins instead of admitting and agreeing that we are wrong and that God is right.

Hebrews 12:1

*Therefore, since we are surrounded by so great a cloud of witnesses, let us also **lay aside every weight, and sin** which clings so closely, and let us run with endurance the race that is set before us.*

The author of Hebrews paints the picture of life as an endurance race. And in this race, we are instructed to lay aside every weight and sin. It is obvious that weights and obstacles inhibit our ability to run a physical race, so it is with weights and sin - they inhibit our ability to run our spiritual race. Let us lay these obstacles aside and live the miraculous life we are designed to live.

As a side note to this entire chapter: Everything that is going on "wrong" in a believer's life isn't because of some sin or something they've done. Remember, they could be in a testing season like Job. And on the other side of the test lies the miraculous.

Let's Be Honest – Self-Evaluation:

1. Have you been truly repenting for past sins, or have you been simply sorry and feeling guilty? Is there an issue that you constantly fight time and time again?

2. Is there some issue/sin that is keeping you from receiving the miraculous results in your life?

3. Do you truly believe that God loves you in spite of your sin? Or have you adopted a mentality that you can't come to God because of your sin?

4. When you ask for forgiveness, do you truly believe that you are forgiven? Or do you feel that you have to earn forgiveness (be good for a week, 2 months, give extra money, be nice to people, etc.)?

5. What can you do to implement changes in your mentality to lead to true repentance?

OBSTACLE II: Immaturity/Lack of Management

"I'll just ask you again tomorrow…"
- Every child after their parents tell them 'NO'

God is known by many titles in the lives of the Believer. He is Jehovah - Righteous Judge - Lord (or Owner) - He is our Provider - Healer - an Ever-present Help in our time of need - our Strength in times of weakness. The Prophet, Jeremiah, even called Him a "Battle-axe". Yet, the most powerful aspect of Who God is in our lives is Our Father. The Hebrew word for Father is the term "Abba," which means "Source." He is our Source – the One who sustains us. Jesus nearly always referenced Him from this aspect in accordance to their Father - Son relationship.

One of the responsibilities of being a parent is to put your children in the best possible position to succeed. Proverbs 22:6 teaches us, *"Train up a child in the way he should go: and when he is old, he will not depart from it."* Part of this responsibility is giving children all the knowledge, resources, and tools needed to succeed. The other part (and maybe much more significant) is knowing your children and what they can/cannot handle. Every parent (I would hope) has an innate nature to want what's best for their children, to give their children a better life than they had when they were growing up, and to protect their children at all costs (even if it's protecting them from themselves).

Being the gracious, loving, and awesome Father that I am, I wanted to give my children the best that I could give them. I wanted them to have things that I didn't have growing up. **I can remember when my children were growing up and they started to go crazy; I don't know what it is about kids, but when they reach the age of 10-13 years old, they think they automatically know how to drive a car.** I don't know if it's their years of experience watching from the back seat or if a switch goes off in their brains, but every child thinks about or has the desire to drive their parent's vehicle. My wife and I had vehicles. It would have been easy to just throw them the keys and say, "Have at it; make sure you put on your seat belt and be back by 9 o'clock." It would have been easy to get them to praise and love me by giving in to their desires, but (as a parent) I knew my children. At such a young age, they weren't ready for the responsibility of driving a vehicle. They could not only have hurt themselves in an accident, but they could have potentially killed someone else – Not to mention damaging my credibility and reputation as a good parent.

Why am I using this example? God, OUR FATHER, does not give us certain blessings/miracles because we are not ready for the responsibility. We may think we can handle millions of dollars, but how many of us honestly have a plan in place for such wealth? We may think we can handle a spouse, but how many of us honestly are ready to make the sacrifices and changes that are needed in marriage? We may think we can handle healing, but how many of us would honestly end up right back in the hospital because we failed to take care of our bodies? God, being the Awesome, Loving, and Gracious Father that HE is, would love to give us whatever we desire. The scriptures even tell us as much...

Luke 11:9-10

9And I say unto you, Ask, and it shall be given you; seek, and ye shall find; knock, and it shall be opened unto you. 10For every one that asketh receiveth; and he that seeketh findeth; and to him that knocketh it shall be opened.

God **WANTS** to bless us with the miraculous – I can't stress this enough. He wants to give us the desires of our hearts. He even goes on to even compare Himself to us....

Luke 11:11-13

11If a son shall ask bread of any of you that is a father, will he give him a stone? or if he ask a fish, will he for a fish give him a serpent? 12Or if he shall ask an egg, will he offer him a scorpion? ***13If ye then, being evil, know how to give good gifts unto your children: how much more shall your heavenly Father give the Holy Spirit to them that ask him?***

However, just as we as parents know our children, God knows us. He knows what we are ready and capable of managing AND what responsibilities we are not ready to handle just yet. Just like a child isn't ready for the responsibility of driving, some of us aren't ready for certain miracles because the responsibility could lead us to harming ourselves. It could even be a danger to others. And most importantly, it would damage the credibility of God as a Father. If a 10-year-old has a car accident, the first thing people are going to ask is, "Where were his/her parents?" ... "Why did they let that child drive a car?" And so, it would be with God, Our Father.

Personally, I don't believe God ever tells us "No" when we ask for something unless it is outright against His Will or not in His Purpose for our lives. For example, "God, please kill my neighbor" or "God, please give me her husband." [I once prayed for God to make me a fireman.... God knew good and well that I wasn't jumping into a fire to save anyone.] I believe He tells us "Yes," especially concerning His promises (*for the promises of God are yea and amen*), and I truly believe that He tells us "Not Yet." Now, if you've ever been a child... "Not Yet" isn't a "Yes,"...but it also isn't "No." It means that there are things that need to be in place prior to that "Not Yet" becoming a definite "Yes." Once you become of age and take a few lessons, demonstrate that you can manage the responsibility...Okay – yes, you can drive.

It is likewise with God. When we pray, we may sometimes attract "storms," "tough situations," or even "just-so-happen-to-meet certain people." These "tests," "trials," and "temptations" aren't always from the Enemy. Some of our "chance meetings" and "happenstance encounters" aren't just coincidences. These are tactics, tools, and pieces of the blueprint that God utilizes to develop character (or reveal character flaws that we need to work on correcting) – that enable us to handle the miracles we ask of Our Father.

The Shunammite's Son

2 Kings 4:18-25, 32-37

¹⁸When the child had grown, he went out one day to his father among the reapers. ¹⁹And he said to his father, "Oh, my head, my head!" The father said to his servant, "Carry him to his mother." ²⁰And when he had lifted him and brought him to his mother, **the child sat on her lap till noon, and then he died.** *²¹And* <u>*she went up and laid him on the bed of the man of God and shut the door behind him and went out.*</u> *²²Then she called to her husband and said, "Send me one of the servants and one of the donkeys,* <u>*that I may quickly go to the man of God and come back again."*</u> *²³And he said, "Why will you go to him today? It is neither new moon nor Sabbath."* <u>*She said, "All is well."*</u> *²⁴Then she saddled the donkey, and she said to her servant, "Urge the animal on; do not slacken the pace for me unless I tell you." ²⁵So she set out and came to the man of God at Mount Carmel.*

³²When Elisha came into the house, **he saw the child lying dead on his bed.** *³³So* <u>*he went in and shut the door behind the two of them and prayed to the Lord. ³⁴Then he went up and lay on the child, putting his mouth on his mouth, his eyes on his eyes, and his hands on his hands. And as he stretched himself upon him, the flesh of the child became warm.*</u> *³⁵Then he got up again and walked once back and forth in the house, and went up and stretched himself upon him. The child sneezed seven times, and* <u>*the child opened his eyes.*</u> *³⁶Then he summoned Gehazi and said, "Call this Shunammite." So he called her. And when she came to him, he said,* **"Pick up your son."** *³⁷She came and fell at* *his feet, bowing to the ground. Then she picked up her son and went out.*

The Shunammite woman welcomed Elisha, the man of God, into their home during his travels. Elisha inquired of her deepest desires, and it was revealed that she was a widow. God gave her the miracle of having a child. Why? Because she blessed the man of God; but also, because she could manage and handle the responsibility.

[The worst thing that can happen after you've obtained a miracle is for your miracle to die: Your business you prayed for ends in bankruptcy.... Your marriage dies in divorce.... The cancer you were healed from returns.... You are fired from the job that just gave you a promotion and a raise. Do you question God? Get angry? What do you do??]

The Shunammite woman's son – her miracle – was DEAD. She didn't panic. She didn't fall to pieces. She didn't run to her husband and cry. She didn't accept "the death of her miracle." She knew what to do: she went to find God or someone that could get in touch with HIM - in this case, Elisha. She wasn't entertaining anyone's questions. Her response was, "All is well." She wasn't taking anyone else's advice: "All is well." She may not have known how to revive her son, but she knew enough to get in touch with the Source of the miracle. Elisha came to the house and revived the son.

[Are you ready for the responsibility of maintaining your miracle? When the miracle appears to die, do you believe that "All is well"? Can you handle the pressure and the weight that comes with that responsibility? Or will you just give up?

Response of Joseph

In Genesis, we have the story of Joseph.... He was the youngest of 11 at the time, and he was his father's favorite – he even got a special robe. In addition to being the favorite, Joseph began to have dreams that his older brothers and parents would bow to him. Of course, this made his brothers jealous, so they cast him into a pit and sold him into slavery. God kept and blessed Joseph: however, Joseph endured years of heartache and pain because of what his brother did to him. He needed a miracle to get out of slavery, out of prison. **[Could you handle the miracle of being delivered if it came with the responsibility of saving the very ones that threw you in a pit and sold you into slavery?]** Let's look at Joseph's response when he faced his brothers years later....

Genesis 45:4-7

*4So Joseph said to his brothers, "Come near to me, please." And they came near. And he said, "I am your brother, Joseph, whom you sold into Egypt. 5**And now do not be distressed or angry with yourselves because you sold me here, for God sent me before you to preserve life.** 6For the famine has been in the land these two years, and there are yet five years in which there will be neither plowing nor harvest. 7**And God sent me before you to preserve for you a remnant on earth, and to keep alive for you many survivors.***

Joseph was sold into slavery, put in prison, lied on for doing the right thing, forgotten by those he helped. But –

by God's grace – he received the miraculous elevation to become 2nd-in-Command to Pharaoh. He could handle the responsibility that came with the miracle. He knew what to do when he faced his brothers who had sold him into slavery. He knew what to do in years of plenty and in the years of lack. [Are you ready for the miracle of promotion? Could you handle such a miracle? Or once you have a position of power, would you seek revenge against those that had wronged you? Would you abuse the money and resources that come into your possession? Can God trust you with more, with greater?]

Jesus, the Christ

Jesus walked on water. Jesus cast out devils. Jesus fed thousands. Jesus healed people of incurable infirmities. Many of us want to walk in the miraculous powers that Jesus walked in. Could you handle the responsibility of being obedient, even unto death? You're famous; everyone loves you…would you die for everyone? Could you handle the burden of taking on the sins of the whole world?

While Jesus was being crucified these were his last moments:

Luke 23:34-37

*34 And Jesus said, "**Father, forgive them, for they know not what they do.**" And they cast lots to divide his garments. 35 And the people stood by, watching, but the rulers scoffed at him, saying, "He saved others; let him save himself, if he is the Christ of God, his Chosen One!"*

36 The <u>soldiers also mocked him</u>, <u>coming up and offering him sour wine</u> 37 and saying, <u>"If you are the King of the Jews, save yourself!"</u>

Could God trust to raise you from the dead without you seeking out those religious leaders that killed and wronged you? Would you ask God to forgive those that you've helped, but in your hour of need, they only stood watching? Would you ask God to spare the people you're dying for as they gamble for your clothes, mock you, questioning who you really are? This is the level of responsibility, discipline, and love in which Jesus had to walk to obtain his level of power and authority in the miraculous. Are you ready for such responsibility? Do you have such discipline? Could you love others at such depths?

The Rich Fool

One day, when Jesus was teaching the masses, he told them a parable of someone who wasn't able to handle the responsibility of the miraculous.

Luke 12:16-21

*16And he told them a parable, saying, "**The land of a rich man produced plentifully**, 17and he thought to himself, 'What shall I do, for I have nowhere to store my crops?' 18And he said, 'I will do this: I will tear down my barns and build larger ones, and there I will store all my grain and my goods. 19And I will say to my soul, "Soul, you have ample goods laid up for many years; relax, eat, drink, be merry."' 20But God said to him, 'Fool! This night your soul* *is required of you, and the things you have prepared, whose will they be?'* ²¹*So is the one who lays up treasure for himself and is not rich toward God."*

This rich man received a miraculous harvest. He had so many crops that he didn't even have room to store them. He had overflow that would last him for years to come. Instead of becoming a blessing to others, establishing a legacy that would generate wealth for his children, or even giving a "first-fruit" offering to God, he told himself that this was enough. He couldn't handle the responsibility of receiving the overflow from God. He didn't manage God's resources well. He tore down his barns, built larger ones, and decided to live the rest of his days using the miracle only for himself.

[When we are not able to handle the miraculous, God removes it from our possession. Can God trust you with the miraculous?]

I see people all the time praying for healing from high blood pressure, diabetes, lung cancer, etc. If God healed them miraculously, I wonder if they could maintain or manage the Healing. If God healed a person from high blood pressure, would they stop eating recklessly? ... Would they manage their diet? ... Would they begin to exercise more to maintain their Healing? If God healed you from Diabetes, are you capable of managing normal sugar levels by giving up so many sweets, bread, carbohydrates, and other foods that taste so good? Are you ready for that responsibility? Could you give up smoking if you were healed from lung cancer?

Is there something that you're praying to God for that you're not ready to handle? Let's change God's "Not Yet" into a "Yes" by addressing our flaws, inadequacies, mindsets, strongholds, and shortcomings. Let's demonstrate to God that we understand that we're asking for the miraculous and that we're able to manage the responsibility that comes with it. Let's first prepare – and allow ourselves to be prepared – for that miracle for which we are asking God; otherwise, we have a perpetual "Not Yet" stamped on the ticket to our miracle.

(As an aside, let me say this. I know that some sicknesses, diseases, etc. happen to people. People who exercised and took care of their bodies have ended up with cancer. Good people that ended up with autoimmune diseases like Multiple Sclerosis, Lupus, Rheumatoid Arthritis, etc. Young people who have type 1 Diabetes and other ailments that keep them from living like other young kids. It doesn't seem fair. And I won't patronize nor act like I have the answers why some things have happened. I truly don't know. But I am praying, fasting, interceding, and agreeing with you that the miraculous healing occurs. I am seeking God with you for answers to understand WHY these things happened to you or your loved ones. If there is something that needs to be addressed from our ancestral lineage, something we're not in alignment with, or some other greater purpose - I'm asking God to reveal it. I know the older religious generation told us, "You don't question God." But God is not afraid of our questions. He's the one with answers.

Let's Be Honest – Self-Evaluation:

1. Are you ready for the responsibility that comes with the blessing / miraculous?

2. Have you been denied blessings / miracles because you were not ready? What did you do to prepare yourself?

3. What is God able to trust you with? What is He unable to trust you with?

4. Have you been told "Not Yet" from God? Did you take that as a "No"?

OBSTACLE III: Lack of Communication/Prayer

"The single biggest problem in communication is the illusion that it has taken place." - George Bernard Shaw

There have been many books written on the topic of prayer. If you asked every "Believer," they would say that it's important to pray. However, as the late Dr. Myles Munroe said, "Prayer is the least attended meeting and least practiced component in the body of Christ." Most of us (yes, myself included before I was taught better) don't pray because of our past experiences. We needed miracles. We prayed for things for ourselves, and we prayed for other people. But alas, we saw no results. We were sincere. We had faith. However, to be honest…over time, we just gave up on prayer altogether because prayer didn't seem to work for us. (I've been there. I know the feeling of disappointment all too well.)

But if you're ever going to get your miracle from God, prayer is ESSENTIAL. The Bible says, "Ye have not because ye ask not." We have replaced intimate time in prayer with God with the "all-inclusive prayer": "God, just give me what You want me to have!" ... "God, just do what You want to do!" ... "God, I accept whatever You have for me!" I think everyone generally understands what people mean when they make such proclamations – However, if you're not more specific or more intentional, how will you know that your prayers have been answered?

If your life is average and mediocre, do you really believe this is all your Heavenly FATHER has for you?? Don't allow the past failures, disappointments, and heartaches to instill fear and cripple you from even participating in your citizenship right of communication through prayer. Don't allow seeds of doubt to keep you from asking God for the desires of your heart.

Requests/Asking of God

James 4:2-3

²*You desire and do not have, so you murder. You covet and cannot obtain, so you fight and quarrel.* **You do not have, because you do not ask.** ³*You ask and do not receive, because you ask wrongly, to spend it on your passions.*

Matthew 7:7-8

*7"**Ask**, and it will be given to you; seek, and you will find; knock, and it will be opened to you. 8**For everyone who asks receives**, and the one who seeks finds, and to the one who knocks it will be opened.*

God sees and knows where you are in your life. He knows what you are in need of and what you desire. However, we don't trust God. Therefore, when we want money, we steal (even kill) for it. We want what others have, so we fight to take it from them. We want a better life; but we settle for the temporary escape in illegal drugs, immoral sex, and mindless distractions.

If we want the miraculous life, God is telling us how to obtain it: ASK. I know, I know, I know…. you're thinking, "But I did ask, and nothing happened" … But did you ask the way God tells us to ask? What does God mean when He tells us to "ask"? How or what am I supposed to "seek"? What does God mean by "knocking"? Is there some door I'm unaware of? These are the kinds of questions that bring clarity to understanding prayer and communication.

Case in point, when God instructs us to ask, it doesn't mean to beg. It doesn't mean to cower and hope that God "works things out on our behalf." No! "Ask" in the Hebrew language is translated "to demand" – of course, not in a disrespectful manner, but rather a self-assured knowing that you have a right to what you're asking.

Asking is intricately tied to your knowledge of your rights. If your lights are turned off and you've paid the bill, you call the power company and demand that your power is restored – you don't beg or plead: you have a right to the service. You have a right to walk down the street and not be harassed by strangers, the police, or even fellow citizens – you shouldn't have to beg. If you have a valid driver's license, you have the right to drive the car for which you're paying the note and insurance – you don't have to plead with anyone for permission. Whatever you have a right to, you don't beg or plead…You demand.

If the police arrest someone, and don't inform them of their "Miranda Rights" (You have the right to remain silent…. You have the right to an attorney…. Etc.), contrary to popular opinion, they don't automatically escape punishment. However, much of the evidence gathered from anything the suspect says or during the arrest CANNOT be used against the suspect during a trial.

Why is all this important? God informed us that "we have not, because we ask not." However, many of us don't ask because we don't know how. We don't ask properly because we are ignorant of our rights. We don't have the miracles because we don't demand and command Him to give us what is rightfully promised. We don't see the miracles because we aren't effectively communicating with God.

Effective Communication vs Talking

Although I won't get into the depth and nuance that is prayer, I do think we need to understand some important aspects of prayer. (Jesus' Teachings in scripture – as the Source – and Dr. Myles Munroe's book on Prayer, "The

Power and Purpose of Prayer"– an excellent resource – would both be excellent places to start a study on prayer.)

WHAT is prayer? ... Prayer is simply communication with God. That sounds simple, but there is some depth to that statement. Prayer is how, when, and where we do the "asking." Prayer is COMMUNICATION with God – you see, a lot of us TALK TO God or TALK AT God, but we don't **COMMUNICATE WITH** Him. There is a difference between talking and communicating.

I learned this lesson all too well in marriage. I would talk to my wife, and she would talk to me; however, there were times when the messages weren't received or fully understood. We were raised in two different environments. I was raised in downtown Mobile, Alabama. My father was a gambler. I had umpteen siblings that I didn't know. We weren't raised in Church. I didn't know a thing about God. I'm from what many would call "the streets." My wife, on the other hand, was raised just a little bit differently... her father was a Pastor of five different locations. They were raised to love and respect God. She knew all her brothers and sisters. They were raised to go to college and be successful. We would interpret each other's words from a completely different basis of experiences.

There would be times when she would say something to me, and I'd interpret it in a completely different way than the way she intended. There would be times when I'd talk to my wife, only to find out years later that she didn't understand the message I was trying to convey.

I can remember driving one night with her, and we stopped to get a snack: stage planks, cheese, and soda. We just rode around and talked. She then said, "You know what... this is all I ever wanted." I felt all warm and good inside. "OHHH, I'm with my Baby...and she's happy. She LOVES ME. WOW!!! I'm the Luckiest Man in the world," I thought to myself. Then my mind got to working: "Hold on... you mean to tell me that to make you happy, it only took a quarter tank of gas, stage planks, cheese, and soda???" To really understand my frustration, you have to realize that I was buying my wife vehicles, clothes, fur coats, jewelry - thinking that was going to make her happy. To this day, sometimes I jokingly tell her, "I could have been RICH...all it took was a quarter tank of gas, stage planks, cheese, and soda."

How did this happen? There was talking, but no communication. In talking, you understand what the other person says (their words - the 'what' they said). In communication, you understand what the other person means (the 'why' they said it). Talking comes by imitation (a form of teaching): place a baby in any environment (regardless of culture/race/ethnicity/gender/genetic predisposition) and he/she will eventually learn to speak the language of that environment (whether it be English, Spanish, Dutch, French, etc.).

Likewise, we have to be taught how to communicate with people because we're all different. We understand things differently. In order to learn how to communicate, I have to be in the other person's environment or their mind to learn what they mean when they are talking. Not only were my wife and I raised differently, but she is also of the opposite sex - so that communication is on a different level altogether. Whereas I may be thinking logically, she may be thinking emotionally. Whereas she may be thinking details, I may be thinking "big picture." Whereas she may be thinking for the present, I may be thinking for and about the future.

And so, it is with God; Whereas GOD may be speaking Spiritually or prophetically, we may be thinking from a worldly standpoint. We have to get on the same "wavelengths" in order to communicate effectively and get the results to our prayers.

Prayer goes beyond talking to God into the depths of communication with God. This doesn't come by simply going to church or watching other people pray. Isn't it interesting that the disciples walked with Jesus, saw him perform many, many miracles (walk on water, turn water to wine, show them where to fish, raise the dead) and the only thing they asked Him to teach them was how to pray? They asked Jesus, "How do you communicate with the Father? What are the steps to this activity you do every morning without us?" (If it had been me... I'd want to know how to heal eyes, how to walk on water, how to feed thousands. I'd be more enamored by the miracles.) However, the disciples noticed something about Jesus. They noticed that He spent a lot more time praying than He did performing miracles or anything else. So...by deductive reasoning, they concluded that prayer was more important than any other activity. Let's examine Jesus' response to their request...

Luke 11:1-2

*Now Jesus was praying in a certain place, and when he finished, one of his disciples said to him, "Lord, **teach us*** *to pray, as John taught his disciples."* ²*And he said to them, "When you pray, say:"*

I'll just stop right there. The disciples recognized Jesus' prayer life and asked Him to teach them how to do it. The first words to His response are important: "When you pray..." There is an expectancy in His response. Not *"If you pray"* but *"When you pray"* denotes that prayer isn't a choice for the Believer. To live effectively and to experience the miraculous, you should be praying and in communication with God. In Luke, He even tells you how often you should pray...

Luke 18:1

*And he told them a parable to the effect that they **ought always to pray** and not lose heart.*

Paul reiterates this in 1 Thessalonians:16-18
¹⁶*Rejoice always,* ¹⁷***pray without ceasing***, ¹⁸*give thanks in all circumstances; for this is the will of God in Christ Jesus for you.*

We are told to pray always. Does this mean that we're supposed to be in prayer – head bowed, eyes closed – 24 hours a day? No, of course not. But we should be in constant contact, in constant communication with Heaven at all times. There should be time devoted to meditation and prayer (daily!); yet, as we travel, work, interact with other people, and go about our daily lives – our intentions, actions, speech, thoughts should be in alignment with Him. If we come to a difficult situation or face a tough decision, we should take it to God in prayer - ask for His insight and wisdom.

In communication through prayer is often where Jesus was taught and instructed what to do. Jesus would make statements such as, "I only do what I see my Father do" ... "If you've seen me, you've seen the Father" ... "I and the Father are One" ... How could He make such bold proclamations???

As we stated earlier, Teaching is a reproduction of the Teacher's mind into a vessel (student, disciple, person) who wants to learn. Once the vessel knows and understands what the Teacher knows and understands (regarding that information), they are the same. The Teacher and the student are One through communication. Because the student now thinks like the Teacher, their actions are going to be the same concerning a particular topic, subject, or agenda.

Keys to Unlocking Effective Communication

I. Environment

The first important step in communication is often the most overlooked. Where are you having this conversation? What kind of atmosphere is this conversation taking place? The environment sets the tone and is the first impression as to the nature, seriousness, or intimacy of the conversation. If you want to talk to me, and we're having the conversation at a loud party with music and other people - I'm going to assume that this isn't a serious or intimate conversation. On the other hand, if you ask to block off hours of my schedule and take me somewhere secluded and exclusive - I'm going to assume the conversation is going to be more detailed and intimate than "I just wanted to say hello" or "What did you eat for lunch today?"

Jesus took this very concept into consideration when discussing prayer. In Matthew 6:6, Jesus instructs:

But when you pray, go into your room and shut the door and pray to your Father who is in secret. And your Father who sees in secret will reward you.

Alone...Quiet...Secret places. For Jesus this was often in the mountains. For others it may be a prayer room or closet. [Corporate prayer (prayer meeting, prayer in church) is fine, but it should never substitute for one's personal prayer time with God.] Jesus seems to suggest that the environment and atmosphere when we communicate with God should be one in which there are very little distractions. *"Go into your room and shut the door...secret"*. There's an intimacy that is suggested by the environment that you can be honest, open, "naked and not ashamed". You can have communications that you couldn't have with anyone else. I wouldn't talk about **my fears** that paralyze me, **my anger thoughts** that could land me in prison, or some of **my deep-rooted insecurities** that people could take advantage of; I wouldn't discuss these things in a public forum or in a crowded restaurant - the atmosphere wouldn't be appropriate for such.

II. Audience

The next step in communication is to have an understanding of your relationship to your audience. Jesus instructs us to *"Pray to Your, Father..."* I would talk and communicate differently with my father than I would with a president or dignitary of a foreign nation. I would talk more informally with my friends than I would if I were in a court of law or business meeting. The relationships are different, thus the communication would be different.

God is our Father, our Source – Christ: our Savior – the Holy Spirit: our Comforter/Teacher. Because it depends on the relationship, you would be more open with someone whom you're close to as opposed to strangers. Therefore, when we communicate with God, we can be open and honest about what's bothering us – He already knows about it anyway: "I'm distraught because my mother has cancer – I want her to be healed" ... "My business is failing (or I need to pay bills) – I need financial resources" ... "God, I'm on drugs and depressed – Help me."

God is Father, yet He is also the King, the Lord, and the Righteous Judge. To effectively communicate with Him, you have to bring Laws, His Words, and His Teachings to correlate with your honesty. "I desire healing for my mother – You said 'healing is the children's bread'; You said, 'By My stripes, you're healed'" ... "I need financial resources – You said I'd be the lender and not the borrower; You said, 'I've never seen the righteous forsaken nor his seed begging bread.'" ... "I'm depressed/on drugs – You said that I'm made in Your image and your likeness; ... You said that You'd never leave me nor forsake me."

Notice Jesus did not tell us to pray to him...or to Mary...or to the Holy Spirit...or to Peter or anyone else. I've seen this error many times during church services; people are praying to other persons than God. Jesus is our Savior: He's our big brother, and we are thankful that he's the reason we can communicate with the Father—But Jesus isn't the Father; He is the Son. Mary was the Mother of Jesus—But she's not the Father. When we pray, we should direct our communication to God, our Father.

III. Responses

The final, and often most overlooked, element of communication is Allowing/Receiving Responses to make sure you both understand the assignment.

So many times, we think we're communicating, but we're just talking. There have been many times that I've been having conversations with my wife, my family, or my friends and thought we were really communicating. What I was actually doing was listening enough to what they were saying to craft a response or reinforce my position. I really didn't care what they had to say...I just needed to be ready to talk when it was my turn. I wanted to be heard and understood yet hardly granted them the same respect.

This "Hear me - Understand me - Glad we had this conversation" mentality is WRONG. Never did I take the time to pause and pursue further inquiry into what they meant when they said particular things, used certain words, or evoked certain expressions. When my wife said

"Love," I just assumed that she meant it in the same shape, form, and fashion that I was thinking in my head. Never did I try to get in her head and extrapolate what she meant. When my friends said "Trust," I (in my unknown arrogance) did not for one second think they could possibly have a meaning different from my own.

Unfortunately, and to our detriment, we do the same with God. We read scriptures and think we know what God means instead of actually trying to get into His mind. We "say" our prayers, not giving Him a chance to respond, to correct, to reprove, to confirm or show us error in what we've attempted to articulate. Just as in our relationships with people…we think we have communicated, we think that we have an understanding with God, when we actually don't. And it isn't until things seem to fall apart or don't work in our favor that we look to God as if to say, "God, why are You doing this to me? … I'm your boy…or I thought I was your girl…. I thought we had an understanding."

Often because we don't communicate effectively, we miss when God does answer our prayers. You may not get a check in the mail, but you may get instructions – you may get a business idea or opportunity – you may get Teaching on tithing and management. But if you're still looking for a check or cash from someone…you'll miss out on the miraculous that God has for you.

There's an old familiar story that comes to mind…

*A fellow was stuck on his rooftop in a flood. He was praying to God for help. Soon a man in a **rowboat** came by and the man shouted to the fellow on the roof, "Jump in. I can save you."*

The stranded fellow shouted back, "No, it's Okay. I'm praying to God, and He is going to save me." So, the rowboat went on.

*Then a **motorboat** came by. "The woman in the motorboat shouted, "Jump in. I can save you."*

To this the stranded man said, "No, thanks. I'm praying to God, and He is going to save me. I have faith." So, the motorboat went on.

*Then a **helicopter** came by and the pilot shouted down, "Grab this rope and I will lift you to safety."*

To this the stranded man again replied, "No, thanks. I'm praying to God, and He is going to save me. I have faith." So, the helicopter reluctantly flew away.

Soon the water rose above the rooftop, and the man drowned. He went to Heaven and finally got his chance to discuss this whole situation with God. At this point he exclaimed, "I had faith in You, but You didn't save me; You let me drown. I don't understand why!"

To this God replied, "I sent you a rowboat...a motorboat...AND a helicopter!! What more did you expect?"

Like the man stuck on the roof, we miss God's responses because we're expecting Him to answer in a particular way, instead of being open to how He chooses to respond. Are you going to stay stranded in a dire situation because you're unable to recognize how God communicates with you? You may get instructions to forgive someone that wronged you … to give your last … to sacrifice your time. These may be God's responses/answers to your prayers. Are you hearing Him clearly? Are you able to "see" God in these responses? Will you participate in obtaining your miracle? Or will you just continue to wait for God to answer in the manner you think He should? (We'll get more into obedience later in this book.)

Asking Amiss

The last components of prayer and communication that I want to discuss are our intentions and motives – to put it more plainly: the "why," or "reason," or purpose of your prayers. Let's study James' account once again...

James 4:2-3
²You desire and do not have, so you murder. You covet and cannot obtain, so you fight and quarrel. You do not have, because you do not ask. **³You ask and do not receive, because you ask wrongly, to spend it on your passions.**

The third verse in this scripture tells us that we ask and don't receive because we ask with wrong motives and intentions. You ask ... but you're going to misuse and abuse that which we've asked of God. Does this describe you? Have you asked yourself "why" you wanted that miracle? Why do you want healing miracles? ... So that you won't die? ... So that you'll feel better? Why do you want financial miracles? ... So you can brag to your family and friends? ... So you can buy a lot of expensive things? ... So you can travel the world? Why do you want to be off drugs to be spared from going to jail? What is your motivation and intention? Why do you want a miracle to save your marriage? ... So that you don't get embarrassed by a divorce? ... For the kids' sake?

These may be your reasons, but these rarely (if ever) move God. You want your miracle... show God how He is a Priority in your request: "I want healing because I can't do Your will effectively if I'm sick or ill" .... "I want a financial miracle because it would be a stain upon Your reputation if my needs aren't met; I need finances to carry out the Purpose and Plans You have for my life" .... "I want to be off drugs (not depressed) because that's not who You created me to be; You created me to have dominion, not to be dominated; In order for me to be useful to you, I need to be sober and of sound mind" .... "I want a miracle to save my marriage because it would reflect poorly on You that we profess to be Your Children but can't make the institution that You ordained work; Help us."

As you make God a priority in your motivations for prayer, just watch the miraculous responses.

I want you to know two things about prayer and communicating effectively with God:

1. It doesn't come overnight. Just like any activity that is learned through Teaching, it has to be practiced before being perfected.

2. Not everyone's methods of communicating will be the same. There may be similarities, but we are all different. We have different callings, different assignments, different communication styles, yet the overarching theme should be the same – intimating my desires to Him and receiving responses to understand how and if this plays a role in His grand Will/Plan/Purpose for my life.

Please let me reiterate... Prayer is Essential. The disciples saw the miracles constantly. They were impressed, inspired, and amazed by them, yet they asked to be taught how to pray. I believe that they got a Revelation: "Perhaps, it's what He's doing, hearing, seeing, receiving in prayer alone with God that allows Him to be so powerful when He is among the people." Prayer is time invested, not time wasted. Jesus spent hours praying, communicating with God, and only minutes performing miracles, solving the problems of man.

Again, I say... Prayer is Essential.

Let's Be Honest – Self-Evaluation:

1. Do you pray to God? Do you know how to pray? How often do you pray?

2. Do you get results when you pray?

3. Did anything happen to make you give up on trying to communicate with God?

4. Have you been communicating with God effectively? What are some ways that your communication can be improved?

5. Do you demand your rights or are you begging?

6. What are your motivations when you pray? Are you selfish in your motives? Or do you desire God's Will?

OBSTACLE IV: Lack of Faith

"To one who has faith, no explanation is necessary. To one without faith, no explanation is possible."
- St. Thomas Aquinas

Another common obstacle that prevents us from seeing the miraculous is a lack of faith. If we examine ourselves when we pray and ask God for miracles in our lives, we may find that we really don't believe that God will keep His Word. I know this is often the case because we buffer our requests with statements like: "If it be the Lord's Will..." or "I know God is in Control and that He is going to do what He wants to do..." These statements put the responsibility on God rather than on us if we feel that our prayers have failed. So, when we are let down because the miracle didn't occur ... because the family member died of the disease ... because the house or apartment was taken ... because the child went to jail... we have an excuse or reason that it didn't occur – that it's not our fault: "It was God — He's the reason it didn't happen" or "It must not have been His Will." All the while, we bear no blame at all with this type of mentality.

Most of us have an idea of what faith is. Some of us can quote the scripture found in Hebrews 11:1 – *"Now Faith is the SUBSTANCE of things hoped for, the EVIDENCE of things not seen."* The writer tells us that Faith is **substance** and **evidence**.

Take the wind for example: Can you see the wind? Do you know when the wind is present? I may not be able to physically see it with my eyes, but on a hot, sweltering day I can **feel** the presence of the cool, refreshing wind against my skin. Even if I'm inside and looking out the window, I can **see** the majestic, powerful effects of winds as they nearly break and bend tree branches and leaves to their whim. There are even some settings in which I can **hear** the howling of the winds as if they were a pack of wild animals migrating to a distant unknown. Do you understand? Even though the wind can't be seen (per se), it is a physical presence.

The same goes for Faith. My faith is the substance and evidence that what I'm believing for exists. Faith is like transitional matter because faith is what "transitions" something from the **unseen realm** into the **seen realm** – from the spiritual world into the natural world – from the crevices of dreams and imaginations into reality.

(Continuing with the theme of correlating Faith to the winds) Before a cloud in the sky is seen, before a roar of thunder or a flash of lightning, even before a drop of rain is felt…you feel the winds first. And that is how Faith operates: the winds of Faith often blow before the rains of miracles are manifested in our lives. All throughout scripture, before the miracle of healing can be felt…before the miraculous wealth transfer can be seen… before you see your prayer for your miracle come to fruition… there must be a measure of faith.

Mustard Seed Faith

Luke 17:5-6

[5]*The apostles said to the Lord, "**Increase our faith!**"* [6]*And the Lord said, "If you had faith like a grain of mustard*

seed, you could say to this mulberry tree, 'Be uprooted and planted in the sea,' and it would obey you.

The disciples asked Jesus to increase their faith. Their question inherently shows they believed that they didn't have enough faith or that they needed more. I've often heard this scripture preached and taught. However, I've gotten a slightly different revelation that it's not about the **quantity** (or size) of your faith. But rather, it's about the **quality** of your faith – that if you believe with "**faith LIKE a grain of mustard seed**" you could speak and things would happen. The scripture never puts emphasis on the size, but rather the type of seed. Though a mustard seed is definitely a small seed, the mustard seed has other unique qualities.

One such unique quality is that the mustard seed **cannot be hybridized** – that means that it cannot be mixed with another plant species. It will not grow into a variant species of plant like other seeds. The mustard seed only grows when it is pure and uncontaminated. The same is true of Faith. Your faith in God can't be mixed with doubt, or worry, or contaminated with concerns of "what people might say." Like the mustard seed, your faith won't grow in those conditions. (We'll discuss contamination later.)

Secondly, the way the disciples asked the question seemed to imply that more Faith could be given to them...like asking for a raise on the job: "Increase our pay" Or turning up the volume on the television: "Increase the volume." The disciples asked Jesus: "Increase our faith; turn it up; give us more!" Jesus answered them in a manner that doesn't seem to take into account their preconceived notion of Faith: He addressed Faith differently. He talks of Faith in the manner of seed, which implies that Faith isn't given, but rather it is grown. Jesus implies, "I can't give you faith; rather, the faith you possess has to grow and mature like a mustard seed."

Now if you know anything about Jesus, you know that He would have a difficult time explaining Kingdom (Spiritual) principles in an earthly environment. One such barrier in communicating spiritual truths is the concept of time. **God exists in eternity**, outside of time; however, **mankind lives in time**. The disconnect is obvious. However, this is why God can call someone or something beyond what he/she/it presently appears to be. For instance, God called David a king when he was only a shepherd boy. He changed Abram's name to Abraham which means "father of many nations" even though he had no children. He called Gideon a mighty warrior even when was acting like a coward. (You get the picture.) Time is irrelevant to God. He doesn't have to wait to call the person or thing what it will become. To God it is already in the mature form—even though it is in seed form presently.

Where most would only see a mustard seed, God sees an entire forest. So even though you only have "one mustard seed of faith" ... God sees a "forest of faith." You have what you need to grow and mature to the point of being able to speak to trees and mountains and cast them into the sea. You have the faith to speak to a storm and it will cease – to speak to an illness and healing will take place – to speak to any situation and have it manifest according to the words you've spoken. This ability comes from growing and maturing in your faith.

A baby may not be able to talk or walk in their current form, but as they grow and mature, they learn to talk, sing, walk, and even run. You don't have to add legs or alter their tongues or anything. When they are simply in an environment of teaching and encouragement, these abilities and capabilities develop. So, it is with Faith.... You may speak and nothing happens right now...but keep growing, keep maturing, keep speaking, keep being in environments of teaching and encouragement... and watch the miracles (fueled by your faith) manifest.

Faith is Neither Good nor Bad

Faith is simply belief. It is a power unlike anything you're likely to experience. Power (in and of itself) is not good or bad; it simply exists. Now the wielder of the power can use it for good (to help others, to make the world a better place), or the wielder can use the power for bad or with negligence (to destroy, for selfish ambitions, etc.). Faith is of the same ilk: Faith can be used with good or bad intentions.

*Positive Thought of what God has spoken
—develops—>Faith in God
*Faith in God —leads to—>Positive Manifestation

I begin with positive thoughts on God's Teaching that I'm healed: "Healing is the children's bread" – I constantly confess and am reminded of healing; I constantly remind myself of how God healed the people in the scriptures—

My faith in God's ability to heal grows—Healing manifests.

Or the Contrary...

*Negative Thought of what God has spoken
—-develops——> Lack of Faith in God
(Faith in the Negative Report)

*Lack of Faith in God (Faith in the Negative Report)
——leads to ——> Negative Manifestation

I don't believe that I can be healed – I believe the doctor's report that I have only 3 months to live; Whenever asked, I say that "I only got three months". I'm reminded of others in the same situation that only had 3 months to live and died in 1 month – My faith in God is absent; My faith in the doctor's report grows – Healing cannot manifest.

This is why God tells us what to think. It's not that He's trying to control you; He's trying to grow your faith and the positive manifestations in your life. In Philippians 4:8, we are instructed:

Finally brethren, Whatsoever things are true, whatsoever things are honest, whatsoever things are just, whatsoever things are pure, whatsoever things are lovely, whatsoever things are of good report; if there be any virtue and if there be any praise, **think on these things**.

Seven Levels of Faith

Bishop Tudor Bismarck teaches that there are Seven Levels of Faith.

Faith to Salvation – At this level of Faith, the individual believes and accepts that Jesus was the Ultimate Sacrifice for our sins and that we are once again connected back to our Father. This Faith enables the Believer to accept the indwelling of the Holy Spirit, the saving of our Spirit Man.

Ephesians 2:8,9

*8For by grace you have been **saved through faith**. And this is not your own doing; it is the gift of God, 9not a result of works, so that no one may boast.*

Paul here explains to the Church at Ephesus that they received salvation through Faith. It was a gift by the grace of God and not of our own doing. We weren't so clever, so holy, or good enough to come up with the faith to receive God's gift of salvation.

Faith to Works – At this level of Faith, your faith will have accompanying actions.

James 2:14-17

14What good is it, my brothers, if someone says he has faith but does not have works? Can that faith save him? 15If a brother or sister is poorly clothed and lacking in daily food, 16and one of you says to them, "Go in peace, be warmed and filled," without giving them the things needed for the body, what good is that? ¹⁷***So also faith by itself, if it does not have works, is dead.***

Faith has to have the accompanying actions to be effective. You can believe and have faith for a million-dollar miracle; however, if you don't put forth the energy, effort, or accompanying actions to acquire and prepare for such, it will never come to pass. So many of us have faith for dreams and desires that will forever lie dormant because we never put the works to our faith.

Faith to Sacrifice – This level of faith is transitory, but it describes a level of Faith and belief at which many people remain. This is the level of faith to which people had to develop once Adam disobeyed and abdicated his Kingdom Dominion on the earth. Once this occurred, Sin entered the earth thereby activating Death (separation from God).

Genesis 3:21 – The First Sacrifice

And the Lord God made for Adam and for his wife garments of skins and clothed them.

To satisfy the Death requirement, one had to rectify Sin. There could be no remission of sin without the shedding of blood (*Hebrews 9:22*). Therefore, this is where the Faith to Sacrifice comes in: In order to keep Death from activating in their lives spiritually, God's people were required to sacrifice certain animals and shed the blood thereof for their sins (as noted in the example given by God once Adam disobeyed). Unfortunately, the sacrifice of animals was limited and couldn't cover every sin that the people would commit. This is where Faith to Salvation enters the equation - and Jesus becomes the Ultimate Sacrifice for our sins.

However, we continue to try to function in God's system in this manner. If we do wrong, we feel that sacrificing a big offering (or something valuable) will make us right with God. If we mistreat our brothers, we feel as if going to church will rectify the initial mistreatment and make us okay with God. If we cheat on our spouse, we feel as if treating her to the spa or buying him nice gifts will rectify the sin. If we sin against God, we feel that we have to do something good or "offer some sacrifice" in order to be placed back in right-standing with Him.

This is no longer the reason we operate in Faith to Sacrifice. Instead of sacrificing animals, we should sacrifice our will for God's Will. Instead of big financial sacrifices, we should sacrifice our plans, ideas, and strategies for God's Purposes. At this level of faith, we have no problem giving anything to God, because we understand it all belongs to him anyway.

Faith to Obedience – This is a progression of the Faith to Sacrifice - At this level of faith, **YOU** are essentially the offering; **YOU** become a living sacrifice (Romans 13:1). Your mind, behavior, motivations, intentions are in congruence to God's Will.

1 Samuel 15:22

And Samuel said, "Has the Lord as great delight in burnt offerings and sacrifices, as in obeying the voice of the

Lord? Behold, **to obey is better than sacrifice***, and to listen than the fat of rams.*

Faith to act in accordance with God's instructions and teaching negates the need to sacrifice because of disobedience. This scripture is from when Samuel was about to tell Saul that God was taking the kingdom from him because of disobedience. God needs us to get to this level of Faith to bring a manifestation of His Will into the earth realm. (We will discuss more about obedience, and its connection to faith later.)

Faith to Prosperity – At this level of Faith, you prosper and see fruit from the seeds of your faith.

3 John 1:2

Beloved, I wish above all things that thou mayest prosper and be in health, even as thy soul prospereth.

You are successful. You are living a life connected to God. God's Will, agenda, purpose, plans and intentions are fulfilled in your life. Because of you, other people will be successful in their purpose. This could come in the form of great wealth, or it could be peace that surpasses all understanding. It could be happiness and joy or having passion and doing what you love every day. Living life according to God's Word, instructions, and teachings – instead of the limited vision of our eyes and senses – will place us in a position to prosper and be in good health.

Faith to Healing/Miracles – At this level of Faith, one has the faith to believe that miracles will occur and even graduate to become the person that performs miracles in the lives of others.

1 Corinthians 12:8-11

*⁸For to one is given by the Spirit the word of wisdom; to another the word of knowledge by the same Spirit; ⁹To another **faith by the same Spirit**; to another the **gifts of healing by the same Spirit**; ¹⁰**To another the working of miracles**; to another prophecy; to another discerning of spirits; to another divers kinds of tongues; to another the interpretation of tongues: ¹¹But all these worketh that one and the selfsame Spirit, dividing to every man severally as he will.*

All throughout scripture, we see Faith intricately tied to the miraculous. It was the Centurion Soldier's faith that Jesus noted when He healed the servant on his behalf. Jesus highlighted the faith of four friends that tore through a roof to help their friend. It was the faith of the Syrophoenician woman (a.k.a. the Canaanite Woman) that Jesus acknowledged prior to healing her daughter. It was this same Faith to Healing and the Miraculous that Jesus groomed the disciples and that many other patriarchs in the faith demonstrated.

Faith to Victory – This is the level of Faith that allows one to overcome trials, tribulations, circumstances, temptations, etc.

1 John 5:3-5

³For this is the love of God that we keep his commandments. And his commandments are not burdensome. ⁴For everyone who has been born of God overcomes the world. ***And this is the victory that has overcome the world—our faith.*** *⁵Who is it that overcomes the world except the one who believes that Jesus is the Son of God?*

Faith to Victory is the belief that we can be successful no matter what arises. It is the Faith to Victory that allowed Jesus to tap into the power of authority over situations, circumstances, challenges, trials, demonic forces, etc. Therefore, we saw Him speak to the weather, walk on water, defeat the enemy in the wilderness, conquer death, hell, and the grave, etc. And because Jesus demonstrated the Faith to Overcome, we have this same faith and ability to overcome and lead victorious lives as well.

Now, when I first heard about the Levels of Faith, I looked at them as a certain progression that everyone must go through. The first step is Faith to Salvation, then Faith to Works, etc. … with the last step being Faith to Victory. I thought that everyone proceeded in this manner. However, that is not the case. It's true that this may be the outline for some, while others may have a completely different progression in their faith experience. While some may start with Faith to Salvation, others may end with it. Some may start with Faith to Miracles or Faith to Prosperity, and others may have to build up to Faith to Sacrifice. Some people may have grown up in an environment where business, finances, and wealth-building were normal, so their Faith to Prosperity comes much easier than Faith to Works or Faith to Salvation. Most people who grew up in "religion" were accustomed to an environment where people received salvation, so the

Faith to Salvation may have come easier than the Faith to Victory.

Paul wrote in Romans 12:3, that we were all given a measure of faith that God assigned. Therefore, just because one has the faith to believe for Healing and Miracles, it doesn't make them better than the person who has the faith to receive Salvation. Having the Faith to Victory doesn't make one better than the person who has the Faith to Sacrifice. We may start with "a measure," but the objective is to encourage one another in faith, unite and agree in faith, and to most importantly grow in the progression of faith.

Growing in Faith

We are often told to have faith in God, to have faith for blessings and miracles, but few people actually TEACH us how to have faith or grow our faith in God.

Maybe this example will help.... I have a chair in my home; it's been there for years. I walk in the house sometimes and just plop down in it. I sleep in the chair. I watch TV in the chair. I can find the chair in the dark and just sit down and rest. Every time I sit in the chair, I'm confident and have faith that the chair will hold my weight. I don't check the chair to see if it's sturdy.... I don't pray before sitting in the chair.... I don't sit down slowly.... I just sit. Why? ... **The chair and I have history.** I have tried the chair for years, and it has never failed me. I wake up from a nap in the chair, and I'm not on the ground. I watch movies, sports, game shows – and I never wonder to myself, "Will the chair let me down today?"

This is how we develop faith in God. Just like I've tried the chair... try God and His Way. When it comes to finances – do what God says with the money. When it comes to dealing with conflict and relationships – forgive and live in peace with all men. When we face any adversity, any circumstances – what does God say about them? The more successes, peace, increases, miracles, and fulfillment we experience doing things God's Way, the easier it will be to place our faith/confidence/trust in HIM.

We must read, study, and learn about Him and His Kingdom Government system. We have to spend time communicating with Him in prayer and meditating on His Word to be able to know Him. Sadly, many of us can't try God's Way because we don't know Him. We attempt to "try Him," using errors taught to us by religion, our parents, our friends, the World, social media, etc. This actually causes us to lose faith in God and place it in unwarranted people and things.

Misplaced Faith

For some of us, it is not our lack of Faith that is the problem, but it is the placement of our faith that prevents us from experiencing the wondrous works of God. We put our faith in our jobs, wealth, spouses, pastors, the media, our heritage, friends, our talents and abilities, doctors, even our youth and experiences. This is why we are so frustrated: We can be fired from our jobs.... Our wealth can be stolen.... Your spouse may cheat and leave you or at the very least not like you very much on a given day.... Pastors have acted contrary to what they have taught their congregations (lied, cheated, committed adultery, even killed), and people have left "the church" scarred and bruised never to return again.... The media can lie to push a certain agenda.... There are times that we feel our closest friends may not be there when we need them most.... Our talents and abilities can be nullified with an illness or a motor vehicle accident.... Your youth eventually fades to joint cracking pains, and your experience and expertise can become obsolete with the advent of the latest technology.... Yet, we put our faith in these and many others that can change in the blink of an eye. It's not until an unexpected change occurs that our faith is shaken, and we are left to pick up the pieces. If a stranger lies to us – so what, no big deal. But if our close friend or trusted spouse lies to us – we can't function for weeks. Why? ... It is because we gave them something we shouldn't have: our faith.

In Mark 11:22-24, when teaching His disciples, Jesus gives insight into this problem that we run into:

*22And Jesus answered them, "**Have faith in God.** 23Truly, I say to you, whoever says to this mountain, 'Be taken up and thrown into the sea,' and does not doubt in his heart, but believes that what he says will come to pass, it will be done for him. 24Therefore I tell you, whatever you ask in prayer, believe that you have received it, and it will be yours*

David echoes these sentiments in Psalm 20:7-8.
*7Some trust in chariots and some in horses, **but we trust in the name of the LORD our God**. 8They collapse and fall, but we rise and stand upright.*

Your faith is equivalent to your trust. We trust what/whom we have faith in, and we have faith in what/whom we trust. They are synonymous. Jesus and David both agree on where to put faith - **HAVE FAITH IN GOD**. Many people agree with this sentiment in theory, but not in reality. Your trust shouldn't be in others or objects. Jesus didn't even tell them to have faith in him (Jesus). He didn't tell them to have faith in the miracles – but rather put your faith in the One who performs the miracles. So, if your pastor falls… your faith is not shaken. If your friends leave you or disappoint you, it's okay … your faith or trust wasn't in them from the beginning. You can lose jobs, wealth, health, talent, or whatever change in circumstances and you will not fall apart … your faith is in the One that doesn't change.

The instructions for where to put your trust/faith do not have any limitations: HAVE FAITH IN GOD, period. We were not even told to trust our spouses or those that we are in relationships with. (Paul instructs husbands to love their wives as Christ loved the church; and wives to respect their husbands. But nowhere are they instructed to put their faith in each other.) This is a big issue because the first thing many relationship books, relationship experts, friends, or our experiences teach us is to place high priority in finding people to trust. This is why, when our expectations aren't met or the relationship dissolves (resulting in emotional PTSD or divorce), we may fall to pieces and find it difficult to recover and enter relationships again.

Taking the concept even further… we are not advised to have faith in OURSELVES. I love me; I have confidence and am not fearful; **but I don't trust me.** I have never cheated on my wife, nor do I have a desire to do such a thing. I have never used drugs for anything other than medicinal purposes. I have never stolen money from the ministry or anything of the sort. I am confident that I have no desire to do such things, but my faith isn't in myself...Anymore.

Call the Right Play

I can think back to my days of coaching and see examples of how I had more trust in myself than in God. When I was coaching football, there would be times that the Holy Spirit would give me the aptitude and feel about which play to call.

Now, before I joined the coaching staff, Natchez had lost to Gulfport the previous year by 66 points...in FOOTBALL!! So, the next year – as you can imagine – everyone wanted to avenge this embarrassment. I was just hired as the Offensive Coordinator for the team, which meant that I would be in charge of calling the offensive plays. The atmosphere was filled with electricity and excitement.

We started off the year 2-0; both teams came in undefeated. Somebody had to lose; however, we felt that it wasn't going to be us. It was a hard-fought game, and we were ahead in the fourth quarter...with about a minute left in the game. We had the ball. If we could get a first down, we would be able to run out the clock and win the game.

Now, usually when God gave me promptings about which play to run, it was usually general in nature: "Run on this play" ... "Pass on this play" ... "Go for it on fourth down," etc. However, for this next play, I was urged to run a specific play. Now, this was a play that we had NEVER run in a game before. The only time we ran the play was a few times during practice. I wasn't even sure if the players could make the play work. I instead trusted myself and went with a play that had worked in game situations before: a play that I knew that the players were comfortable running.

We ran the play and... It didn't work. We failed to get the first down.

They got the ball back. They moved the ball downfield. We got a penalty on defense (a pass interference penalty), and they ended up scoring a touchdown as time expired: We lost by one point.

That was one of my toughest losses as a coach because I had the answer. God had given me the teachings and promptings. But because I had more faith in myself, my plays, and my experience, we lost the game. I felt as if I had let the players, the fans, and the entire city of Natchez down. Most importantly, I let God down. It showed me that I didn't trust Him like I thought I did.

Which plays are you calling in your life? Are you trusting God to make the right decisions, or are you trusting yourself and your knowledge of the situation? I'm bringing up the issues of having faith in other people or having faith in ourselves because they can hinder the miraculous. The more faith we have in ourselves, our spouse, the pastor, our jobs, our skills – the less faith we have in God. This hinders the miraculous because instead of bringing the issue to God or trusting in what He instructs, we run to our "trusted friends" – We tend to formulate a plan without consulting God.

We ask God to "help us" but operate in a manner more consistent with the World's system. For example, we need money to pay bills and fund visions, so we listen to "successful" businesspeople who teach us how to cheat on our taxes. We need time to run errands or get some of our business ideas off the ground, so we listen to our co-workers and "go to our grandmother's funeral" for the fourth time in order to get time off. Our brother or sister teaches us to save money by stealing cable and movies by "breaking a Firestick" or illegally downloading your favorite shows. Is any of this okay with you? Do you not trust God enough to come through for you?

Free people and yourself from the weight of expectations that come with your trust. You will at some point be disappointed. The IRS just might audit you, and you'll end up owing more money.... You might run into your boss, when you're supposed to be at the "funeral" .... The Government may levy fines or jail time for your illegal access of copy-written material.... And where will those people be who gave you that "good advice"? Will they pay the money you lost? Give you a job? Will they even answer your phone call?

But rather put trust in God, who can "make all things work together for your good…" Misplaced faith is the equivalent of having no faith at all. It produces the same results: utter disappointment, frustration, confusion, a longing for "something more," and no miracles to show.

The Power of Faith in Teaching

In an atmosphere or environment where teaching is going forth, there is nothing more powerful than your faith. On one occasion, Jesus told Peter that he was a target for Satan.

Luke 22:31-32

[31] *"Simon, Simon, behold, Satan demanded to have you, that he might sift you like wheat,* [32] ***but I have prayed for you that your faith may not fail.*** *And when you have turned again, strengthen your brothers.*

Notice: Jesus didn't say that He prayed that Peter wouldn't get sifted. He didn't pray to destroy Satan. He didn't pray that Satan's demand wouldn't be allowed by God. He didn't "cancel the plans of the enemy." He didn't pray that Peter receive "power from on high." The one thing that Jesus prayed for on Peter's behalf was that his "faith not fail."

I mean, personally, I would have had more questions for Jesus: "When is this supposed to happen? What do you mean by "sift like wheat" – is that a parable? You sure you didn't mean John? Do I need some extra power to handle this? You sure you didn't mean that "you prayed that this wouldn't happen to me?""

Jesus didn't appear to be too concerned. Why? Because Peter had received Teaching. Peter wasn't ignorant concerning spiritual matters – all he had to do was have faith in what he was taught. Jesus didn't even pray that he receive "more faith." The faith that Peter had was apparently sufficient. How powerful must Faith be if this is the ONLY thing Jesus knew Peter would need to combat the enemy!!

Let's look at an example of what happens when Teaching goes forth, but there is no faith in the teaching. Matthew 13 records this account...

*⁵³And when Jesus had finished these parables, he went away from there, ⁵⁴and coming to his hometown he taught them in their synagogue, so that they were astonished, and said, "Where did this man get this wisdom and these mighty works? ⁵⁵Is not this the carpenter's son? Is not his mother called Mary? And are not his brothers James and Joseph and Simon and Judas? ⁵⁶And are not all his sisters with us? Where then did this man get all these things?" ⁵⁷And they took offense at him. But Jesus said to them, "A prophet is not without honor except in his hometown and in his own household." ⁵⁸**And he did not do many mighty works there, because of their unbelief.***

We have seen time and time again the formula where Jesus taught and then miracles followed. He was putting the blueprint into practice. However, this was His hometown – this was His homecoming. He had healed and helped all the other towns, now this was His chance to give back to the community that He was raised in. The people recognized the power and wisdom of what He was teaching, but their faith in the teaching was choked away because they took offense at who He was. They knew His parents, His family. Perhaps, they likely knew the gossip that Joseph wasn't His "real" father and thought that Mary had cheated on Joseph – that this Jesus was the product of an adulterous relationship: "Who does he think he is? What gives him the right to teach and instruct us?"

Have you ever rejected truth and wisdom because of where it came from? Are we too familiar with some people, that we don't recognize that God is trying to use them to get the miraculous to us?

Let's Look at a few examples of faith in conjunction with the miraculous:

John 4:46-53 – The Official's Son

46 So he came again to Cana in Galilee, where he had made the water wine. And at Capernaum there was an official whose son was ill. 47 When this man heard that Jesus had come from Judea to Galilee, he went to him and asked him to come down and heal his son, for he was at the point of death. 48 So Jesus said to him, "Unless you see signs and wonders you will not believe." 49 The official said to him, "Sir, come down before my child dies." 50 Jesus said to him, "Go; your son will live." **The man believed the word that Jesus spoke to him and went on his way.** *51 As he was going down, his servants met him and told him that his son was recovering. 52 So he asked them the hour when he began to get better, and they said to him, "Yesterday at the seventh hour the fever left him." 53 The father knew that was the hour when Jesus had said to him, "Your son will live."* **And he himself believed, and all his household.**

The scriptures say that "the man believed the word that Jesus spoke to Him." – he had faith that his son would live based on Jesus' Word. If he had no faith, there would have been no healing. He confirmed the source of the healing by comparing the time his son improved to the time of his conversation with Jesus.

Notice this: It wasn't even the faith of the sick son that manifested the miracle. It was the faith of the father on behalf of his child.

Mark 5:22-24 – **Jairus' Daughter**

*²²Then came one of the rulers of the synagogue, Jairus by name, and seeing him, he fell at his feet ²³and implored him earnestly, saying, "**My little daughter is at the point of death. Come and lay your hands on her, so that she may be made well and live.**" ²⁴And he went with him. And a great crowd followed him and thronged about him.*

So, we see Jesus was asked to come to heal the daughter of Jairus. Once again, we see a Father interceding for his child. He is desperate. His daughter is "at the point of death"! It was an urgent request. While on the way to perform the miraculous, Jesus was interrupted....

Mark 5:25-34 – **The Woman with the Issue of Blood**

*²⁵**And there was a woman who had had a discharge of blood for twelve years**, ²⁶and who had suffered much under many physicians, and had spent all that she had, and was no better but rather grew worse. ²⁷<u>She had heard the reports about Jesus</u> and came up behind him in the crowd and touched his garment. ²⁸**For she said, "If I touch even his garments, I will be made well."** ²⁹And immediately the flow of blood dried up, and she felt in her body that she was healed of her disease. ³⁰And Jesus, perceiving in himself that power had gone out from him, immediately* turned about in the crowd and said, "Who touched my garments?" *31*And his disciples said to him, "You see the crowd pressing around you, and yet you say, 'Who touched me?'" *32*And he looked around to see who had done it. *33*But the woman, knowing what had happened to her, came in fear and trembling and fell down before him and told him the whole truth. *34*And he said to her, **"Daughter, your faith has made you well; go in peace, and be healed of your disease.** "

While Jesus was on the way to heal the daughter of Jairus, He was interrupted by the faith of a woman who had "an issue of blood" for 12 years. She was determined to reach Him. Jesus told her, "Your faith has made you well." Faith in what? Perhaps she too had heard of Malachi 4:2 - which speaks of healing being in the "Sun of Rigteousness' wings." That word "wings" translates to *hem, border, garment corners* in Hebrew. Or perhaps it was her faith in the reports/teachings about what Jesus had done. It wasn't the touching of His garment that healed her, but it was her faith that Jesus was a Source of healing. Many people touched Him, as His disciples pointed out; however, only she received the miracle she needed.

All too often, we put emphasis on what a person did when they obtained the miracle result. And people try to imitate those particular actions or deeds; however, Jesus highlights that it wasn't her actions, but rather it was her faith.

Mark 5:35-42 - **Healing of Jairus's Daughter**

35While he was still speaking, there came from the ruler's house some who said, **"Your daughter is dead.** *Why* *trouble the Teacher any further?" ³⁶But overhearing what they said, Jesus said to the ruler of the synagogue, "**Do not fear, only believe.**" ³⁷And he allowed no one to follow him except Peter and James and John the brother of James. ³⁸They came to the house of the ruler of the synagogue, and Jesus saw a commotion, people weeping and wailing loudly. ³⁹And when he had entered, he said to them, "Why are you making a commotion and weeping? The child is not dead but sleeping." ⁴⁰And they laughed at him. But he put them all outside and took the child's father and mother and those who were with him and went in where the child was. ⁴¹Taking her by the hand he said to her, "Talitha cumi," which means, "Little girl, I say to you, arise." ⁴²**And immediately the girl got up and began walking** (for she was twelve years of age), and they were immediately overcome with amazement.*

Jesus finally arrived at the house of Jairus. Even though people had come and informed him that the child was dead, Jesus gave Jairus the key to his daughter's healing: *"Do not fear, only believe that your daughter will be healed."* Upon arriving, there were people who believed that the child was dead. When Jesus told them that she wasn't dead, they laughed. Jesus needed people of faith for this miracle – He put all fear, doubt, and unbelief out the room. He didn't even take all of His disciples – only Peter, James, and John, and the child's parents. Once again, we see faith unlocking the miraculous.

Because faith unlocks the miraculous and it is very powerful, it is often the target of the enemy's attacks. Let's look at a few examples:

The Deception of the Woman

The Enemy has no new tricks – the same shenanigans he used back then are the same ones that he's recycling now. Deception through man's ignorance is one of his main tactics. The Enemy deceived the Woman in the garden of Eden by causing her to doubt, questioning her belief/faith in God's Word.

Genesis 3:1-6

He said to the woman, "Did God actually say, 'You shall not eat of any tree in the garden'?" ²And the woman said to the serpent, "We may eat of the fruit of the trees in the garden, ³but God said, 'You shall not eat of the fruit of the tree that is in the midst of the garden, neither shall you touch it, lest you die.'" ⁴But the serpent said to the woman, "You will not surely die. ⁵For God knows that when you eat of it your eyes will be opened, and you will be like God, knowing good and evil." ⁶So when the woman saw that the tree was good for food, and that it was a delight to the eyes, and that the tree was to be desired to make one wise, she took of its fruit and ate, and she also gave some to her husband who was with her, and he ate.

Satan questioned Eve's faith just like he attempts to question your faith: "Did God really say...?" ... "Do you really believe that what God said applies to your life/your situation?" ... "Are you sure you're understanding God correctly?" ... "Can you be healed?" ... "Can your financial situation improve?" ... "Can you get out of this situation?"

The questions that the serpent asked may have seemed harmless. I mean... the woman was not forced to do anything against her own will. However, these questions hit their intended target – her faith, her belief, her trust in what God had instructed. Her faith was being attacked with doubt. She went from believing God's words to believing the words of the serpent/Satan. Perhaps, she thought, "Maybe God is keeping something from me."

If your faith is manipulated, it can make you change your perspective and viewpoint. By questioning her faith, the Woman went from seeing the Tree as forbidden and untouchable to seeing it as "good for food," "a delight to the eyes," and "to be desired to make one wise." Once her faith was manipulated, the serpent didn't have to say or do anything else. He didn't tell her to eat.... he didn't tell her to give it to her husband.... he didn't tell them to hide from God.... they did that all on their own once their faith was no longer in God's words/teaching.

Adam and Eve forfeited Eden as a result of the attack on their faith. I can only wonder what miracles, blessings, wonders we have forfeited because our faith was not in God's words.

The Wilderness Test

When Jesus was tested in the wilderness, the first thing Satan did was question how God defined and identified Him. In the third chapter of Matthew, God had just spoken, "This is my beloved son, with whom I am well pleased." The attack occurs in the very next chapter...

Matthew 4:1-4

*Then Jesus was led up by the Spirit into the wilderness to be tempted by the devil. ²And after fasting forty days and forty nights, he was hungry. ³And the tempter came and said to him, "**If you are the Son of God**, command these stones to become loaves of bread." ⁴But he answered, "It is written, "'Man shall not live by bread alone, but by every word that comes from the mouth of God.'"*

Satan's attack was the same as it was on the Woman in the Garden of Eden, an attack on the faith in what God had spoken. He questioned, "If you are the Son of God..." as to place doubt or apprehension that there is a possibility that it wasn't true: "Maybe you heard wrong" ... "You're not really the Son of God...if you were the Son of God, then you could do x, y, and z."

Notice Jesus' response: He didn't respond with what He thought, or felt, or wanted. He responded with God's Teaching: "It is written, 'Man shall not live by bread alone (natural, physical nourishment), but by every word that comes from the mouth of God" (Words from the mouth of God are laws/teaching). This is similar to another scripture found in 2 Corinthians 5:6-7 ...

*⁶So we are always of good courage. We know that while we are at home in the body we are away from the Lord, ⁷***for we walk by faith, not by sight.***

Paul assessed that we walk by (live, move, have our being, perform actions, make decisions, etc.) by faith and not by sight (our senses, physical realm, natural elements). This statement is in accordance with Jesus' teachings.

Jesus responded that we shall live by "every word that comes from the mouth of God," while Paul taught that we live by faith.

As noted, our faith has to have an object, an idea, a person, etc. We live by our faith in every Word that comes from the mouth of God. Or more plainly... we live by our faith in God's teaching.

Faith Pleases God

Hebrews 11:6

And without faith it is impossible to please him, for whoever would draw near to God must believe that he exists and that he rewards those who seek him.

I don't know about you, but if I desire something from someone, I want them to be pleased with me before I ask. Oftentimes, when my children wanted money, or to use the car, or to go out, they wanted to make sure that I was in a good mood. They wanted to make sure that I was "pleased with them" – they would clean up around the house, be nice to one another in my presence, cook dinner or bring me something to eat, compliment me, etc. They understood that I was more likely to say "yes" if I was pleased with them as opposed to when I was displeased or disappointed with them.

It is the same with God; however, God is NOT moved or easily pleased by compliments and flattering words. He's not moved by how well you clean your house or car. He's not moved by you being nice to people just before you're about to pray to Him. These actions don't move

God. Neither is God moved by your tears, yelling, worry, anger, nor by reminding him of your problems, going to church, long prayers, speaking in tongues, etc. (especially from those who are/should be spiritually mature). God is pleased with your faith in His Word...period. If you have no faith, He is not pleased.

James 1:5-8

*5If any of you lacks wisdom, let him ask God, who gives generously to all without reproach, and it will be given him. 6But let him ask in faith, with no doubting, for the one who doubts is like a wave of the sea that is driven and tossed by the wind. 7**For that person must not suppose that he will receive anything from the Lord;** 8he is a double-minded man, unstable in all his ways.*

    James says that the person who asks not in faith (asks but has worry/doubt) will not receive anything from the Lord. God is not pleased if there is no faith. Even if you ask, beg, plead... if there is no faith in His Word there will be no results. This is where many of us are. We ask God for the miracles, but either we lack Teaching (Word of God), or we lack faith in the Teaching. Either way... God is not pleased, and we are often disappointed.

    As you can see... Faith is intricate to the miraculous and our lives as citizens in God's Kingdom. Faith in God is our "compass" always pointing and directing us in the direction of the plans, purposes, vision, and miracles of God. God told us that He would never leave us nor forsake us. Let us be people of Faith and not of our senses. Faith in the Teachings of God is key in unlocking the miraculous in our lives.

Let's Be Honest – Self-Evaluation:

1. When you ask God for the miraculous, do you believe that it will happen?

2. Have you ever felt that you needed more faith? What situation was being faced that made you feel this way?

3. Is your faith in God? ... in others? ...in yourself? ... in money?

4. Do you have faith for some things and not others? For example: Faith to believe in salvation, but not miracles? Faith to believe in not cheating or stealing, but not to believe in tithing or other aspects about God's teachings? If so, why?

5. Has the enemy attacked your faith in what God has promised? What are you doing to prevent attacks on your faith?

OBSTACLE V: Faith Contaminants

"Once something is contaminated, the natural inclination is to throw it away. Well, when we were contaminated with sin, God didn't throw us away..."
   - Bishop Robert Cade

[By definition a "contaminant" is a polluting or poisonous substance that makes something impure (Definition from *Oxford Languages*). In this chapter, when I speak of "contaminants," I'm referring to things like u*nbelief, doubt, worry, anxiousness, suspicion, confusion, indecision, paranoia, hesitancy, wavering, distrust, uncertainty, cynicism, depression, low self-worth, etc.*]

Flint, Michigan

Many have heard about the water crisis that occurred in Flint, Michigan. For the sake of saving money, neglectful officials decided NOT to properly treat the water and update the piping system. Lead from the pipes leaked into the drinking water supply, and the water of Flint, Michigan became poisonous. It's not that there wasn't any water or all of a sudden there was less water – the water was rendered useless because it was contaminated. Many children became sick, got diseases, suffered neurological damage; some even died.

I didn't bring up the situation in Flint, Michigan to stoke anger, but rather to give insight on Faith. The issue the people in Flint had was not an issue of the quantity of water – they had water but…it was contaminated water. Likewise, for many of us, our problem isn't that we have no faith – we have faith. But the question I have to ask is, "Is your faith contaminated?"

The contamination of the water in Flint didn't decrease the amount of water, but it made the water useless; it turned life-giving water into a dangerous, toxic, poison. Our faith can be contaminated by many things: doubt, anxiousness, unbelief, etc. The contamination doesn't decrease our faith, but it makes our faith ineffective, hazardous, and unstable. We often view these entities as if they are on the same spectrum with faith - meaning that we often think, "If I have doubt or unbelief, then I have no faith" and vice versa – or that the two cannot co-exist. However, it is possible to have faith and unbelief at the same time. Let's look at the scriptures closely....

Mark 9:20-24 – **Help My Unbelief**

*[20]And they brought the boy to him. And when the spirit saw him, immediately it convulsed the boy, and he fell on the ground and rolled about, foaming at the mouth. [21]And Jesus asked his father, "How long has this been happening to him?" And he said, "From childhood. [22]And it has often cast him into fire and into water, to destroy him. But if you can do anything, have compassion on us and help us." [23]And Jesus said to him, "'If you can'! **All things are possible for one who believes.**" [24]Immediately the father of the child cried out and said, "**I believe; help my unbelief!**"*

Jesus had just come down from the mountain where He was transfigured, and His disciples were attempting to cast a demonic force out of a young man. Now, let's look at this scripture from a different angle than it is usually dissected and focus on the father....

Jesus gave the father the key to the miraculous: All things (even miracles) are possible for those who have faith in God. The father responded, "I believe; help my unbelief" ... "I have faith in what you're saying Jesus, but I also have doubt." The father had faith; it was just ineffective because it was contaminated with unbelief. So, essentially, this man was telling Jesus, "I need my faith decontaminated." ... How does one decontaminate faith?

The Refiner's Fire/The Fuller's Soap

When it comes to decontamination or purification, the scriptures make reference to the refiner's fire or fuller's soap. (A Fuller was one who cleaned raw sheep's wool and made it thicker - his soap was harsh and chemical in nature). In reference to purifying His people (into "pure gold" or "pure silver" or "removing impurities"), God uses the analogy of putting us "into the fire" or "cleansing with fuller's soap".

Malachi 3:1-3

*"Behold, **I send my messenger**, and he will prepare the way before me. And the Lord whom you seek will suddenly come to his temple; and the messenger of the covenant in whom you delight, behold, he is coming, says the Lord of hosts. 2 But who can endure the day of his coming, and who can stand when he appears? For **he is like a refiner's fire and like fullers' soap**. 3 He will sit as a **refiner** and **purifier of silver**, and **he will purify the sons of Levi and refine them like gold and silver**, and they will bring offerings in righteousness to the Lord.*

Malachi notes that God will send his messenger to prepare the people. Perhaps this is a reference to John the Baptist; or a reference to Malachi 2:7 - *For the lips of a priest should **guard knowledge**, and people should **seek instruction** from his mouth, for he is **the messenger of the Lord of host**.* "The Messenger" is a teacher, bringing instructions, preparing the people. Thus, the teaching is like a refiner's fire that burns away impurities in precious metals (people)—making them soft, malleable, moldable, teachable...or Fuller's soap—cleansing them of their impurities. God doesn't desire to get rid of His people; He would much rather just decontaminate or purify them.

In the case of Flint, Michigan, the solution was not to throw away the contaminated water but to decontaminate it. **The most important step in decontamination is finding the source of the contamination.** In this case, it was the old pipes causing lead contamination, so the government had to replace pipes and remove the lead.

Decontaminating faith is similar in approach. First, we must realize or discover the source that is contaminating our faith. This is often **exposed** by "the messenger" - it can be the situations, circumstances, and challenges that God allows us to go through to learn valuable lessons; teachers that teach us the error in our ways; or the Holy Spirit that reveals our mistakes. No matter what the method that God uses to teach, the goal is always the same: to expose areas of flaws, weakness, ignorance and contamination.

Sources of Faith Contamination

There are three main sources of faith contamination: ignorance, bad teaching, and sight/natural senses.

Contamination Due to Ignorance: People don't believe because they don't have True Teaching. They lack the Experience, Information, or Revelation of True Teaching.

Contamination due to bad teaching: People don't believe because they've received incorrect information.

Contamination due to sight/natural senses: People don't believe because they are placing trust in what they can see, hear, etc.; or because of circumstances in the natural realm.

Each source of contamination (ignorance, bad teachings, relying on our natural senses) can lead to any number of manifestations: confusion, doubt, worry, anxiety, depression, hopelessness, fear, self-doubt, low self-worth, etc.

Once the contamination source has been identified, then we can start the process of decontamination. If fear is caused due to ignorance, I need to decontaminate with information, teaching, and revelation. If doubt is caused due to bad teachings, I have to decontaminate by (a) letting the bad teachings go and then (b) supplementing them with the correct teachings of God. If confusion is caused by reliance on my senses, then I have to decontaminate by coming to the understanding that what I see isn't more influential or powerful than what is unseen or what God has spoken.

Let's examine the scriptures and dig deeper, shall we:

Matthew 16:5-12 – **Contamination of Confusion**

[5] *When the disciples reached the other side, they had forgotten to bring any bread.* [6]*Jesus said to them, "Watch and beware of the leaven of the Pharisees and Sadducees."* [7]*And they began discussing it among themselves, saying, "We brought no bread."* [8]*But Jesus,*

aware of this, said, "***O you of little faith***, why are you discussing among yourselves the fact that you have no bread? ⁹***Do you not yet perceive?*** Do you not remember the five loaves for the five thousand, and how many baskets you gathered? ¹⁰Or the seven loaves for the four thousand, and how many baskets you gathered? ¹¹***How is it that you fail to understand*** that I did not speak about bread? Beware of the leaven of the Pharisees and Sadducees." ¹²***Then they understood*** that he did not tell them to beware of the leaven of bread, but of the teaching of the Pharisees and Sadducees.

Let's examine the warning of the "leaven" of the Pharisees and Sadducees once again. Jesus was teaching them a lesson and giving them warning about bad teaching. The disciples couldn't comprehend the lesson and focused on their mistake of forgetting to buy bread from the trip. Jesus notes the disciples' faith ("O, ye of little faith") but also notes their contaminant ("do you not yet perceive" ... "how is it you fail to understand"). The quality of their faith was depreciated by their confusion.

The contamination of confusion appears to have been a product of <u>ignorance</u> and <u>lack of revelation</u>. However, once Jesus brought to their remembrance that physical "bread" wasn't an issue (remember how God five thousand with five loaves? Or four thousand with seven loaves?), then they got the revelation that He was referring to the bad teachings of the Pharisees and Sadducees. Jesus spoke to them concerning erroneous teaching – they thought He was speaking about bread.

Matthew 6:30-34 – Contamination of Anxiety

*³⁰But if God so clothes the grass of the field, which today is alive and tomorrow is thrown into the oven, will he not much more clothe you, **O you of little faith?** ³¹Therefore **do not be anxious**, saying, 'What shall we eat?' or 'What shall we drink?' or 'What shall we wear?' ³²For the Gentiles seek after all these things, and your heavenly Father knows that you need them all. ³³**<u>But seek first the kingdom of God and his righteousness, and all these things will be added to you.</u>** ³⁴"Therefore do not be anxious about tomorrow, for tomorrow will be anxious for itself. Sufficient for the day is its own trouble.*

Here, we have a lesson on priorities. Jesus was teaching His disciples not to be concerned with what they will eat, drink, and wear to the point of anxiety. But rather, He instructed the disciples to put their faith in God. Once again, Jesus notes their faith ("you of little faith") and the contaminant ("do not be anxious"). The quality of their faith was restricted by the contamination.

Their contamination of anxiety seems to have been induced by <u>erroneous teaching</u>. Many of us were taught to "take care of ourselves." Even in school… we're taught to obtain the basic needs (food, water, shelter, clothing, etc.). However, Jesus redirects these priorities – instead, make **the Kingdom of God** (God's teachings, the way that God operates in His Kingdom system) and **His Righteousness** (being in right standing and good relationship with God) the priorities. THEN all the things that you've been desiring – food, water, shelter, money, healing, prosperity, promotion, elevation, help in time of need, strength, peace, ALL THESE THINGS…even the miraculous – will be ADDED unto you. **If it's being added, you don't work for it.** You don't make it happen for yourself. God does it because the right priorities place you in the right position to receive what you need right on time.

Matthew 14:28-33 – **Contamination of Doubt**

²⁸And Peter answered him, "Lord, if it is you, command me to come to you on the water." ²⁹He said, "Come." So Peter got out of the boat and walked on the water and came to Jesus. ³⁰But when he saw the wind, he was afraid, and beginning to sink he cried out, "Lord, save me." ³¹Jesus immediately reached out his hand and took hold of him, saying to him, **"O you of little faith, why did you doubt?"** *³²And when they got into the boat, the wind ceased. ³³And those in the boat worshiped him, saying, "Truly you are the Son of God."*

We always talk about how Jesus walked on water, but we forget that there was another person in the scriptures who also walked on water – It was Peter. Peter asked Jesus for a Word, an instruction: "Lord, if it is you, COMMAND ME to COME to you on the water." Jesus responded, "Come." Peter had faith in that one Word from Jesus. He got out of the boat; and Peter walked on water just like Jesus. However, his faith became contaminated with doubt because of his **natural senses**. The scripture says that "when he SAW the wind; he was AFRAID; he started to sink." Jesus recognized and noted his faith ("O you of little faith") and his contaminant ("Why did you doubt?"). The quality of his faith was inferior in comparison to the faith of the Centurion Soldier *(Matthew 8:5-15)*.

Matthew 8:23-26 – **Contamination of Fear**

²³And when he was entered into a ship, his **disciples** *followed him. ²⁴And, behold, there arose a great tempest in the sea, insomuch that the ship was covered with the waves: but he was asleep. ²⁵And his disciples came to him, and awoke him, saying,* **Lord, save us: we perish.** *²⁶And he saith unto them, Why are ye* **fearful***, O ye of little faith?* <u>**Then he arose, and rebuked the winds and the sea; and there was a great calm.**</u>

In this instance, it was the disciples that experienced the miraculous: their lives were saved from a great storm at sea. These were men who were watching miracles being performed and receiving teaching from Jesus the Christ. They had left all to follow Him and to be baptized under His school of thought and teachings. But when the storm came…they panicked.

Jesus pointed to the contaminant of their faith – fear: "Why are ye fearful?" He acknowledged that they had faith ("O ye of little faith"). Jesus even said Himself that "a little faith" is enough to move mountains – However, the quality of their faith was diminished. Their contaminant of fear was caused by what they SAW: a great storm, the crashing waves, and a sleeping Jesus. Fear kept them from activating their own faith and speaking to the storm themselves. Yet, they did have enough faith in Jesus to awaken Him to save them.

Get Rid of Your "But"

We have to address the contamination of faith at the source.... This has to be a self-evaluation: You believe...but you have some doubts! You trust God...but in the back of your mind you remember what happened the last time! You have faith...BUT...! You believe God...BUT...! You have confidence that God can do what He says...BUT...! Whatever "IT" is...get your "BUT" out of the way! Your "BUT" is killing the quality and effectiveness of your faith, which in turn is disqualifying you for the miracles that you otherwise have the right to obtain as a Kingdom Citizen.

Why are you Afraid? ...Let the fear go! ... Leap!

Why are you Hesitant? ... Make a decision! ... Make a move!

Why are you Anxious? ... God is our Father! ... Relax!

Why are you Uncertain? ... God knows what He's doing! ... Resolve it in your Heart!

Why are you Distrustful? ... God didn't hurt you! ... He didn't take anything from You! ... He's trying to get something TO you, something OUT of you, and something THROUGH you!!!

Why are you Cynical? ... God LOVES YOU!!!...Trust in HIM!

Why are you wavering? ... God has equipped you with everything you need!!...Settle Yourself!

Let's get the Teachings of God. Let's incorporate the revelations of God in our lives. And let's decontaminate our faith so that we can experience the miraculous life that God desires for us to live.

Let's Be Honest – Self-Evaluation:

1. Is your faith contaminated? If so, by which contaminant(s)? How did this happen?

2. Is there something you're believing God for; however, doubt has crept in?

3. Are you afraid that you won't receive the miracle? Are you not sure that God will do as He promised?

4. In what areas of your life has your faith been contaminated: finances, education, relationships, weight loss, work/entrepreneurship, etc.?

5. Are you stressed out? Are you Anxious? Cynical? What is it that is keeping you from moving forward in faith?

6. Is your past holding you back?

OBSTACLE VI: Disobedience

"Obedience is an act of faith; Disobedience is the result of unbelief." — Edwin Louis Cole

I'll begin by defining obedience as "actions that align with instructions and/or teaching from someone in a position of authority." Jesus phrases it more simply as being a "doer" of the Word, not just a "hearer." Many scriptures place an emphasis on the power of obedience and the perils of disobedience:

1 Samuel 15:22

And Samuel said, Hath the LORD as great delight in burnt offerings and sacrifices, as in obeying the voice of the LORD? Behold, **to obey is better than sacrifice***, and* **to hearken** *than the fat of rams.*

1 Kings 2:3

And keep the charge of the Lord your God, **walking in his ways and keeping his statutes, his commandments, his rules, and his testimonies***, as it is written in the Law of Moses,* that you may prosper in all that you do *and wherever you turn.*

Exodus 19:5

Now therefore, if you will indeed **obey my voice and keep my covenant***,* you shall be my treasured possession among all peoples*, for all the earth is mine.*

Don't Tell Me What to Do!

No one likes being bossed around. We want to do what we want to do… when we want to do it. This attitude was captured by the Isley Brothers when they crooned,

"It's your thang, do what you want to do..." Even in the younger generation, this same attitude was captured in Lil Nas X's song "Old Town Road": "Can't nobody tell me nothing, you can't tell me nothing."

I have found that most people hate being told what to do...even if they realize it will benefit them. From little children being told to eat their vegetables and do their homework...to adults being told to exercise or take better care of themselves, we hate feeling "ordered" or "bossed around." We hate being instructed on our jobs. We hate when our spouse, loved ones, or family attempt to give us advice. Men hate getting directions from their wives. Wives hate being told they spend/shop too much by their husbands. We just want to live our lives, "do what we want to do," and have "nobody tell us nothing" – free from criticism and consequences.

The miracles of God, however, are intricately tied to our obedience. Often, when we think of obedience, we think of it in terms of a reward: <u>If I'm obedient, then God will reward me with miracles.</u> <u>If I'm good enough, then I'll get healed.</u> <u>If I'm faithful enough in going to the church, I'll be blessed financially.</u> That is not truly the case. It is your obedience that positions you properly and presents you with the opportunity to take part in God's Kingdom system.

Obedience isn't something that we do to get God to act on our behalf. Rather, obedience to God's Word is mostly for our benefit. God is our Creator, and as Creator, He knows what is in our best interest, what we need, where we function best.

Obeying God's teaching and commands is similar to following the instructional manual to any product provided by the manufacturer: It's in the car's best interest to get the oil changed regularly.... It's in the cell phone's best interest to charge it once or twice a day.... It's in the elevator's best interest not to go beyond the capacity weight limit.... By default, every manufacturer benefits from the creation's ability to operate effectively because it bolsters the reputation of the manufacturer.

Mankind functions the same way; By listening to the teaching and instructions from our Manufacturer (God Almighty), we function best. God tells us to forgive those who have wronged us, treat our fellow man with love and compassion, abstain from sinful acts, honor father and mother, do not lie, cheat, or steal, etc. Obedience to these teachings allows us to function at our maximum capacity. By default, God benefits when we function properly because He's able to accomplish His agenda through us and it bolsters His reputation.

Obedience Unlocks Miracles

It is our obedience to the Word of God that will even unlock the miraculous (we'll view some examples later). I know this may sound controversial, but... **Obedience to Teaching negates the need for prayer!** If I obey, there's no need to pray. This is because prayer is often answered in the form of Teachings: Experimentation, Information, Revelation. If I don't apply what I've learned or the answers received in prayer, I won't get miraculous results. I don't care how much I keep praying, begging, crying...If I don't obey and apply the principles... nothing happens.

If you don't tithe, you don't need prayer...you need obedience to the teaching of God's financial system. If you're cheating on your spouse, you don't need prayer...you need obedience to God's teachings on marriage. If you're unforgiving, you don't need prayer...you need to obey God and forgive. Prayer won't work in these situations anyway because you're breaking His principles.

Let's look at a more practical analogy: **You** may like coffee. It tastes really good, and it gets **you** up and going in the morning. If you put coffee in your car, the car cannot function. It doesn't matter how much you pray. It doesn't matter how loud you beg God or articulate the need to get to work on time—<u>The car will not start.</u> Why? Because you've <u>violated a principle or teaching from the manufacturer</u> concerning the kind of fuel the car needs. You don't need prayer – you need obedience to the principle put in place by the creator: Cars need Gasoline (or if it is an electric vehicle, it needs to be charged).

Unfortunately, many people think prayer is the answer to their problem; it IS NOT the answer when they already have the teaching or instruction. When teaching and instructions are known, obedience is the key to unlock the miraculous.

"But Ma...the Rent Is Due!"

I can remember reading an article about Oprah's interview of comedian Kevin Hart published on *beliefnet.com*:

Hart's mother saw the talent within her son and agreed to pay Kevin's rent for a year while he worked his way through show business. She told Hart that she wouldn't be a dream killer and gave him a year to make his dreams come true.

Despite the small success during his first year of comedy, Hart was running low on funds and asked his mother about the contribution she agreed to pay. His mother's only response was, "Have you been reading your bible?" Hart told Oprah that he would tell his Mom that he didn't have time to talk about religion and really needed the rent money. To which his mother replied, "When you read your Bible, then we'll talk about your rent."

These conversations went on for weeks on end, until Hart eventually received an eviction notice on his door. With nowhere else to turn, Hart decided to take his mother's advice and open up his bible. Hart told Oprah, "I go home and say, 'Man let me open this Bible up.' Open the Bible up, six rent checks fell out. She put all my rent checks in the Bible." (Guzman 2020)

Hart had received instructions and teachings from his mother: "Read your Bible" – Simple. He talked to his mom; perhaps even prayed to God. But the answer to his needs… the answer to his problem…the miracle he desired could only be revealed when he followed the teachings of his mother. She had made provisions for him contingent upon his obedience.

I believe that God does us the same way…. He has "checks already written for us": healing, houses, protection, salvation – already prepared for us. And it's all predicated on our obedience.

Obedience in the Kingdom of God

God's Kingdom operates according to His Word and teachings. God's Word as King becomes "Law" (a political type of teaching). As a Kingdom Citizen, you are expected to obey these Laws, just as you are expected to obey the laws if you are a citizen in the United States. Adherence to the Laws doesn't grant you anything magical, no special prize, or great miracle reward; however, it does give you something very important. Let's dissect a parable Jesus gave to the people....

Luke 17:7-10

7"Will any one of you who has a servant plowing or keeping sheep say to him when he has come in from the field, 'Come at once and recline at table'? 8Will he not rather say to him, 'Prepare supper for me, and dress properly, and serve me while I eat and drink, and afterward you will eat and drink'? 9Does he thank the servant because he did what was commanded? 10So you also, when you have done all that you were commanded, say, 'We are unworthy servants; **we have only done what was our duty.***'"*

In this passage, Jesus gives insight into the Kingdom Citizen concept of Obedience through the parable of a servant. He explains that the servant does what is required of him. You don't give him anything special or extra for doing his/her job. You don't invite them to relax at the table.... You don't give them more money.... You don't make a big deal that they did their job.... You don't even give them special thanks; they were just being obedient. The servant also has the mindset that they don't want to receive special thanks: "I'm just doing my job."

However, the servant's obedience places him/her in a position to be blessed. The servant's obedience places him/her in a position of usefulness and benefit to the lord. As a result, all the servant's needs are met: shelter is provided.... the servant has access to the food ("and afterward you will eat and drink") ... clothing is provided (he was instructed to "dress properly").

If the servant were to get sick, the lord would find someone to help cure their ailment. [Remember the Centurion Soldier *(Luke 7:2-3)*? He sought help to heal his valued servant.] If the servant needed money, the king would give him money. [Remember the parable of the king who forgave the servant a great debt *(Matthew 18:24)*? He apparently had loaned him money because the servant was in need.] Even if the servant were to be sad, the king would attempt to end his sorrow. [Remember Nehemiah *(Nehemiah 2:2)*? The King noticed Nehemiah's countenance had changed.]

Any need that the servant had, the lord would help meet it. It's not because the lords and kings were always so good and kind. It was not even because they loved the servants all the time. The reason is because it served the lord's own interest. If the servant were sick, upset, hurt, or had any need, he/she would be unable to perform his/her duties effectively. Therefore, the lord would meet the servant's needs so that the servant could be effective in accomplishing the lord's agenda.

So, if a human king or lord would do this for their servant – how much more would God do for HIS sons, daughters, and citizens of His Kingdom. David put it this way:

Psalm 23:1

The Lord is my shepherd, I SHALL NOT WANT.

Psalm 37:4

Delight yourself in the Lord, and He will give you the desires of your heart

Consequently… if you break the law, you run the risk of having your rights and privileges revoked…even if you didn't know you were breaking the law. If you break driving laws (drinking and driving, speeding, reckless driving), you may forfeit your right to drive. If you break the law by stealing or committing murder, you may forfeit the right to freedom / liberty due to incarceration. Also, people who are imprisoned due to breaking the law may lose other rights and privileges permanently (i.e., the right to vote, to bear arms, etc.).

It is the same way in the Kingdom of God - When are disobedient or break the Law of God, we may forfeit certain rights, privileges, and benefits: the right to be healed… the right to access to HIS resources (finances, land, buildings)… the privilege to serve in your area of gifting (preaching, teaching, singing, etc.)… the benefits from the teachings of the Holy Spirit… the advantage of casting your cares on HIM (no worrying)… and yes, even the miraculous.

Teaching prevents us from breaking the Law of God unintentionally. Many rob God because they were never taught about tithes and offering. Many abuse their spouses because they were never taught how to treat them according to the Law of God. Many don't forgive or hold grudges because they were never taught about forgiveness in the Kingdom of God. Oftentimes, the miraculous is inhibited due to our "unintentional" disobedience.

However, where there is obedience to God's teachings and commands, the miraculous is often present. Let's look at a few examples….

Obedience to Teaching and Miracles
Luke 6:46-49 – **Parable of Hearers vs Doers**

[46] *"**Why do you call me 'Lord, Lord,' and not do what I tell you?** [47]Everyone who comes to me and **hears my words and does them**, I will show you what he is like: [48]he is like a man building a house, who dug deep and laid the foundation on the rock. And when a flood arose, the stream broke against that house and could not shake it, because it had been well built. [49]But the one who **hears and does not do them** is like a man who built a house on the ground without a foundation. When the stream broke against it, immediately it fell, and the ruin of that house was great."*

Jesus essentially explains the difference between hearing His teachings and obeying them versus hearing

His teachings and not obeying them. In both scenarios (for obedience and disobedience), there was a man building a house (symbolic of a person's life) and there was rushing water and crashing waves due to an overflooded stream (situations/ circumstances of life that arise). The difference between the two was the foundation: Jesus equates the person who is obedient to His teachings as building a foundation on a rock (something solid, dependable), while the person who does not obey is seen as having no foundation.

I assume a storm occurred or a dam broke because a flood and raging stream arose for both individuals. The stream beat upon both houses. Basically...they both were going through a tough situation in which a miracle was needed. They had the same type of house, same flood, same stream, yet the results were totally different. The person who obeyed His teachings wasn't shaken, while the disobedient person's house fell to great ruin.

Obedience to the teaching and Word of God doesn't prevent the storm and flood from occurring, but it enables you to stand when all others fall. It allows you to have health and healing when others are sick and dying around you. Obedience allows you to have peace when there is chaos. Obedience to a particular teaching is intricately tied to faith in that teaching. If I believe in it, then I will do as the teaching, or the Teacher, instructs.

Matthew 9:9-15 – "Stretch Forth Thine Hand"

*9And when he was departed thence, he went into their **synagogue**: 10And, behold, there was a man which had his hand withered. And they asked him, saying, Is it lawful to* *heal on the sabbath days? that they might accuse him. ¹¹And he said unto them, What man shall there be among you, that shall have one sheep, and if it fall into a pit on the sabbath day, will he not lay hold on it, and lift it out? ¹²How much then is a man better than a sheep? Wherefore it is lawful to do well on the sabbath days. ¹³Then saith he to the man,* **Stretch forth thine hand. And he stretched it forth***; and it was* <u>*restored whole, like as the other.*</u> *¹⁴Then the Pharisees went out, and held a council against him, how they might destroy him. ¹⁵But when Jesus knew it, he withdrew himself from thence: and great multitudes followed him, and* <u>*he healed them all*</u>*;*

Jesus told him to stretch out his hand. And he stretched it forth. Something as easy as following a simple command can be the difference between the miraculous and continuing to go about life in the same mundane, debilitating condition.

Genesis 6:13-22 – "Build the Ark, Noah"

¹³And God said to Noah, "I have determined to make an end of all flesh, for the earth is filled with violence through them. Behold, I will destroy them with the earth. ¹⁴Make yourself an ark of gopher wood. Make rooms in the ark, and cover it inside and out with pitch. ¹⁵This is how you are to make it: the length of the ark 300 cubits, its breadth 50 cubits, and its height 30 cubits. ¹⁶Make a roof for the ark, and finish it to a cubit above, and set the door of the ark in its side. Make it with lower, second, and third decks. ¹⁷For behold, I will bring a flood of waters upon the earth to destroy all flesh in which is the breath of life under heaven. Everything that is on the earth shall die. ¹⁸But I *will establish my covenant with you, and you shall come into the ark, you, your sons, your wife, and your sons' wives with you. ¹⁹And of every living thing of all flesh, you shall bring two of every sort into the ark to keep them alive with you. They shall be male and female. ²⁰Of the birds according to their kinds, and of the animals according to their kinds, of every creeping thing of the ground, according to its kind, two of every sort shall come in to you to keep them alive. ²¹Also take with you every sort of food that is eaten, and store it up. It shall serve as food for you and for them." ²²***Noah did this; he did all that God commanded him.**

Because of man's rebellion and sin, God was going to destroy the earth with flood. God instructed Noah to build an Ark. He gave Noah specific instructions: "This is how you are to do it…" Noah received teaching from God. Verse 22 says, "Noah did all that God commanded." He was obedient. This obedience unlocked a miracle for Noah and his family. Noah and his family and the animals were spared from the destruction caused by the flood. If Noah was disobedient, he would have forfeited the miracle, and he and his family would have died. [God may even have chosen someone else who would have been obedient to the instructions and teachings.]

While in Prayer

One day I was praying and meditating, and I heard God (more clearly than I had ever before) say, "Cade, will you speak for me?" I was hesitant and reluctant, giving excuses – variations of "I can't be a preacher … I'm the coach." I eventually got to "Yes, Lord." I was a bit ashamed of myself that this wasn't my initial response. I was sorrowful and apologetic.

God told me, "That's ok, you weren't my first choice, anyway. You were my sixth choice." I was stunned and amazed...**One**: that God was even talking to me this clearly – **Two**: that He had chosen me – **Three**: that there were 5 other people before me that said "No" to God's request to speak for HIM (**I was number six!**) – and **Four**: that those other people may not realize the benefits and miracles that they had forfeited.

It may be the same way with you.... What have you forfeited by saying, "No" to God? How different could your life have been if you'd only believed and trusted Him and said, "Yes, Lord."

Mark 10:17-23 – **Rich Young Ruler**

*17And as he was setting out on his journey, a man ran up and knelt before him and asked him, "Good Teacher, what must I do to inherit eternal life?" 18And Jesus said to him, "Why do you call me good? No one is good except God alone. 19You know the commandments: 'Do not murder, Do not commit adultery, Do not steal, Do not bear false witness, Do not defraud, Honor your father and mother.'" 20And he said to him, "Teacher, all these I have kept from my youth." 21And Jesus, looking at him, loved him, and said to him, "**You lack one thing: go, sell all that you have and give to the poor, and you will have treasure in heaven; and come, follow me.**" 22<u>Disheartened by the saying, he went away sorrowful, for he had great possessions.</u> 23And Jesus looked around and said to his disciples, "How* *difficult it will be for those who have wealth to enter the kingdom of God!"*

This is a well-known passage of scripture about a rich young ruler. He came before Jesus and asked a question about obtaining eternal life. Jesus directed him to the teachings/commandments: Don't murder, don't steal, etc. The young ruler noted that those were not a problem for him. He said, "I've been OBEDIENT to these things all my life." Jesus looked at him and loved him. [I want to emphasize that loving someone isn't always praising and accepting what they do; If I truly love you, I have to tell you the truth.] Jesus pointed out the one thing that this young ruler lacked – Jesus told him to sell his possessions and come, follow him. The thing that he lacked wasn't necessarily his love for his possessions; his issue was the attitude that the possessions and wealth had created. His possessions owned him, instead of him owning them – he couldn't let them go. **He lacked obedience to the teaching Jesus gave Him.**

Wealth doesn't always mean possessions, money, and resources. Wealth could be information and teaching you received before coming into the knowledge of Jesus' message of the Kingdom. Some people have a "wealth" of Religious Doctrine. Others may have a "wealth" of experience. Do these things prevent you from being obedient to God? If God asked you to sell what you have… let what you have go…forget what you think you know…Would you be able do it? Could you be able to do it?

By exposing this young man to himself, it was revealed that he wasn't teachable concerning matters of his wealth. Murder was not an issue. Adultery was not an issue. Honoring mother/father is not an issue. But when asking him to give up his wealth, it showed that he had more faith, more trust, more confidence in his wealth than in the teachings of Jesus. It is impossible to serve God and money. One will be Master in your life.

2 Kings 5:1-15 – "Go, Wash in the Jordan River"

Naaman, commander of the army of the king of Syria, was a great man with his master and in high favor, because by him the Lord had given victory to Syria. He was a mighty man of valor, **but he was a leper.** *²Now the Syrians on one of their raids had* **carried off a little girl from the land of Israel***, and she worked in the service of Naaman's wife. ³She said to her mistress,* "<u>Would that my lord were with the prophet who is in Samaria! He would cure him of his leprosy.</u>" *⁴So Naaman went in and told his lord, "Thus and so spoke the girl from the land of Israel." ⁵And the* **king of Syria** *said, "Go now, and I will send a letter to the king of Israel." So he went, taking with him ten talents of silver, six thousand shekels of gold, and ten changes of clothing. ⁶And he brought the letter to the king of Israel, which read, "When this letter reaches you, know that I have sent to you Naaman my servant, that you may cure him of his leprosy." ⁷And when the king of Israel read the letter, he tore his clothes and said, "Am I God, to kill and to make alive, that this man sends word to me to cure a man of his leprosy? Only consider, and see how he is seeking a quarrel with me." ⁸But when Elisha the man of God heard that the king of Israel had torn his clothes, he sent to the king, saying,* **"Why have you torn your clothes? Let him** *come now to me, that he may know that there is a prophet in Israel."* ⁹*So Naaman came with his horses and chariots and stood at the door of Elisha's house.* ¹⁰*And* **Elisha sent a messenger to him, saying, "Go and wash in the Jordan seven times, and your flesh shall be restored, and you shall be clean."** ¹¹*But Naaman was* **angry** *and went away, saying, "Behold, I thought that he would surely* **come out to me** *and* **stand** *and* **call upon the name of the Lord his God***, and* **wave his hand over the place** *and* **cure the leper.** ¹²*Are not Abana and Pharpar, the rivers of Damascus, better than all the waters of Israel? Could I not wash in them and be clean?" So he turned and* **went away in a rage.** ¹³***But his servants*** *came near and said to him, "****My father, if it was a great word the prophet has spoken to you; will you not do it? Has he actually said to you, 'Wash, and be clean'?***" ¹⁴<u>*So he went down and dipped himself seven times in the Jordan, according to the word of the man of God, and his flesh was restored like the flesh of a little child, and he was clean.*</u>

This story of Naaman illustrates the key aspects of obedience to teaching and the subsequent miraculous. Notice: it was a "captive maid" (a slave girl) from Israel that gave them teaching/information/knowledge that there was a prophet in Samaria that could heal leprosy. If they didn't have this information, Naaman would never have gone to see the prophet in the first place. So, he obviously had some level of faith in the information about God and the prophet in Israel.

The issue that Naaman ran into was an issue that many of us run into. We receive a Word from God or instructions through prophecy, prayer, study of the scripture, a word of knowledge, etc., but because it does not come in the form we thought it would, we forfeit our miracle. Naaman THOUGHT that the prophet would heal him in a certain way. (Perhaps come out to greet him, stand and call on the name of the Lord, waive his hands over him, and heal him.) When the miracle didn't come the way he thought it would, he went away angry.

It was the servants who brought him back to reality. They noted that he (Naaman) would have obeyed if he was asked to do something big or grand. (It is often the simple instructions that are ignored and rejected that prevent us from having the miracles we seek.) In Naaman's case, he relented and washed as instructed. He experienced the miraculous because of obedience. [I truly believe that if he had never washed, Naaman would have died with his leprosy.]

Luke 5:3-9 – "Cast Out Your Nets"

*³And he entered into one of the ships, which was Simon's, and prayed him that he would thrust out a little from the land. And he sat down, and **taught the people out of the ship**. ⁴Now when he had left speaking, he said unto Simon, **Launch out into the deep, and let down your nets for a draught.** ⁵And Simon answering said unto him, Master, we have toiled all the night, and have taken nothing: nevertheless <u>at thy word I will let down the net</u>. ⁶**And when they had this done, they inclosed a great multitude of fishes: and their net brake.** ⁷And they beckoned unto their partners, which were in the other ship, that they should come and help them. And they came, and **filled both the ships**, so that they began to sink. ⁸When Simon Peter saw* *it, he fell down at Jesus' knees, saying, Depart from me; for I am a sinful man, O Lord. ⁹For he was astonished, and all that were with him,* **at the draught of the fishes which they had taken:**

In this passage, the only thing preventing the miraculous was the obedience of Simon Peter. Jesus gave the instructions: "Let down your **_nets_**" (more than one net, plural). Peter proceeded to do what we do – tell Jesus what we have done before and how it didn't work: "We have been fishing all night long and caught nothing." However, Peter acquiesced and obeyed...partially. Instead of letting down all the nets like Jesus instructed, He let down **_the net_** (one net, singular). Even in partial obedience, he experienced the miraculous. However, he missed out on many fish because he didn't put down all his nets.

How much do we miss out on because we don't fully obey?

Isaiah 1:18-20 – **Willing and Obedient**

¹⁸*"Come now, let us reason together, says the Lord: though your sins are like scarlet, they shall be as white as snow; though they are red like crimson, they shall become like wool.* ¹⁹***If you are willing and obedient, you shall eat the good of the land;*** ²⁰***but if you refuse and rebel, you shall be eaten by the sword;*** *for the mouth of the Lord has spoken."*

Here we have Isaiah prophesying to the children of Israel…. Israel had rebelled and not followed the commands of God. God spells it out plainly: "If you willingly are obedient to my commandments and teachings, <u>You shall eat the good of the land</u>" (resources, real estate, financial blessings, favor, healing, prosperity, miracles etc.) Obedience to God's teachings places you in a position to receive all of these amazing blessings from God. However, the opposite is true as well. Disobedience (refusal and rebellion) to God's teachings, places you in a position to be "eaten by the sword" (financial ruin, no favor, no miracles, things "just not working out" in your life, sickness, family crisis, even death).

The two choices are made plain for you to make a decision. God doesn't decide to bless you with the miraculous – you must make a decision to eat the "good of the land." Neither does God curse you or cause bad things to happen to you – you decide that as well. So, which will you choose?

Luke 17: 11-19 – "Go Show Yourselves to the Priests"

[11]*On the way to Jerusalem he was passing along between Samaria and Galilee.*[12]*And as he entered a village, he was met by* ***ten lepers****, who stood at a distance* [13]*and lifted up their voices, saying, "Jesus, Master, have mercy on us."* [14]*When he saw them he said to them,* ***"Go and show yourselves to the priests."*** <u>***And as they went they were cleansed.***</u> [15]*Then one of them, when he saw that he was healed, turned back, praising God with a loud voice;* [16]*and he fell on his face at Jesus' feet, giving him thanks. Now he was a Samaritan.* [17]*Then Jesus answered, "Were not ten cleansed? Where are the nine?* [18]*Was no one found to return and give praise to God except this foreigner?"* [19]*And*

he said to him, "__Rise and go your way; your faith has made you well.__"

In actuality… obedience is an extension of faith: you generally put into action what you truly believe. As addressed earlier, faith is believing and trusting in someone or something. So, if my faith is in God and what He has said in His Word, it will be demonstrated and manifested through my obedient actions. In essence… if I trust God, I will obey His Word. When He instructs me to tithe – I will give 10 percent of my earnings. When He says that my body is His temple – I won't fornicate… I won't smoke tobacco or do anything which poisons or is detrimental to this body…. I won't overindulge with poor eating habits…. I will exercise. When He tells me to forgive others – I won't hold grudges.

Likewise, when He tells me to "go show myself to the priests," – I don't sulk that He didn't lay hands on me…. I don't cry that He didn't say, "Be healed." I obey His instructions and get to walking towards the priests…even though it was against the law for lepers to do so!

Jesus seemed disappointed when only the Samaritan returned to offer thanks and praise. He asked, "Were not ten cleansed, where are the other nine?" Jesus is interested in not only getting us the miracle (healing, in this instance), but also teaching us how to get the miraculous result. Now… all of the Lepers may have received their healing; however, only one received the key ingredient – the teaching on how the healing occurred: "Your faith in what I told you to do is what made you well."

Genesis 22:1-2, 9-13, 15-18 – **The Sacrifice of Isaac**

After these things God tested Abraham and said to him, "Abraham!" And he said, "Here I am." ²He said, "**Take your son, your only son Isaac, whom you love, and go to the land of Moriah, and offer him there as a burnt offering on one of the mountains of which I shall tell you.**"

⁹When they came to the place of which God had told him, Abraham built the altar there and laid the wood in order and bound Isaac his son and laid him on the altar, on top of the wood. ¹⁰<u>Then Abraham reached out his hand and took the knife to slaughter his son.</u> ¹¹But the angel of the Lord called to him from heaven and said, "Abraham, Abraham!" And he said, "Here I am." ¹²He said, "**Do not lay your hand on the boy or do anything to him, for now I know that you fear God, seeing you have not withheld your son, your only son, from me.**" ¹³And Abraham lifted up his eyes and looked, and behold, behind him was a ram, caught in a thicket by his horns. And Abraham went and took the ram and offered it up as a burnt offering instead of his son.

¹⁵And the angel of the Lord called to Abraham a second time from heaven ¹⁶and said, "By myself I have sworn, declares the Lord, because you have done this and have not withheld your son, your only son, ¹⁷<u>I will surely bless you, and I will surely multiply your offspring as the stars of heaven and as the sand that is on the seashore. And your offspring shall possess the gate of his enemies,</u> ¹⁸<u>and in your offspring shall all the nations of the earth be blessed, because you have obeyed my voice.</u>"

This is the account of Abraham being asked to sacrifice Isaac: His ONLY Son, whom HE LOVED. [Now if he had 10 or 20 children, maybe…then he could probably have chosen the one who gave him the most trouble, the one who he didn't like and sacrifice that one… *(I'm kidding)*] But God asked for his ONLY son and for something He loved.

[Could you have been obedient? Would you trust God enough to give up your only, your last, or something that you love? Will you hold on to the resource or will you put your faith in THE Source?]

Abraham trusted God and was willing to sacrifice Isaac. I believe Abraham had faith to believe that if He killed Isaac, God would do something: raise him from the dead, heal him, perform some miracle. This great level of sacrifice and obedience caused God to bless not only Abraham (for Abraham was very rich), but also his children and offspring, and also all the nations of the earth. [Verse 18 is a reference to the miracle of Jesus coming to the earth to die for Man's sin and reconnect us back to our Father.] All nations are blessed and received the Greatest Miracle in history because of the obedience of Abraham.

James 2:14-17 — **Obedience Gives Life to Your Faith**

*[14]What good is it, my brothers, if someone says **he has faith but does not have works?** Can that faith save him? [15]If a brother or sister is poorly clothed and lacking in daily food, [16]and one of you says to them, "Go in peace, be warmed and filled," without giving them the things needed for the body, what good is that? [17]So also faith by itself, if it does not have works, is dead.*

Many of us have faith, but, unfortunately, it is dead. We say that we believe in God and His Word; however, we don't obey. We don't perform the works and actions that line up with our faith. If we were one of the 10 Lepers, we wouldn't go to the priest because we don't understand how that would lead to us being healed. We don't tithe because we don't have faith that God will keep His Word and "open the windows of Heaven and pour out a blessing that we won't have room enough to receive." We don't take care of our bodies because we don't truly believe that God lives in us and has a purpose for us; we don't believe that God will place us on stages and platforms where we will need to be in peak physical conditioning - and not pass out because we can hardly breathe. We lie and cheat to get ahead because we don't believe that God will keep His Word and be a Provider. We don't pray because we don't believe that God watches over His Word to perform it; we don't believe God will answer. We don't forgive others because we don't believe that it will be of any benefit. We don't turn the other cheek because we don't believe that God will keep His Word and vindicate us.

We don't want to obey or submit to God's Authority. However, disobedience is often a major obstacle to obtaining the miraculous for which we cry out to God. When we are disobedient, we are essentially saying, "I'm not willing to participate in doing things Your way, God" … "I don't trust You, God" … "I don't believe You, God" … "I love this more than I love You, God." Whether we speak these words or not is irrelevant – this is the mentality that our actions demonstrate. And as the old saying goes, **"Actions speak louder than words."**

Where there is a lack of obedience, God is hindered. It's not that God does not want to bless us or perform the miraculous; rather, we "put God in handcuffs" and do not allow His blessings to flow. God did not make a decision to withhold the miraculous, we made a decision to not put ourselves in a position to be blessed and receive the miraculous.

Obedience Affirms our Love for God

John 14:15-24

15 "If you love me, you will keep my commandments. 16And I will ask the Father, and he will give you another Helper, to be with you forever, 17even the Spirit of truth, whom the world cannot receive, because it neither sees him nor knows him. You know him, for he dwells with you and will be in you. 18 "I will not leave you as orphans; I will come to you. 19Yet a little while and the world will see me no more, but you will see me. Because I live, you also will live. 20In that day you will know that I am in my Father, and you in me, and I in you. 21Whoever has my commandments and keeps them, he it is who loves me. And he who loves me will be loved by my Father, and I will love him and manifest myself to him." 22Judas (not Iscariot) said to him, "Lord, how is it that you will manifest yourself to us, and not to the world?" 23Jesus answered him, "If anyone loves me, he will keep my word, and my Father will love him, and we will come to him and make our home with him. 24Whoever does not love me does not keep my words. And the word that you hear is not mine but the Father's who sent me.

Here, we see Jesus making a correlation between our Love for God/Him with Obedience (keeping His commandments). This must have great importance because in a span of only 9 verses, He mentions it 3 times – in addition to an antithesis, "whoever does not love me, does not keep my words."

[I've pondered this greatly and often wondered, "How does my obedience equate to me loving God? ... I love God (or at least I say I do) but I haven't always obeyed every commandment. So, what is Jesus saying?"]

"If you love me, you will keep my commandments" means that our obedience is a byproduct, a result, a manifestation of our love for God. How do I evaluate my love for God? ... I check my thoughts and actions to see if they line up with God's teachings. I obey and keep God's commandments BECAUSE I LOVE HIM. I don't obey God to get blessings or miracles – I don't obey Him to get a big house, new car, financial blessings – I don't obey Him to earn my way to Heaven or His favor... I obey Him because I love Him.

To dissect this further, I guess we need to understand Love from God's perspective.... God's form of love is Agape: Unconditional Love. There's nothing that we can do to separate us from the Love of God *(Romans 8:38)*. God loves us unconditionally, in spite of what we do. Unfortunately, when we say "love," we have conditions and reasons: "I love her because she's beautiful" ... "I love him because he makes 6 figures" ... "I love her because she cooks well" ... "I love him because he is physically fit" ... Well, if that's the case – the love dissipates when her beauty fades.... your love vanishes when he no longer makes 6 figures.... there is no love when she doesn't cook.... or your love runs out when he puts on a few pounds – This is NOT God's idea of Love.

True love, the *Agape* type of love is not emotional (for emotions change); it's not intellectual (for information changes). Love is a choice, a decision that you make. How could God love us, in spite of what we've done? He chose to love us without the conditions that we obey Him, praise Him, worship Him, agree with Him, etc. In the same manner...we have the capability to make a decision to love unconditionally. So, when we are mistreated, we can still demonstrate love because our decision wasn't predicated upon if they treated me right. If our spouse is being "a butt" (You can say that about your spouse, but no one else can.), we can still demonstrate love because our decision wasn't predicated upon them always being agreeable.

Therefore, God is saying. "If you make the decision to love Me, it will manifest in your obedience." You'll obey whether you're getting a blessing or not – a miracle or not – a promotion or not — good times or bad times. It doesn't matter, because you've made the decision to truly love God...without conditions, no matter what He does or doesn't do.

The Sacrifice of Obedience

In our obedience to God, there is sacrifice/giving. Better yet, a greater level of sacrifice is required. Sacrifice entails giving of your money, possessions, time, attention, etc. Obedience entails giving of yourself – sacrificing your will, your way, what you want to do, your fleshly desires in favor of God's Will, God's Way, and what God wants us to do.

A common misconception is that Love is automatic; therefore, Obedience is automatic – NOPE!!! I have to make the decision to love God, day by day—sometimes, moment by moment. Inherent in love is priority: "Do I love God enough to be faithful to my spouse; or do I love my fleshly desires, or this other person more?" ... "Do I love God more than stealing?" ... "Do I love God more than lying?" ... "Do I love God more than what I want?" I may make this decision when I wake up in the morning; or I may have to make this decision when situations arise: "Do I love this? ... or ... Do I love God?"

If I choose my desires, my will, to do what I want to do or to act contrary to God's teachings – I don't love Him.... or I don't love Him more than my desires, my will, other people, etc. ... or I don't love Him in the manner that He says I should ("love God with all your HEART, SOUL, AND MIND"). I don't keep His teachings /His commandments/His Words because I have chosen to love (give priority to) something else and not HIM. We say we love God, but if we're not following His teachings, His instructions, His words –- we don't love Him with "ALL." Our love is strengthened by the continual development of our relationship, intimacy, and obedience to his teachings.

If we don't follow God's teachings, we don't even really love ourselves, because (as noted before) God's commandments and teachings are in our best interest. God is not trying to take something valuable from us; He's trying to get something great to us. The miracles you need, the answers to your problems, the solution to your circumstances may be hindered by disobedience to His Words, teachings, commandments, instructions, information, or revelations.

What I want you to understand is that the blessings and miracles don't come because you are obedient. It is the obedience that demonstrates that you love, trust and believe in God's teachings. Even if you don't understand... still trust God enough to obey. Even though the miracle hasn't manifested yet... continue to obey. The motivation for obedience should be built on the foundation of our LOVE for God...not to try to get some blessing or miracle or to earn some reward.

Let's Be Honest – Self-Evaluation:

1. Have you been disobedient to God's teachings? Was it due to ignorance or willful disobedience?

2. Is your obedience predicated on what you can get from God? Are you obeying God to get "stuff"?

3. How has disobedience hindered you/blocked the miraculous?

4. How has obedience been advantageous/advanced you?

5. Do you love God? If yes, does your obedience align with your confession?

6. Do you love God with ALL your heart, mind, and soul?

OBSTACLE VII: Ignorance

"What a culture we live in; We are swimming in an ocean of information, and drowning in ignorance."
- Richard Paul Evans

Whenever my siblings and I were getting ready to do something that wasn't right or something that our parents told us not to do, one of us always reasoned, *"What Mama don't know, won't hurt!"* If our college coach told us specifically not to go out before the game, some of my teammates would override anyone's concerns with, *"What Coach don't know, won't hurt!"* I don't know where this saying originated, but it seemed as if it had the power to override any rule or statement of authority.

Growing up, there were a few similar sayings that I can remember: "What you don't know, won't hurt" … "No news is good news" … "What the eyes don't see, the heart don't grieve over" … and the classic - "Ignorance is bliss." These statements gave the impression that if you didn't know about something or didn't have any information about something, you were insulated from its effects or consequences.

God, however, emphatically disagrees with this sentiment in Hosea 4:6:

My people are destroyed for lack of knowledge;
because you have rejected knowledge,
I reject you from being a priest to me.
And since you have forgotten the law of your God,
I also will forget your children.

You can't get your miracle because there is some information – some revelation – that you don't possess. God is saying, in this particular passage of scripture, that it is not HIS fault that you're ignorant and being destroyed. We're being destroyed...we're missing out on the miracles...we're not living the life that God designed... because we're rejecting knowledge. God has answers, but we fail to "ask." The information/the revelation to solve our problems is out there, but we don't "seek" it. People may have even shared knowledge with us, but we've rejected it.

Kingdom of Darkness vs Kingdom of Light

The devil, the Enemy, desires to steal, kill, and destroy us. Our adversary is called the Prince of Darkness. His "kingdom" is a kingdom of darkness. Now... this doesn't mean that Satan goes around trying to turn off all the lights in your home or sneaking around causing trouble when the sun goes down. **The Hebrew concept for "Darkness" is Ignorance.** Satan has no power except the power that we give him. Therefore, the demonic forces attempt to rule and influence our lives by keeping us in the dark – or better yet, keeping us ignorant. This is why God says, "My people are destroyed for lack of knowledge." Or in laymen's terms... "My people lose in life because they are ignorant and stupid." The less information, knowledge, and teachings from God that we have, the more influence and power we give the enemy. The more information and knowledge that you understand, the less power and influence the enemy has in your life.

It's quite simple: Teaching is an important foundational tool of God. The first thing God did when creating the world was institute knowledge...

Genesis 1:3

And God said, Let there be light: and there was light.

"Light" here isn't referring to the sun, the moon, and the stars; He didn't begin to orchestrate these "lights of the heavens" until Genesis 1:14. Just as Darkness is a symbol of Ignorance, **the Hebrew concept of "Light" is symbolic of Knowledge/ Information.** When the entire world was in chaos, darkness, and disarray...God introduced the most important element first... KNOWLEDGE.

Jesus is referred to as the "Word of God." The believers are referred to as the "light of the world." God does not want us to be ignorant. He even tells us to "**Study** to show yourselves approved" and to "take my yoke upon you, and **learn** of Me." One lesson from God can enable you to be more financially competent.... One lecture from the Father can help you become better in your relationships.... One tutorial from the Master can equip you to be a better employee or entrepreneur.... One class or session with the Creator will always bring you way closer to your miracle.

Acts 26:16-18

[16]But rise and stand upon your feet, for I have appeared to you for this purpose, to appoint you as a servant and witness to the things in which you have seen me and to those in which I will appear to you, [17]delivering you from

your people and from the Gentiles—to whom I am sending you [18]***to open their eyes, so that they may turn from darkness to light and from the power of Satan to God***, *that they may receive forgiveness of sins and a place among those who are sanctified by faith in me.*

In this recollection of his assignment from Jesus, Paul notes that his mission was to take people from darkness to light, to expose their ignorance and transform people with the knowledge of God, to take people from under the power and influence of Satan (darkness) and transfer them under the power and influence of God (knowledge, wisdom).

Even as we evaluate Paul's letter to the Ephesians *(6:17)*, the Word/teaching of God is referred to as the "sword of the spirit." Many of us are unable to "fight" in the spirit realm because we don't have knowledge. We have no "sword." However, when Satan tempted Jesus, Jesus didn't cry.... He didn't beg God to remove the test.... He didn't ask God to take away the tempter.... He responded with the Word of God: "It is Written...It is Written...It is Written...."

We don't have healing because we don't have knowledge about God's teachings on healing. We lack true wealth because we don't know about God's blueprint concerning management of His resources. We don't experience the miraculous power to shape and formulate our environment and world because we are ignorant.

Light, knowledge, God's Words and teachings are our greatest weapon and the greatest threat to our adversary. Satan doesn't care about you going to church. He doesn't care about you being rich. He doesn't care about you singing, praise dancing, or shouting. As long as you aren't receiving God's teachings, He isn't afraid of you.

Let's examine this concept when Jesus explains the parable of the sower...

Matthew 13:18-23

*18 "Hear then the parable of the sower: 19***When anyone hears the word of the kingdom and does not understand it, <u>the evil one comes and snatches away</u>** *what has been sown in his heart. This is what was sown along the path. 20As for what was sown on rocky ground, this is the one who hears the word and immediately receives it with joy, 21yet he has no root in himself, but endures for a while, and* **when tribulation or persecution** *arises on account of the word, immediately he falls away. 22As for what was sown among thorns, this is the one who hears the word, but* **the cares of the world and the deceitfulness of riches choke the word,** *and it proves unfruitful. 23As for what was sown on good soil, this is the one who hears the word and understands it. He indeed bears fruit and yields, in one case a hundredfold, in another sixty, and in another thirty."*

The "evil one" is so deathly afraid of the teachings about the Kingdom of God that he comes himself and snatches away the teachings. But notice, he only comes when you don't understand it. He attempts to keep you ignorant before you learn the truth. He is so afraid of the Word of God that he doesn't come personally once you hear and receive the Word of God. He attempts to use "tribulation, persecution, cares of the world, deceitfulness of riches" to destroy your faith in the teachings.

Satan knows how powerful and amazing God created you to become – that's why he's been fighting you ever since you were a child - even before you were born. He's tried to kill you as a child. He's tried to steal your destiny. He's thrown every enticing thing he can in your path to trip you up and keep you ignorant. He knows that if you ever get God's teachings and understand who you really are, you can change your world, your life, your circumstances. Nothing he tries to do will be able to stop you.

Let's examine the power of ignorance in obstructing the miraculous...

Genesis 19:12-14 – **Lot Warns His Sons-in-law**

12Then the men said to Lot, "Have you anyone else here? Sons-in-law, sons, daughters, or anyone you have in the city, bring them out of the place. 13For we are about to destroy this place, because the outcry against its people has become great before the Lord, and the Lord has sent us to destroy it." 14So Lot went out and said to his sons-in-law, who were to marry his daughters, "Up! Get out of this place, for the Lord is about to destroy the city." But he seemed to his sons-in-law to be jesting.

In this passage the Angels warned Lot of the destruction that was to come. Lot, in turn, passed on the knowledge of this destruction to his future sons-in-law. They thought he was joking, being silly, fooling around. They rejected knowledge. They missed out on the miracle to save their lives due to their ignorance. As a result, they were destroyed with the city.

Ignorance is dangerous. What you don't know won't just hurt you…it can kill you. Ignorance can derail your destiny. Just because you don't know, it doesn't mean that you're not subject to the consequences. Let's look at some real-life examples…

The Story of Carl

Let me tell you a story about a kid named Carl… Carl was smart, athletic, college bound, and destined for greatness. In high school, Carl was one of the few kids with a car. He was popular and was friends with everyone: Teachers liked him; basketball and football teams praised him; the smart kids and special needs kids loved him; the cheerleaders found him attractive; the rich kids and the poor kids, popular and unpopular, all held him in high esteem…Carl was just a cool guy that everyone liked.

One day, one of his friends, "Red," asked for a ride to the store. Of course, Carl gave him a ride – it was right up the street from the school, no problem. It took Red a little while to come out of the store, but when he came out, he was running with two bags, full of snacks. Red got to the car (out of breath) and told Carl, "Let's Go!!! Drive!!!"

Carl puzzled began to drive back to the school. He asked Red, "Is everything okay? Why did you come out of there in such a hurry?"

Red replied, "Oh, it's nothing…we are good…just in a hurry to get back."

The next day the police came to the school. Red and Carl were both arrested. Turns out, Red had robbed the gas station and shot the clerk. Police viewed the video footage and saw the license plate of the getaway car – CARL'S CAR!!! Carl told them that he didn't know that Red was going to rob the store; Heck...he didn't know that he had robbed the store until the police told him.

Carl was charged as an accessory to the crimes. A good kid with a bright future, who did not have any intention of committing a crime, was now being sent to jail because of his ignorance. Because the clerk died, Carl wasn't only an accessory to robbery, but he was also an accessory to murder. His ignorance to Red's plans and actions interrupted the trajectory of his life. Ignorance cost his family legal fees. It cost him college scholarships. It cost him his reputation and many opportunities. But most of all, ignorance cost him his freedom.

This isn't some made up story. This type of scenario occurs in the court systems all the time. Even if a person is involved in illegal activity unknowingly, he/she still has to face the consequences of their actions or the actions of others.

Truancy

As I was listening to a lawyer tell me the importance of knowing the law, he told me a story about one of his clients.... He was a hardworking young man and was up for a promotion at his job. He was a single parent (a widower). He went to work early in the mornings and sent his daughter to school every day.

One day, the police showed up at his office and arrested him. He was puzzled and confused and repeatedly asked what he had done. Apparently, his daughter had been skipping school. After so many days of unexcused absences, the school/city/state officials deem it a crime and make an arrest. However, they don't arrest the one committing the truancy (or absenteeism): No, they don't arrest the child – They place the parent/guardian under arrest. Even though this father didn't know his daughter was missing school... even though he thought he was sending her to school... even though he was ignorant of her actions... he had to face the consequences of HER actions.

Do you still think ignorance is bliss? Similar ignorance keeps us from experiencing the miracles of God. If we don't know how to unlock God's miracles or if we don't know what God requires of us, then we live a life devoid of the miraculous and filled with disappointment and frustration.

Mark 9:17-18, 25-29 – "Why Could We Not Cast It Out?"

[17]And someone from the crowd answered him, "Teacher, I brought my son to you, for he has a spirit that makes him mute. [18]And whenever it seizes him, it throws him down, and he foams and grinds his teeth and becomes rigid. So I asked your disciples to cast it out, and they were not able."

[25]And when Jesus saw that a crowd came running together, he rebuked the unclean spirit, saying to it, "You mute and deaf spirit, I command you, come out of him and never

*enter him again." ²⁶And after crying out and convulsing him terribly, it came out, and the boy was like a corpse, so that most of them said, "He is dead." ²⁷But Jesus took him by the hand and lifted him up, and he arose. ²⁸And when he had entered the house, his disciples asked him privately, "Why could we not cast it out?" ²⁹And he said to them, **"This kind cannot be driven out by anything but by fasting and prayer."***

The disciples were attempting to perform the miraculous. They had seen Jesus cast out demons before. They, themselves, had cast out demons as well. However, for some reason, they were struggling to perform the miraculous. The father of the possessed boy asked Jesus for help and told Him that the disciples couldn't help his son: "They couldn't get me the miraculous result that was needed." This must have been embarrassing, frustrating, and disappointing for the disciples.

When they were alone, the disciples asked Jesus what had been burning in their minds all day: "Why could we not perform the miracle? ...What did we do wrong? ...Why did we fail?" Jesus had taught about unbelief and its importance, but he also gave them a lesson on the power of ignorance: "But this kind never comes out except by prayer and fasting." The disciples were ignorant – they didn't know that "this kind" of demonic force was susceptible to something beyond what they were accustomed to using to defeat the demonic forces in the past. They just didn't know!!!

However, the result did not change because of their ignorance. They could have been there all night, rebuking, crying out to God, saying loud prayers, jumping up and down, playing music, shouting, etc.... The demonic force would not have relinquished the boy. Jesus said, "This kind CANNOT be driven out, EXCEPT by prayer and fasting." If there was no prayer and fasting, this kind of demonic influence would NEVER be defeated.

Jesus had a teaching and understanding about this demonic force that the disciples did not have. Therefore, Jesus could perform miracles that the disciples could not. It was their ignorance that limited them and was an obstacle to the miraculous.

The solution to Ignorance is simple: Knowledge, Information, and Revelation. Many of us are destroyed because of the lack of knowledge. God didn't say it was a lack of miracles, not a lack of prayer, not for a lack of love, not a lack of money, not a lack of whatever it is we think we need. We have a knowledge deficiency because we lack teaching (the Word of God).

This goes beyond "book smarts." It goes beyond being "street savvy." It goes beyond being able to tap into and understand emotions. One Word from God can make a Doctorate degree look elementary. One Word from God can make common sense seem foolish. The teachings and revelation from God should be our very sustenance, our livelihood, our daily bread.

"Man should not live by bread alone, but by every Word that proceeds out of the mouth of God" – If I don't understand or know what Word or teaching has proceeded out of God's mouth, I'm dying in that situation. If I don't know what God has spoken about physical healing, I can be defeated by sickness. If I don't know God's teachings on finances, I'm literally dying financially. If I don't know His protocol about maintaining relationships and love, I'm deficient from a relationship aspect. If I'm ignorant of God's teachings, I'm perishing in that arena.

Let's Be Honest – Self-Evaluation:

1. In what area of your life are you lacking knowledge?

2. How is this limiting you or inhibiting the miraculous power of God in your life?

3. In what area of your life are knowledgeable? How does this compare with the areas of your life in which you're ignorant?

4. Have you ever had to pay the consequences for ignorant actions? Did you think it was fair or unfair? How did this impact you moving forward?

OBSTACLE VIII: Tradition

"The less there is to justify a traditional custom, the harder it is to get rid of it." —Mark Twain

Pot Roast

I remember a story that my spiritual mentor once told me: There was a young couple that had recently gotten married. They went through all the trials that married couples go through, and for the most part, they enjoyed being married – that is except for when the wife made pot roast. It tasted delicious and quickly became one of the young husband's favorite dishes. But it befuddled him every time she made it. She would cut off about a quarter of the roast and throw it away. Her husband didn't understand why she would throw away good (expensive) meat.

The husband couldn't cook, so the young wife largely ignored him. Her usual response was, "This was the way my mom taught us to cook it. If you don't like it, I can cook something else." The husband would usually pipe down after the threat because that meant he'd be eating a ham sandwich for dinner.

One day, while she was preparing pot roast, they called her mother: "Hey, Mom", the wife greeted. "Could you settle something for us?"

"Sure, Honey...I'll try," the mom responded.

The young wife began, "Would you explain to my NON-COOKING HUSBAND that when cooking pot roast, you have to cut away some of it before seasoning it?"

The mom affirmed, "That's right, Baby. That's just how I taught all of you girls how to cook it. Does it not taste good?"

The satisfied wife gestured towards her husband to speak up, "Hi, Mom...no, the pot roast is delicious. I was just wondering – why do you have to cut so much meat off and throw it away?"

Silence emanated from the other end. Finally, the mother gave a response that the husband had heard all too often: "Well, it was the way that mom taught me how to cook it."

For the next year or two, the husband had to endure the unanswerable question about the pot roast. He'd asked the other sisters, only to be told the same thing - "That's just how we were taught". After a long and enduring trail of dead-ends, he saw a glimmer of hope. The next Saturday, the family was having a gathering in honor of his wife's grandmother's "100th Birthday." He hoped that she would have the answer to his question.

As the celebration was winding down (after the music, after the cake, after the presents), the young husband found an opportunity to have a conversation with the Matriarch of the family. After some small talk, he eased his question into the discussion. "Grand-Ma," he started, "I love the pot roast that my wife makes. They tell me that it is an old recipe of yours."

"Yes, it was passed down to me by Momma," the elderly woman explained.

The husband was heartbroken. "Oh no...not again..." he thought. He'd heard how this story was going to end, but he asked the question anyway: "Why did you cut so much meat off and throw it away before seasoning it?"

Silence exuded from the elder as she seemed to be in deep thought. She finally answered, "Oh... we did that because we didn't have a pot big enough to cook all the roast. So, we had to cut some of it off so that it would fit inside of our small pots. We threw it away because we didn't have a fancy freezer to keep meat...it would just spoil, so we threw it away." With a laugh she exclaimed, "I'm sure they have pots big enough now to cook two or three roasts at the same time."

Feeling vindicated, the young husband walked toward his wife with a wry smile. "What did you do?" She asked him.

"Who, me? I've done nothing…but come with me," he retorted.

He led her to the table of the 100-year-old woman. With a satisfied smile, he said "Now, Grand-Ma, could you explain to my wife why you cut off a portion of pot roast before cooking it?"

Tradition/Religion

Some of us fall into the trap of the young wife - When attempting to follow God and understand Him and what He is doing, we have to make sure that HE is the priority. Sometimes, we are unable to accept what God is trying to do in our lives TODAY because we are still fixated on how He has done things in the PAST. We are unable to see God for who He is because we are constantly viewing God from the prism of yesterday.

God is Progressive. If you're not progressing, you're stagnant or dying. Unfortunately, the "way we've always done things" has hindered God's progressive plans in our lives and stifled his agenda. Let's look at a few examples:

Mark 7:1-13 – **Making Void the Word of God**

Now when the Pharisees gathered to him, with some of the scribes who had come from Jerusalem, ²*they saw that some of his disciples ate with hands that were defiled, that is, unwashed.* ³*(<u>For the Pharisees and all the Jews do not eat unless they wash their hands properly, holding to the tradition of the elders,</u>* ⁴<u>*and when they come from the marketplace, they do not eat unless they wash. And there are many other traditions that they observe, such as the washing of cups and pots and copper vessels and dining couches.*</u>*)* ⁵*And the Pharisees and the scribes asked him, "Why do your disciples not walk according to the tradition of the elders, but eat with defiled hands?"* ⁶*And he said to them, "Well did Isaiah prophesy of you hypocrites, as it is written,*

"'This people honors me with their lips,
    but their heart is far from me;
⁷**in vain do they worship me,**
    teaching as doctrines the commandments of men.'

⁸*<u>**You leave the commandment of God and hold to the tradition of men.**</u>"* ⁹*And he said to them, "<u>**You have a fine way of rejecting the commandment of God in order to establish your tradition!**</u>* ¹⁰*For Moses said, 'Honor your father and your mother'; and, 'Whoever reviles father or mother must surely die.'* ¹¹*But you say, 'If a man tells his father or his mother, "Whatever you would have gained from me is Corban"' (that is, given to God) —* ¹²*then you no longer permit him to do anything for his father or mother,* ¹³<u>*thus making void the word of God by your tradition*</u> *that you have handed down. And many such things you do."*

The Pharisees were a religious group renowned for their knowledge of the scriptures. They had a tradition of not eating unless they washed their hands. This tradition was passed down and held great importance in their lives. It was such a priority and had such authority in their lives that they questioned Jesus when His disciples did not wash their hands before eating. To them, the disciples had committed a great atrocity and disrespect to God.

Jesus addressed their commitment to tradition. He quoted Isaiah and told them that they "teach as doctrines the commandments of men. You leave the commandment of God and hold to the tradition of men." In other words, "you give your traditions equal weight with the Word/teachings of God. Sometimes, you even place a greater importance on your traditions than God's own words."

He noted that because they were so loyal to the traditions of the elders/men, they were neglecting the commandments (teachings) of God. He gave the example of the teaching to "Honor your father and mother." However, this teaching was voided, made of no effect, negated because of their tradition. They established a tradition called "Corban" – that is, whatever they had was a gift to God; therefore, they were not allowed to do anything for their mother and father. Helping father or mother would "violate their vow of Corban."

Because of our traditions we "make void" (negate/cancel) the Word of God (the teachings of God). I've heard that women shouldn't be in the pulpits. Some "churches" don't allow musical instruments. Others demand that women dress a certain way with head covering, no makeup, long dresses, no elbow showing, etc. Some religious institutions are accustomed to paying dues. Others don't allow dancing or speaking in tongues. These and all other traditions make the True Teachings of God powerless and ineffective. So, if God desires to use a woman, He can't because of the tradition of that particular religion. If God desired to bring healing through music, He can't because of the tradition of no musical instruments. If God is leading someone to accept Christ's sacrifice, He can't because she may not be wearing the right clothes according to man's traditions and religious rituals. Our traditions can put "handcuffs" on what God wants to do.

Peter and the Gentile

Peter was a Jew, and the Jewish tradition was that they didn't associate or interact with the Gentiles. Even Jesus' instructions to the disciples was that they "feed the lost sheep" – basically, meaning to teach and save those Jews who didn't know of Christ's sacrifice. Their target audience, their assignment as far as they were concerned, was teaching the Good News (the Gospel) to the Jews.

However, God interrupted the Jew's and Peter's tradition. In Acts 10, Peter had a dream and was instructed to not call anyone common or unclean; he also went to the house of Cornelius – a GENTILE, not a JEW. Cornelius and his family received the Holy Spirit and received Salvation. Peter was shocked and amazed but couldn't deny that God was doing something contrary to Peter's traditional beliefs. Upon being questioned about what had happened by the other apostles and Jews, Peter recounts:

Acts 11:15-18

*¹⁵As I began to speak, **the Holy Spirit fell on them just as on us at the beginning**. ¹⁶And I remembered the word of the Lord, how he said, 'John baptized with water, but you will be baptized with the Holy Spirit.' ¹⁷<u>**If then God gave the same gift to them as he gave to us when we believed in the Lord Jesus Christ, who was I that I could stand in God's way?**</u>" ¹⁸When they heard these things they fell silent. And they glorified God, saying, "<u>**Then to the Gentiles also God has granted repentance that leads to life.**</u>"*

Peter and the other Jews realized that God was operating differently from their traditions, their preconceived notions, what they had been taught all their lives, and what their religion demanded of them. [What are we holding on to that is preventing us from experiencing the miracles of God?] If Peter had held onto his traditions and religious beliefs, Cornelius and his family would have missed out on the miracle of Salvation. Peter himself would have missed out on the Revelation of God's plan for redemption for all of mankind.

Some of us are so loyal to our traditions that we limit God. Will you continue to go to a "church building" because "Big Mama" and "MeeMaw" went there... even though you aren't learning or growing Spiritually? Will you continue to pay dues and building fund payments rather than tithes and offerings because that's what your church has always done? Will we continue to put homosexuals out of the church, instead of teaching them the Word of God, showing them the error in their ways with no condemnation, and demonstrating the LOVE of God at the same time? Will we continue to turn a blind eye to the infidelity, adultery, hypocrisy of our leaders because that is what we've always done; or will we hold them accountable? It seems as if we'd rather DIE in traditions than LIVE apart from them.

Tradition reared its ugly head once again when Paul confronted Peter. Let's read Paul's account in Galatians....

Galatians 2:11-14

11But when Cephas came to Antioch, I opposed him to his face, because he stood condemned. 12For before certain men came from James, he was eating with the Gentiles; **but when they came he drew back and separated himself, fearing the circumcision party** *13<u>And the rest of the Jews acted hypocritically along with him, so that even Barnabas was led astray by their hypocrisy.</u> 14But when I saw that <u>their conduct was not in step with the truth of the gospel</u>, I said to Cephas before them all,* **"If you, though a Jew, live like a Gentile and not like a Jew, how can you force the Gentiles to live like Jews?"**

Peter seemingly was beginning to understand and accept that the Gentiles were extended the same gift of Salvation as the Jews. He apparently had begun to fellowship with many of them. Traditionally, the Jews wouldn't interact with the Gentiles – it would have been an atrocity to eat with them. When James returned to Antioch with other Jews, Peter separated himself from the Gentiles according to tradition. Paul notes that Barnabas and the other Jews also began to separate themselves. This hypocrisy was dangerous. Paul could see how detrimental this was to God's agenda.

If our conduct doesn't line up with God's teachings, we pass on error, ignorance, and inhibition to the miracles of God. We can't make our traditions greater than the Truth of God.

Matthew 17:1-6 – **Transfiguration**

*And after six days Jesus took with him Peter and James, and John his brother, and led them up a high mountain by themselves. ²And he was transfigured before them, and his face shone like the sun, and his clothes became white as light. ³And behold, there appeared to them Moses and Elijah, talking with him. ⁴And Peter said to Jesus, "**Lord, it is good that we are here. If you wish, I will make three tents here, one for you and one for Moses and one for Elijah.**" ⁵He was still speaking when, behold, a bright cloud overshadowed them, and a voice from the cloud said, "This is my beloved Son, with whom I am well pleased; listen to him." ⁶When the disciples heard this, they fell on their faces and were terrified.*

This is the story of the transfiguration of Jesus, but I want to focus on Peter's response. Peter, James, and John were witnessing a Spiritual meeting. This was a moment of epic proportions – an encounter of Heavenly leaders on the earth. Whenever there is a move of God or a move of the Holy Spirit, people tend to formulate traditions, religions, and religious doctrines surrounding the experience. Peter wanted to build tents. He wanted to live there and keep Jesus, Moses, and Elijah there. That's what religion and traditions do…they attempt to put God in a box that they can understand, always visit, and have access to on their terms.

God interrupted Peter as "as he was still speaking." God did NOT place the focus on the meeting, the glory of the transfigured, the Heavenly power; but rather on Jesus and His Teachings: "This is My Beloved Son...listen to Him." Listen to His words. Hear His teachings. Watch what He does. Pattern yourselves after Him.

Unfortunately, we are not that different from Peter. Many focus on the great movements of God, the miracles of God, the way He did something great in the past, instead of listening to God Himself. So, we often miss God and His miracles when He "does a new thing" or operates in a different manner.

Titus 1:10-14 – **Paul's Instructions to Titus**

*[10]For there are many rebellious people, full of meaningless talk and deception, especially those of the circumcision group. [11]They must be silenced, because they are disrupting whole households by **teaching things they ought not to teach**—and that for the sake of dishonest gain. [12]One of Crete's own prophets has said it: "Cretans are always liars, evil brutes, lazy gluttons." [13]This saying is true. Therefore rebuke them sharply, so that they will be sound in the faith [14]and will **pay no attention to Jewish myths** or **to the merely human commands** of those who reject the truth.*

Paul is instructing his son in the Gospel, Titus, to rebuke those that teach things that cause disruption, especially those that were initially chosen by God (the

Jews aka the "circumcision group"). Paul admonishes Titus to not allow the incorrect teaching of some of these traditions to go unchallenged: "Rebuke them sharply, so that they will be sound in faith." [However, we are not to rebuke, to embarrass, to embellish our authority and position, or to act out of frustration or anger.] The reason Paul instructed Titus to rebuke these traditional teachings was so that the people would be solid and stable in what they believed.

Note: he tells Titus to not pay attention to "Jewish myths or to the merely human commands." It was the Jewish myths and human commands that caused many to be confused. God says one thing, but the traditions teach something different.

God is Too Big for Your Box

God refuses to be placed in a box. That's why I believe Jesus would heal people in different ways…so that you couldn't put Him in a box. He healed by speaking to them; He spat and made mud; He put fingers in ears; He went to their homes and laid hands; He spoke to the demonic spirits; some touched His garment, some he told to wash. These various methods point to the importance of, not the method but, faith and trust in the God of the methods. I should be ready and open to whatever method He wants to use: It may be medicine for you…. It may be laying on of hands for your sister…. It may be instructions to follow (to forgive someone, to sow a seed) for your father.

Once the people were accustomed to the healing of people, He stepped out of that box of their understanding and raised the dead. Not just raising the dead, but Lazarus who had been buried for 4 days. The Jewish traditions were that if a person was dead for 3 days, then they were truly dead. Jesus referred to death as only sleep. He further damaged their traditions by Himself being resurrected.

I'm not saying that all traditions are bad. I'm not even saying that all our experiences with religion have been detrimental. They have served their purpose. However, we can't be so attached, so interwoven, so stagnated in the traditions and religions that we place them before God. We have to be mindful that just because God "did it like that in the past," doesn't automatically mean that He wants to do it the same way presently and/or in the future.

Let's Be Honest – Self Evaluation:

1. Have you done or take part in "church activities" because "that is the way it has always been done"?

2. Where did these traditional exercises originate?

3. Are these activities/actions in alignment with God or with man-made tradition?

4. How have traditions of man been beneficial and/or detrimental to your life?

5. What traditions do you realize you must let go of in order to progress further in God?

OBSTACLE IX: Unforgiveness

"Unforgiveness is like drinking poison yourself and expecting the other person to die"
- Marrianne Williamson

One of the most common obstacles to the miraculous is unforgiveness because we all have been wronged, mistreated, or taken offense to what someone has said or done. We still don't like some people because they were mean to us in high school 20 years ago. Some of us still aren't talking to some family members because of what they said at the family reunion 15 years ago. We're still upset that Mama didn't give us the attention we felt we needed; or that our Dad walked out on the family. We are still wounded that our best friend betrayed us.... We are still hurt that our spouse, fiancé, boo cheated on us with that same best friend. We find it hard to love again because we were raped as a child – sexually and mentally abused by those who were supposed to love us. We are holding on to anger, disappointment, brokenness, and hurt; We are bleeding from wounds that are 5, 10, 15, 20, 30 years old and for some, even longer.

Unforgiveness keeps these wounds open. Unforgiveness keeps these offenses fresh. Unforgiveness makes what happened 20 years ago feel like it happened 20 seconds ago. We can't heal with unforgiveness in our hearts. Unforgiveness is dangerous because it disconnects us from God, thus shutting down our power source and connection to experience the miraculous. Let's see what Jesus says…

Mark 11:24-25 – **Forgive**

²⁴Therefore I tell you, whatever you ask in prayer, believe that you have received it, and it will be yours. ²⁵And whenever you stand praying, forgive, if you have anything against anyone, so that your Father also who is in heaven may forgive you your trespasses."

Now, I mentioned that in order to receive from God, we have to ask in prayer. Jesus reiterates this point by saying "<u>Whatever</u> you ask for in prayer, <u>even the miraculous</u>, if you have <u>faith</u> that you've received it…it will be yours." You have faith and communication, two key teachings in obtaining the miraculous.

However, unforgiveness can override your faith and communication. God says, "Don't talk to me if you haven't forgiven someone." The reason Unforgiveness disrupts the miraculous is because it ties God's hands. God CANNOT forgive you if you refuse to forgive others.

Matthew (5:23-24) records another time Jesus gave the same teaching when discussing anger and murder:

²³Therefore if you bring your gift to the altar, and there remember that your brother has something against you, ²⁴leave your gift there before the altar, and go your way. **First be reconciled to your brother,** *and then come and offer your gift.*

This is essentially the same teaching: however, the subtle difference is that you are NOT the one with the issue or the unforgiveness. Jesus says that if you're aware that "your brother has something against you." I know what you're thinking: "Wait a minute!! I'm not upset. I'm not mad. I'm not the one that's holding a grudge. Someone has an issue with ME. And I'm the one that has to INITIATE the reconciliation? I have to ask for forgiveness or make it right before I can communicate with God in faith for the miraculous???" According to God: YES, Exactly.

Unforgiveness keeps you in sin because you are not accurately representing God, nor are you following HIS commandments. The wages of sin are not life, blessings, and miracles – The wages of sin is death.

God said in Genesis 1:26 (paraphrasing), *"Let man have dominion over the earth..."* We are the managers and stewards over the earth realm. We have the same creative power and potential to create, shape, and form our personal world like God did when He created the Earth.

Think of it in terms of sowing seeds and reaping.... If I want financial blessings, I should sow financial seeds. If I want help, I should be helpful to others. If I want friends, the Bible teaches that I should show myself friendly. If I want to receive grace and mercy, I should sow seeds of grace and mercy. If I want reap forgiveness, I should sow seeds of forgiveness. The opposite is true as well.... If I sow seeds of unforgiveness, I'll reap unforgiveness.

This is important and gives insight into the way Jesus taught His disciples to pray....

Matthew 6:11-12

[11]*Give us this day our daily bread,*
[12]***and forgive us our debts,***
as we also have forgiven our debtors.

"Forgive us our debts, as we also have forgiven others" … Or more plainly: "God, forgive us the same way that we forgive the people that have wronged us." You dictate and determine the way that God forgives you. If you are slow with forgiving, God will be slow. If you are unforgiving, God is unforgiving to you. If you forgive freely and quickly, God will forgive freely and quickly. **Forgiveness is more about your freedom and access to God than it is about letting someone else off the hook.** I forgive mainly because I want to keep the lines of communication and miracles open with God.

Colossians 3:13

Bearing with one another and, if one has a complaint against another, forgiving each other; **as the Lord has forgiven you, so you also must forgive.**

Paul taught the Colossians to use God as the blueprint for forgiveness. "As the Lord has forgiven you, so you also must forgive" … Or more plainly: "The way that God forgives you; you must forgive in the same way." Paul did NOT leave it up for debate. He told them, "You **MUST** forgive in this manner." Why? … Let's examine a parable Jesus told His disciples….

Matthew 18:23-35 – **Parable of Unforgiving Servant**

[23]*"Therefore the kingdom of heaven may be compared to a king who wished to settle accounts with his servants.* [24]*When he began to settle,* **one was brought to him who owed him** **ten thousand talents**. [25]*And since he could not pay, his master ordered him to be sold, with his wife and*

children and all that he had, and payment to be made. ²⁶*So the servant fell on his knees, imploring him, 'Have patience with me, and I will pay you everything.'* ²⁷**And out of pity for him, the master of that servant released him and forgave him the debt.** ²⁸*But when that same servant went out, he found one of his fellow servants who owed him* **a hundred denarii**, *and seizing him, he began to choke him, saying, 'Pay what you owe.'* ²⁹*So his fellow servant fell down and pleaded with him, 'Have patience with me, and I will pay you.'* ³⁰**He refused and went and put him in prison until he should pay the debt.** ³¹*When his fellow servants saw what had taken place, they were greatly distressed, and they went and reported to their master all that had taken place.* ³²*Then his master summoned him and said to him,* **'You wicked servant! I forgave you all that debt because you pleaded with me.** ³³**And should not you have had mercy on your fellow servant, as I had mercy on you?'** ³⁴**And in anger his master delivered him to the jailers, until he should pay all his debt.** ³⁵*So also my heavenly Father will do to every one of you, if you do not forgive your brother from your heart."*

Jesus taught His disciples an interesting parable. A king forgives one of his servants a great debt. (This translation values it as ten thousand talents – this equated to about 20 years of wages for an average laborer.) After having his great debt cancelled, the same servant runs into one of his fellow servants who owes him a hundred denarii (about a day's wage for an average laborer). The servant who was forgiven the great debt was **unwilling to forgive** his fellow servant. When the king heard what happened, he reversed his decision to forgive the debt and treated the servant like he treated his fellow servant.

The servant dictated how the master treated him. He was unforgiving to his fellow servant; therefore, the king was unforgiving to him. He put his fellow servant in prison until he repaid the debt; the king put him in prison until he repaid his debt. This parable clearly illuminates the power of forgiveness.

Locked Up

This brings back memories of one of the worst losing streaks in my coaching career: we lost the last 7 or 8 games of a season in basketball. It was even more disappointing because we had a pretty good team that year. I couldn't figure out what had gone wrong or what I could have done to be a better coach.

Months later my wife came to me and apologized. She said, "Man, I'm sorry."

I was scared because my wife never apologizes. I was confused because my wife (at least in her mind) was never wrong. I was puzzled: "Why are you apologizing to me? You haven't done anything wrong to me?"

I'll never forget these words: "I'm sorry because I had you locked up..." She explained to me. After the first game of our losing streak, she had come up to be supportive, and (she said) I "snapped" at her. (I don't even remember doing it or exactly what was said.) She took offense and internalized what happened.

I went on with life not thinking that there was an issue; however, I went on to lose game after game, after game, after game. I didn't even know that she was upset. If so, I would have readily apologized.

But because she was offended and holding unforgiveness in her heart, God was unable to prosper our union in marriage, our prayers, our desires, etc. Not only was I not prospering, but she wasn't either. God was unable to work on either of our behalfs until we reconciled and handled the issue.

This is how dangerous and hazardous unforgiveness can be. Not only will it affect you, but it can have a negative impact on others.

Forgiveness is a Process

I'm not going to sit here and say that forgiveness is easy. If you're not mature, forgiveness can take days, weeks, months, and even years depending on the severity of the wound. Some children have grown-up and now have families of their own; and yet, they have never forgiven their parents (father / mother) for the wound of abandonment inflicted upon them when they were children. Some women have remarried, but they have never forgiven their first husband for the cheating that led to the divorce. Some people have been fired, but they have never forgiven their former employer for the wrongful termination.

Forgiveness doesn't come easy for most people. I think in part because we have quite a few misperceptions about forgiveness. Forgiveness has been reduced to one person saying he/she is sorry, and the other person accepting the apology. But forgiveness is a much more intricate process. Oftentimes, the apology and the acceptance thereof are just the first steps in the healing process.

Let me share a story with you....

She Hurt Me

I can remember when I felt that a close friend betrayed me.... I was hurt. I cried. It cut me deep to my core. I knew what the Word of God said about forgiveness; however, I wasn't willing to forgive her. I wanted her to hurt just like she hurt me. I wanted to hurt her by withholding my friendship...not returning her phone calls...trying to convince mutual friends of this person's lack of integrity and poor friendship etiquette by recollecting the hurtful events. I didn't want to be around this person. I didn't want to see her face. I didn't want to hear her voice. I wanted to fight her, hurt her, make her feel my emotional pain.

After a few weeks of distance, we spoke over the phone. She was apologetic, and I was still hurt. I said the obligatory, "I forgive you" to accept her apology; however, I still didn't want to see or hang around her.

Time went on, and I didn't see her for quite a few months. I didn't remember or think about the incident very much. I didn't get sad when reminiscing. It didn't hurt to breathe like it used to. It didn't hurt in my chest at the thought of her. "Time heals all wounds," I told myself, "I'm actually okay."

I went to the store one day and just happened to run into her. I got mad all over again – I was NOT okay. Those feelings ... That hurt ... That hatred ... That unforgiveness flooded my mind. I thought I was over it. I thought I was fine. I thought I was better. I WAS NOT!!

I gradually put more effort into forgiving – Learning about God's teachings on forgiveness was the key for me. As months passed, we talked and I would see her every now and then. I still had no desire to be as close as we once were, but I could function in her presence without wanting to leave the room. With time, more honest conversations, and a whole lot of God, the relationship became close to what it once was.

For a period of time, however, I had to make a conscious decision to forgive daily, or sometimes moment by moment. I never forgot how she hurt me, but that hurt doesn't control me – that hurt doesn't dictate how I respond or show God's Love.

I know this example doesn't fit everyone's experience of forgiveness, but it illustrates some key points I wanted to make. The main point being that **forgiveness is a process**. It may start where you need time and space to process your feelings - You may not be able to stand to hear that person's name! It's okay; You were hurt, you were damaged, you were wounded. Pain (no matter if it's emotional, physical, spiritual) can be debilitating. However, the issue comes when we set up camp and begin to live in the hurt – Yes, you had a reason to be upset! Yes, you have a reason to be angry! Yes, you're entitled to all the feelings that you feel! However, you can't **live** in the pain of unforgiveness and expect to experience the miracles of God.

Gradually, you may progress to the next stage and be able to have some interaction or communication: Text message, talk on the phone, message in a bottle, pigeon carrier, whatever...This is progress. For some, because the pain was hurtful, the betrayal cut so deep, or the disappointment was so paralyzing, this minute level of communication is all we have to give at this time. However, this progress can turn into stagnation; and a place that was once progress can become your grave. This is only a point of transition. Unfortunately, you can't live at any one stage of improvement; God wants you to continue to progress to the fulfillment of complete forgiveness so that you can experience the limitless benefits God has planned for your life.

Over time with sound teaching, counsel, and meditation, you may be able to progress to personal contact without wanting to kill them – and even evolve to personal communication and contact. Who knows, you may reach the stage of complete forgiveness and reconciliation.

I want to state this point: YOU MAY BE IN THE PROCESS OF FORGIVENESS. Even when you accepted the apology, but you didn't want to see their face - You're in the process. You may not have reached the standard God has set, which is complete forgiveness and perhaps reconciliation, but you're better than you were. Likewise, when you're able to be in the same room with that person; It's not the end of forgiveness, but you're improving. That's not the end, but you're headed in the right direction.

I personally believe that God takes note of where we are in our spiritual journey. I believe He applauds the improvement, while encouraging us to complete the process of forgiveness. As I've noted, how long the process lasts varies - for some people this may take months while for others it may take years. **The length of time in the process of forgiveness is totally up to the individual.**

As I've mentioned, the issue most people have is that they accept the apology and think they have forgiven. No effort is ever made to reconcile. They can't be in the same room as their father. They can't look their friend in the eye. Or they can be in the same room, but it is so awkward and cold. They can't have a conversation with their sister at the family reunion. They can't play a game of cards with their friend. Many stop at a certain level of improvement, but God's standard is complete forgiveness and reconciliation. Stopping before God's standard is a sign of an immature believer.

However, a believer who is mature in the area of forgiveness can forgive instantly. Jesus was dying on the cross and made this statement about those that were actively mocking and KILLING Him:

Luke 23:34

*And Jesus said, "**Father, forgive them**, for they know not what they do."*

As Stephen was being stoned and dying, we see this account:

Acts 7:60

*And falling to his knees he cried out with a loud voice, "**Lord, do not hold this sin against them.**" And when he had said this, he fell asleep.*

In a parable about the Prodigal Son, Jesus gave insight about how to forgive. When the Son returns, let's examine how the father treats his son…

Luke 15:20-24

²⁰And he arose and came to his father. ***But while he was still a long way off, his father saw him and felt compassion, and ran and embraced him and kissed him.*** *²¹And the son said to him, 'Father, I have sinned against heaven and before you. I am no longer worthy to be called your son.'* *²²But the father said to his servants,* ***'Bring quickly the best robe, and put it on him, and put a ring on his hand, and shoes on his feet.*** *²³And bring the fattened calf and kill it, and let us eat and celebrate.* *²⁴For this my son was dead, and is alive again; he was lost, and is found.'* <u>And they began to celebrate.</u>

This is the point of maturity God desires us to reach: Instant Forgiveness. Forgiveness BEFORE the person even asks for forgiveness. Forgiveness BEFORE they even acknowledge that they wronged you. This is the level God wants us to get to. It's not easy. This doesn't come overnight, but this is the example set by our Father.

Forgiveness/Forgetting

Have you ever burned yourself? Or gotten a deep scrape or cut as a child? Though the body healed, a scar may have developed. Years may have passed. You can't remember the last time you felt the pain or agony from the trauma. You had no more bleeding or lingering complications from the wound. However, when you look at the scar, you may remember exactly what happened as if it were yesterday. When you look at the burn marks, you can recollect the temperature of the fire. It all comes rushing back to the forefront of your mind.

Forgiveness doesn't mean that you must forget what happened. You may never get the offense or the act of being wronged out of your memory. You may always remember how you felt, how it hurt, how it affected you. That may never go away from your remembrance.

However, mature forgiveness is where you're not debilitated by what happened. Advanced, God-like forgiveness is where you're not constantly bringing up the offense to justify your bad attitude and rude behavior. Your ability to be who God called you to be and to do what God called you to do aren't encumbered by what happened. You can demonstrate the genuine Love of God in spite of what happened. That, my friend, is true forgiveness.

What If God....

When I get beside myself and want to hold people accountable in my "self-righteous prison of unforgiveness," I remember how God forgave me over, and over, and over, and over, and over, and over, and over, and over, and over again. I remember how God sacrificed His Son and that Jesus died for me so that I could be forgiven. When I think about how far God went to forgive me, what it cost Him to forgive me, and how readily He forgives me...I have no right to be unforgiving to others.

What if God had the same attitude as some of us? What if God didn't forgive us for our sins? What if God was "so hurt" that we turned our backs on Him that He just couldn't talk to us anymore? What if God was "so disappointed" that He couldn't look at us anymore ... couldn't love us anymore? What if God was "cut so deeply" that He just couldn't forgive us?

Paul teaches in Romans 12:17-19

*17Repay no one evil for evil, but give thought to do what is honorable in the sight of all. 18**If possible, so far as it depends on you, live peaceably with all.** 19 Beloved, never avenge yourselves, but leave it to the wrath of God, for it is written, "Vengeance is mine, I will repay, says the Lord."*

You can't force anyone to forgive you, accept your apology, desire to reconcile with you, etc. But God requires you to do your part: "If possible, so far as it depends on you..." – this means that we are to do our part in keeping God's teachings even if they aren't receptive. If they come back later (years, even decades later) and desire reconciliation, we shouldn't say, "Oh NO, you missed your chance. You should have reconciled when I tried to the first time." No...we should be forgiving and willing to reconcile even then.

I know unforgiveness can be a hard topic to tackle. There are so many different reasons not to forgive. I've heard it all - "What about this?" and "You don't know what they did." There are so many difficult details. There are so many intricate dynamics that I and other people "just don't understand." You're right.... I feel you.... He hurt you.... She did you wrong.... They left you.... It is not easy. Some issues hurt so deep that some people may need counseling to help them mature to forgiveness.

Even with all that... God is STILL telling you to forgive – NOT for their sake, Not for God's sake, but for YOUR OWN sake. Forgiveness benefits YOU. Forgiveness is in YOUR best interest. Forgiveness unlocks God to work the miraculous in YOUR life.

I implore you to forgive. If you want to receive the miraculous from God, let go of the pain. God says that He wants to give you "beauty for your ashes, the oil of joy for mourning, the garment of praise for the spirit of heaviness." He'll even trade you the miraculous...if you'll let go and forgive those who have hurt, wronged, abused, misled, mistreated, injured, damaged, and manipulated you.

Forgive Yourself

Last but certainly not least, you have to forgive yourself. We make mistakes and fall flat on our faces sometimes. Sometimes, it wasn't a mistake – we knowingly, intentionally, deliberately, willfully, and consciously did some things. We have hurt people on purpose. We have lied, cheated, manipulated, murdered/killed, slandered, abused other people and even ourselves. We've done things that we're ashamed to even admit to ourselves.

Most of us can ask God forgiveness. "No problem," we think to ourselves. "He's God; surely He'll forgive me." Some of us may even be able to muster up the courage to ask for forgiveness from those that we've wronged. For some, that is a huge step to take.

However, when it comes to forgiving self, we don't give ourselves one iota of grace. I mean, like I stated before… it's hard to be around the person or people that have wronged you, especially if they were close. Well, who is closer to you THAN YOU? When you do things that damage you, how can you take a break from yourself? When you realize the suffering you've caused someone else, how do you get some space from "such a monster"? There are times when this can be the last element of forgiveness, but it can also be the most difficult.

Not forgiving ourselves makes receiving forgiveness impossible. For instance: I ask God for forgiveness; however, if I haven't forgiven myself, I don't see myself as "worthy" of being forgiven and I don't receive His love and forgiveness. Even though I may ask my friend for forgiveness… if I haven't forgiven myself, I don't see myself as being good enough to be forgiven.

Forgiveness unlocks love, communication, and relationships. Let's not only forgive others, but also forgive ourselves so that we can embrace the life that God has designed for us to live.

Let's Be Honest - Self Evaluation:

1. Are you holding a grudge or unforgiving to someone that hurt or disappointed you? What did they do? How did it make you feel? Did they even apologize? Would an apology have even mattered?

2. The way you forgive dictates the way God forgives you. How do you forgive others? Quickly? Begrudgingly? After making them beg? After lashing out at them? Etc.

3. Have you begun the forgiveness process, but realized that you've stopped in the process? What level / stage of forgiveness are you currently at?

4. Have you hurt / disappointed / offended someone and desired forgiveness? Was it difficult to take responsibility or your wrong / fault? Were you wrong or did you apologize for the sake of the relationship?

5. Have there been points in your life that you've not forgiven yourself? What did you do that was so disappointing? Did you forgive yourself? How did you do it?

CHAPTER 9: THERE'S NO SUCH THING...

"It is possible to be different and still be all right. There can be two-or more-answers to the same question, and all can be right" - Ann Wilson Schaef

Throughout this entire book, I've been stressing the principles of teaching and their relationship to miracles. There is so much about God and the miraculous that we don't know and even more that we fail to understand. It is often this ignorance that leads to our disappointment. However, teaching and gaining an understanding can alleviate these frustrations.

Allow me to impart this critical truth. God is All-knowing and has infinite Knowledge and Wisdom – suffice to say, **there are some things that we are NOT going to know or understand**. It's not because God is trying to keep something from us, but rather because we don't have the capacity to understand.

A car can only hold so much gasoline in its tank. A battery can only contain so much power. A cloud can only hold so much water. There is a limit to the capacity; not because there is no more gasoline, power, water…but because these containers can't accommodate anymore past a certain point.

God gives us as much of Himself as we desire and are able to handle. You may desire more of God, but you may not be able to handle the more. Therefore, you're limited. In Exodus, Moses desired to see God's face; but

God told Him that he wasn't able to handle it: "No one can see my face and live."

The inverse is true as well: You may be able to handle more, but you lack the desire; once again, you're limited. Take the Israelites for an example: When God came to speak to the Israelites directly, they trembled and were fearful. God wanted to give them a more direct relationship; however, they would rather have Moses speak to them than God. They couldn't handle God speaking to them directly.

How much of God do you want? How much of God's teachings do you desire? How much of God can you handle?

The answer to being limited by capacity is not to force more into the container. No!!... The answer is to increase the size of the container. Increase your capacity to receive more from God. God has been limited throughout history because of our capacity. Let's look at Abraham as an example of limited capacity. Abraham only wanted a son, but God wanted an entire Nation and eventually all Nations. To try to get him to expand his capacity to believe and receive more, God had Abraham look at the stars in the sky and the sands of the earth. He had Abtaham focus on things that he couldn't put a number or restriction on. Similarly, this is what I believe God is screaming to us today - "DON'T PUT A LIMIT ON WHAT I CAN DO IN YOUR LIFE!!"

Teaching Provides the Key to Your Miracles

Peter was told by Jesus that He would give him the keys to the Kingdom. These keys are principles, concepts, teachings about the Kingdom. It is useless to be in a building but have no keys to open any doors. It is just as useless to have keys and not know which key goes to the corresponding door. You're just going to be trying random keys until one works.

This is essentially what many of us have been doing in our spiritual journey. We've been trying random concepts, random teachings, random "keys" trying to open the miraculous. Teaching not only provides the key, but it should instruct you on HOW, WHEN, AND WHERE to use the key effectively.

Many people know scriptures. There are many that can quote the book, chapter, and verse, word for word; however, they don't know how to implement and utilize the scripture ("key") in their daily lives. So... they know Psalm 23, "The Lord is my shepherd, I shall not want," yet they live a life of worry and anxiety. They can quote Genesis 1:26, but they're waiting to die and go to Heaven, living a life on Earth below God's intention. They have read where Jesus says, "And greater works than these shall you do," but they don't believe that this applies to them...Now!

The Miracle of Flight

Flying had often fascinated man. Many people were involved with contributing to the discovery of flying. Some even risked their lives attempting to verify theories and obtain data on the subject. Some people glided a few feet; others jumped off cliffs and broke bones in the pursuit of figuring out the conundrum of flight for mankind.

When most people think of flying, the Wright brothers are often given credit. In the early 1900s, they were the first to develop an engine powered, human-piloted airplane. However, they are not known as the fathers of Aviation – that honor goes to George Cayley. In the early 1800s, it was Cayley who unveiled the forces that would be key to flying (drag, flying weight, lift, thrust). He developed one of the first successful human gliders and correctly predicted that when a more powerful engine was invented, human flight would be possible.

At one point in our history, flying was considered impossible and miraculous...a miracle of epic proportions. However, because engineers and mechanics now understand the concept of flying, we can fly whenever we desire. It doesn't seem so miraculous anymore because it's so common. An entire industry has been formed because man understands the teaching and concept of flying.

The same is true of a lot of things concerning technology and science. Certain diseases have been eradicated – through teachings and revelation, we now know the cause and have a cure for leprosy. Curing leprosy is so common that it's not even considered a miracle to us; however, to individuals in the days of Jesus and prior, people probably couldn't even have fathomed such a thing. The same could be said of the television, cell phone, MRI machine, etc. There was a time that humans could not have even imagined in their wildest dreams being able to see the person they're talking to on the telephone. There was a time people only dreamed of being able to see inside a person's body (their bones, muscles, blood vessels, etc.). People thought it was impossible for people in different parts of the world to be able to experience the same events at the same time. However, through understanding concepts, laws of physics and mechanics, teachings and knowledge of various technology - these once impossible feats, occur at the touch of our fingers and sound of our voices. These are indeed modern-day miracles.

Just like these amazing feats, I believe teaching can open the door to the things that we think are impossible or miraculous today. God used many methods to heal or perform the miraculous. I truly believe that He even uses science and medicine, as well. Our faith is not in the medicine nor is it in the doctor - but rather, our faith is in God, Who has revealed intricate knowledge and revelation concerning man's physical health.

Do you know that they have a medication regimen that can prevent the transmission of AIDS? Do you know that they are on the cusp of curing AIDS? I can remember in the 1980s and 1990s that the diagnosis of HIV/AIDS was a death sentence. Many thought it would be a miracle to live a long and productive life with this disease. However, it's not viewed the same today. God has allowed man to understand the disease process more and develop a cure for healing.

We shouldn't put a limit on God. Healing may come through science and technology... or it may come by simply speaking the words "Be healed" ... or it may come from washing in a stream ... or it may come in some manner that we have yet to even imagine. However, healing (or any other miracle) may manifest, I believe that hearing and understanding teachings from God are intricate in the process.

The more we understand God's teachings, the more we can relegate the miraculous to common and expected events. The more we know and understand about God, the more He is revealed and manifested. Jesus was so intimate with God that He was the embodiment of the Word of God (teaching) – look at the miracles that Jesus performed. Jesus had 12 disciples that walked with and learned from Him – look at the miracles they performed. The miracles were so common that people were no longer amazed. It didn't seem strange for people to be healed, for blind eyes to see, for lame legs to walk. It became expected. **Miracles became normal.**

No Such Things as Miracles

God desires us to see EVERYTHING from His Heavenly perspective. This includes the miraculous; He wants us to see the miraculous like He sees it. He wants miracles to be so common that we don't even look at them as miracles anymore: Healing is normal to God; Wealth is common to Him; Needs being met is the usual; the atmosphere responding to His words is ordinary. It's the way things are supposed to be.

As a matter of fact, **there are no such things as miracles from God's perspective.** To God, what we call miracles... He calls just another day of the week. What we are in awe of, God calls Monday. He's not impressed or caught off guard. I know that may be a shocker for some of you. Heck… it definitely shocked me when I first began to understand it.

Let's take a look at some of the responses of Jesus…

Matthew 8:26

*And he said to them, "**Why are you afraid**, O you of little faith?" Then he rose and rebuked the winds and the sea, and there was a great calm.*

Matthew 9:23-24, 30-31

*[23]And when Jesus came to the ruler's house and saw the flute players and the crowd making a commotion, [24]he said, "**Go away, for the girl is not dead but sleeping.**" And they laughed at him.*

*[30]But when he saw the wind, he was afraid, and beginning to sink he cried out, "Lord, save me." [31]Jesus immediately reached out his hand and took hold of him, saying to him, "O you of little faith, **why did you doubt?**"*

Matthew 21:19-22

*[19]And seeing a fig tree by the wayside, he went to it and found nothing on it but only leaves. And he said to it, "May no fruit ever come from you again!" And the fig tree withered at once. [20]<u>When the disciples saw it, they marveled</u>, saying, "How did the fig tree wither at once?" [21]And Jesus answered them, "**Truly, I say to you, if you have faith and do not doubt, you will not only do what has been done to the fig tree, but even if you say to this mountain, 'Be taken up and thrown into the sea,' it will***

happen. *²²And whatever you ask in prayer, you will receive, if you have faith."*

Luke 9:41-43

⁴¹Jesus answered, **"O faithless and twisted generation, how long am I to be with you and bear with you? Bring your son here."** *⁴²While he was coming, the demon threw him to the ground and convulsed him.* **But Jesus rebuked the unclean spirit and healed the boy, and gave him back to his father.** *⁴³And all were* <u>**astonished**</u> *at the majesty of God.*

Luke 17:12-17

¹²And as he entered a village, he was met by ten lepers, who stood at a distance ¹³and lifted up their voices, saying, "Jesus, Master, have mercy on us." ¹⁴When he saw them he said to them, "Go and show yourselves to the priests." And as they went they were cleansed. ¹⁵Then one of them, when he saw that he was healed, turned back, praising God with a loud voice; ¹⁶and he fell on his face at Jesus' feet, giving him thanks. Now he was a Samaritan. ¹⁷Then Jesus answered, **"Were not ten cleansed? Where are the nine? ¹⁸Was no one found to return and give praise to God except this foreigner?"**

Eventually the Apostles, who were once always amazed as disciples, began to think, act, and become just like Jesus...

Acts 3:12-13

¹²And when Peter saw it he addressed the people: "Men of Israel, **why do you wonder at this, or why do you stare at** *us, as though by our own power or piety we have made him walk?* *¹³The God of Abraham, the God of Isaac, and the God of Jacob, the God of our fathers, glorified his servant Jesus, whom you delivered over and denied in the presence of Pilate, when he had decided to release him.*

Acts 5:12
Now many signs and wonders were <u>regularly</u> done among the people *by the hands of the apostles.*

In these examples and many more in scripture, you never see Jesus caught off guard when faced with someone in need. He never panicked, or stuttered, or attempted to evade people because He was afraid that God wouldn't heal, save, remove demonic forces, or provide answers to hard questions. **He expected results.** He had faith in God that the needs of the people would be met. The events everyone viewed as miraculous were SUPPOSED to occur. Jesus didn't view these things as out of the ordinary. Jesus would marvel at things that were unnatural to Him – like unbelief or great faith demonstrated by non-Jews. The Apostles were taught to adopt this same mentality. The miracles were natural, common, and expected.

Yes, you read that correctly…. No need to check your eyes or write to me asking if I meant to write something else. From God's viewpoint / perspective, there are no such things as miracles.

The Color of the Sky

Two things can be true at the same time. If asked, "What color is the sky?" … How would you answer? On a clear day, most people would say, "The sky is blue." And this is true...from their **visual perspective**, the color they see when they look in the sky is blue. However, there are some people that would be hesitant to answer, or they would say, "The sky is clear" based on their **knowledge perspective**. Some people know that the blue coloration of the sky is due to the gases/particles in the earth's atmosphere that scatter sunlight. Blue light is scattered more (or better) than the other colors; thus, the blue coloration we see in the sky most of the time. The point I'm trying to make is this: whether someone says, "The sky is blue" or "The sky is clear", both answers would be correct depending on the person's perspective.

If you're viewing things from a human perspective, the things that God does are miraculous. However, when seen from God's viewpoint, this is just the way things are supposed to be. This is normal...It's not extraordinary...It doesn't surprise God...It doesn't impress Him...It doesn't amaze Him...He's not shocked or wow-ed.

God's goal is for us to grow and mature. In order for us to mature into the Son/Daughter, the king/queen, the ambassador and His Representative on the earth that God desires us to become, we have to be taught... or better yet, we have to be retrained how to think, act, speak, walk, communicate, etc.

By living a life of following God's teachings, we enter a realm where the supernatural and miraculous become as common as turning on the television or flying on an airplane. Living life according to God's financial principles and teachings will place you in a position to experience wealth. Applying the Heavenly principles of marriage will produce a marriage that most people would think is miraculous or impossible or that "is too good to be true." Utilizing God's teachings on health will diminish so many diseases and self-inflicted health issues. The teachings of God (in every facet of your life) will inevitably lead to a life where the miraculous is common.

"Be Fruitful and Multiply"

In Genesis, God commanded Adam to be fruitful AND MULTIPLY. We focus so much on becoming "fruitful" that I think we forget the "multiplication" – Not just multiply in terms of children, but multiply in terms of teaching someone else how to become fruitful – passing down the knowledge, information, teaching, revelation, experiences, etc. that will position those that come after you to continue God's vision, purpose, fruitfulness in the earth long after you're gone.

The goal is to get teaching and understanding to the point where the miraculous and extraordinary become reproducible. I would love to win the lottery; most would consider this miraculous. But let's compare this method of obtaining wealth versus following sound financial principles and teaching. Let's say that a person scratches lottery tickets for 15-20 years and finally hits the multimillion-dollar winnings. In comparison to another person who utilizes sound financial principles of God for 15-20 years and obtains a multimillion-dollar portfolio. Both have the same amount of money, but who is in the better position moving forward?

Studies have shown that most lottery winners are broke or in worse financial conditions than when they initially won the lottery. Most lottery winners aren't equipped with the knowledge and teachings to handle money on that level; therefore, they squander what many would have thought to have been a miraculous blessing. Also, there is little (if any) multiplication. The odds of someone winning the multimillion-dollar lottery twice in a lifetime are minuscule...if not impossible. If you asked a lottery winner to teach you how to become wealthy - the best teaching he or she could give you from their experience is to scratch lottery tickets or some personal rendition of picking random numbers.

However, people who obtain wealth using sound financial principles, are likely to only increase their wealth and pass it on to the succeeding generations. People like Dave Ramsey and others have produced thousands of millionaires by teaching sound wealth principles. Which financial method would you prefer to implement and entrust your life to? Luck of the draw OR Application of teachings?

Teaching is intricate in the performance of miracles. We see Jesus when He was born; we see Him at 12-years-old in the temple; then we don't see Him anymore until the age of 30 when He starts His ministry. Although this isn't expressly stated in scriptures, I truly believe that during this 18-year period, Jesus was undergoing teaching, studying, training, unlocking mysteries, revelations, developing faith and a relationship with the Father. Therefore, when we see Him on the scene again, He is operating in a level of Power and Wisdom that the world had never seen.

Jesus was able to perform miracles on command; it was not unusual. He was fruitful in the miraculous, and He multiplied Himself: He also taught His disciples how to operate in the miraculous as well. They became disciples (students) whose primary objective was learning the teachings and Words of God. And then they used the teachings to perform miracles.

Teaching was an important, foundational component in their spiritual development.

Teachings vs Teachings

I've heard Myles Munroe say countless times, "The only thing more powerful than an idea is another idea" and "You can't kill an idea with a bullet." Since teachings are the expression of ideas, they have similar properties. The only thing more powerful than teaching...is another teaching. You can kill the teacher, but you can't kill teaching. They killed Hitler; unfortunately, his teachings in the Mein Kempf are still impacting people today. They killed Bin Laden; however, his teachings of terrorism still are a plague to society. They also killed Martin Luther King, Jr., Malcom X, JFK, even Jesus Christ — and their teachings also impact the world today.

Therefore, when God wanted to impact the world, He didn't send His army –He sent His Word (His Teachings, His Ideas). In order to overtake the ideas and teachings of the World, a counter idea and teaching was introduced. Force won't eradicate erroneous doctrine and ignorance; however, God's teachings of Truth will.

The Teachings of God and God's Law are synonymous. However, in the World's systems, there are certain laws that can override other laws. For instance, in the political system, Congress can vote to pass a law; however, the President can veto that law – **the law of veto overrides the law for which Congress voted in favor**. Now, there is another law known as the "**majority of Congress**" that can override the veto. Do you see how this works?

Once you understand the laws and how they function, you can implement them to your benefit. There are some teachings that can override other teachings and reality. God's teachings and laws on health override laws of sickness and disease. God's teachings and laws on self-concept and self-worth override the teachings of the world that lead to depression and dependence on the approval of others. God's teachings and laws on relationships with our fellow man override the teachings of the world to take advantage of those less fortunate.

This isn't to say that problems won't arise in these areas. Following and understanding the teachings of God does NOT exempt us from or negate Life. Tests and trials will come. Circumstances and situations will arise. Storms will occur. Crisis may even happen. However, due to the teachings and faith that develops, you can stand up to Pharaoh like Moses…you can speak to the Storm like Jesus…you can speak to diseases like the Apostles…you can build when the world says otherwise, like Noah…you can defeat giants, like David…you can even raise an opportunity or situation that everyone thinks is dead like Jesus did.

Awareness vs Experience

There are certain things that God wants us to know and other things that He doesn't want us to know. I believe that God wants us to be knowledgeable; however, there are certain things that we have to be able to handle before knowledge is introduced. You want your children to understand sex (its purpose, God's intentions for sex, consequences, benefits, etc.). However, you don't want them to know these things at 5-years-old – they can't handle the responsibility that comes with the knowledge. There are other more important aspects of life they need to obtain before understanding sex.

There are also instances where God wants us to be knowledgeable and aware, but not experience certain things. For instance, you want your children to be knowledgeable and aware of illicit drugs (cocaine, heroin, marijuana), but there is never a point at which you want them to experience the dangerous influence these drugs can have. You want your children to be knowledgeable and aware that people kidnap kids, or about child molestation; but, you never want them to experience such atrocities. You want your children aware of such things to equip them to be in a position to prevent drug abuse or child abuse from happening and/or becoming a victim thereof.

In the Garden of Eden, God commanded Adam NOT to eat of the fruit of the Tree of the Knowledge of Good and Evil. GOD told them about the tree – they were aware and knowledgeable of the tree, but they were not meant to have the experience of eating its fruit. They were not to experience, get nutrition from, operate according to this teaching. It was the tree of **_KNOWLEDGE_** of good and evil. When they ate the fruit thereof, they experienced (their eyes were opened to) something that God didn't want them to experience. The Knowledge of Good and Evil was off-limits for their benefit. Adam and Eve were in the "god-class." They had ACCESS to EVERYTHING. They were just like God - created in His Image and Likeness. God wanted to keep them (and all mankind) to stay that way.

God never wanted you to experience being ashamed. He didn't want you to experience nakedness; He wanted you to be open with Him. He didn't intend for you to experience poverty or lack. He didn't want you to actually be able to explain what hunger felt like. He never wanted you to experience depression or sickness. He didn't intend for you to have knowledge about the concept of divorce. He didn't want you to experience death. He didn't want you to know what life was like without Him. He didn't want you to feel, encounter, endure, face, or have to bear certain things.

In order for God to keep us from these negative experiences, He had to provide. God never wanted us to experience hunger – so He provided Adam with food. He never wanted Adam to experience lack – therefore He had to provide Him with resources. He never wanted Adam to know sickness – so He had to provide Him with a body resistant to death, decay, and destruction. He wanted Adam to not know what failure felt like – therefore God provided Adam with a purpose, plan, and design for success. Adam was so in tune with God spiritually, that he wasn't concerned with physical nakedness; God was their covering – therefore, they never attempted to cover themselves or hide anything about themselves from God.

Unfortunately, due to the actions of Adam, we have experiences that we weren't intended to possess. And we ask questions about things that God never intended us to have experiential knowledge of. We are fearful about somethings that God never wanted to be a part of our reality. We make decisions and act on things that God never desired us to be involved with.

I truly believe God wants us to get back to this "pre-disobedience, Garden of Eden mindset"; this is where the miraculous was normal. If God doesn't want me to experience the effects of sickness, He has to provide Healing and teachings on how to take care of my body – it should be expected. If God does not want me to succumb to poverty, He has to provide His resources or ideas and principles to obtain wealth – it should be normal. If God doesn't want me to experience divorce, He has to provide me with understanding and teaching on how to live with my spouse. If God doesn't want me to suffer from depression, He has to provide me with a sound mind and teachings on good mental health.

If all I know is good health, I expect it – that's the way things should be. If all I know is joy, I expect it –- sadness, worry, anxiety are abnormal. If all I know is that my words have creative power, I expect what I say to manifest – I don't have any reason or capacity for fear or doubt. Let's continue to follow God's teachings and adopt the mindset of God — Miracles should be normal!

Let's Be Honest – Self Evaluation:

1. Do you feel as if your capacity to receive from God has been limited?

2. Have you viewed the actions of God as miraculous instead of normal? What would it take to make you view God's actions as the norm?

3. What ideas have shaped and curated your life: negatively and positively? What ideas could you integrate into your life that would off-set the negative ideas?

4. Have you experienced something God only wanted you to be aware of? Now that you have such experience how has this affected your life and perspective of God?

CHAPTER 10: THE HEART

"Everyone who remembers his own education remembers teachers, not methods and techniques. The Teacher is the heart of the educational system."
- Sidney Hook

Teachings and the miraculous are intertwined. Of course, there are ancillary aspects that are connected to teachings that are important as well: Faith in God (thus faith in His teachings), Obedience/application of the teachings, etc. However, these components have to be in the right place.

For example, batteries are vital to a remote control working properly. I can have the batteries, but if they're not in the right place, then it's just as if I have no batteries. I can place the batteries near the remote – it will not work. I can place the batteries on top of the remote – I will not be able to change the channel or adjust the volume. It is only when I place the batteries inside of the remote control properly that the remote control will function as intended.

In this scenario, we are the remote control; the batteries are teaching, faith, values, conviction; and the various functions of the remote (adjusting the volume, changing the channels, DVR, powering the device, etc.) are the various miracles in our lives. Teaching empowers us to manifest the miracles as God intended. Some of us may have gotten great teaching, but it's not in the right place.

Let's dissect this concept a little further....

The Aspects of Man

We understand that the human being is a three component being: Man is a SPIRIT being, placed in a PHYSICAL body, possessing a SOUL. (See Corresponding Charts at the end of this chapter) Man's Spirit connects to the Holy Spirit (the Governor), which is our connection to God the Father (King). Whereas, Man's Physical Body connects to the earth/physical realm – we have 5 senses that allow us to interact with any physical entity in the earth and with other human beings: sight, hearing, touch, taste, smell. Man's Soul is an intricate component – It is the residence of our mind, will, emotions, intent, intellect, and imagination.

I've studied this and have seen this diagrammed many different ways. However, I think an important entity has been hidden or neglected. That entity is the Heart.

What is the Heart?

I want to be clear because "the heart" has become cliché church rhetoric. When we fall in love, we say that "I gave them my heart." When the relationship ends in devastation, we say "they broke my heart." When being judged for our actions we say, "God knows my heart." However, I've never seen anyone articulate the location of the heart and what the heart actually is. This is important because the bible talks about the heart All. The.Time. But we have overlooked its importance and seemingly talk around it. When mentioned in scripture, the Heart is often not referring to the organ in your chest that regulates blood flow. There are similarities, but the scriptures aren't referring to your physical, beating heart.

The Heart is not your Spirit. The Heart is not the Holy Spirit. The Heart is not your conscious Mind. The Heart is not something that you can give to the person you love. The Heart is not your Soul; however, your Heart is a component of your soul. I know what you're thinking… "How come it's not listed like the will, emotions, intellect and all the others?" That is because the heart is a deeper subcomponent of the soul.

Ephesians 4:17-24

*17Now this I say and testify in the Lord, that you must no longer walk as the Gentiles do, in the futility of their minds. 18They are **darkened in their understanding**, alienated from the life of God **because of the ignorance that is in them, due to their hardness of heart.** 19They have become callous and have given themselves up to sensuality, greedy to practice every kind of impurity. 20But that is not the way you learned Christ!— 21assuming that you have **heard** about him and were **taught** in him, as the truth is in Jesus, 22to put off your old self, which belongs to your former manner of life and is corrupt through deceitful desires, 23and **to be renewed in the spirit of your minds**, 24and to put on the new self, created after the likeness of God in true righteousness and holiness.*

We see Paul writing to the church at Ephesus about the contrast between the Believer and the Gentiles. He tells them that the Gentiles are in the position that they are in because of the "hardness of their hearts." And he encourages a renewal in the "spirit of the mind." This "spirit of the mind" is what we know as the Heart…Yes, your mind has a spirit.

What we deem as "the Mind" is more accurately described as the conscious mind…that which we are aware of, our thoughts that we can actively control. Our conscious mind connects our soul to our physical body. It influences and can be influenced by our environment via our five senses: sight, touch, taste, hearing, smell. Our mind can also be influenced as well as influenced by the other components in our soul (will, emotions, intentions, intellect, imagination).

The Heart is probably more accurately described as our "unconscious mind" or subconscious…that which we aren't always aware of, our thoughts that we don't actively control. It is often found that the unconscious mind drives our actions, emotions, even the way that we think. **Our Heart, the spirit of the mind, is like the thermostat of the mind.** It sets the temperature, the climate, the culture that is you. While the other components can have influence on the mind, the Heart can override them all.

For instance, you say that you love your parents. You know that it is right to honor them and respect them. However, you ignore your mother's calls. You bristle at any advice your father tries to give you. You roll your eyes when they check on you. There is a disconnect between what you know in your conscious mind to be right and what's really in your heart. It's what's in our hearts that dictates what actions ultimately manifest and has the ability to veto what you consciously want to do.

I've seen people that profess to be against racism and "not see color"; however, those same people will clutch their purse or get nervous when I get on the elevator or walk down the same street. I have seen men that say they love their wives, beat them within an inch of their lives. How could this happen? The answer lies deep within their hearts.

Guard Your Heart

For most of us, the Heart has been an issue our entire life, yet we were unaware of its dangerous potential. This is why we have difficulty with sexual immorality, drinking, smoking, lying, cheating, drugs, laziness, low self-value, fear, doubt, etc.

The Heart is the seat and the residence of our values, faith, convictions. It is where our beliefs take root. It is also where fear, doubt, worry, anxiety, hatred, etc. also can reside. It is who we really are. We often quote the scripture, "As a man thinketh, so is he..." However, the scripture in Proverbs 23:7 actually reads, *"For as he thinketh **in his heart**, so is he:"*

It's not just as he thinks…**It is "as he thinks in his heart."** You are what is in your heart. If lying is in your heart, you will lie when under pressure. If fear is in your heart, you will be fearful during the storm. If addiction to drugs is in your heart, you will succumb to the desire of the addiction. If hatred is in your heart, you will be hateful. However, if faith in the teachings of God are in your heart, you will experience the manifestations of God as His child and Ambassador.

Proverbs 4:23 (ESV)

Keep your heart with all vigilance,
for from it flow the springs of life.

Proverbs 4:23 (NIV)

Above all else, guard your heart,
for everything you do flows from it.

Proverbs teaches us to guard our heart, to maintain it, to be watchful, attentive, and protective of it. Why? **Because it gives life to everything.** If faith in God's teachings reside in the heart, it will give life to the miraculous. If the belief in the teachings of health reside in the heart, it will give life to healing. If trust in God's financial principles reside in the heart, it will give life to wealth. But I have to get these things beyond my conscious mind, beyond my emotions, beyond my intellect and my will…I have to get them into my Heart.

What's in the Heart?

Likewise, the same holds true for things that may be negative: i.e., fear, hatred, doubt, etc. Let's study what Jesus said on the topic…

Matthew 15:10-20

*[10]And he called the people to him and said to them, "**Hear and understand**: [11]it is not what goes into the mouth that defiles a person, but what comes out of the mouth; this defiles a person." [12]Then the disciples came and said to him, "Do you know that the Pharisees were offended when*

*they heard this saying?" ¹³He answered, "Every plant that my heavenly Father has not planted will be rooted up. ¹⁴Let them alone; they are blind guides. And if the blind lead the blind, both will fall into a pit." ¹⁵But Peter said to him, "Explain the parable to us." ¹⁶And he said, "**Are you also still without understanding?** ¹⁷Do you not see that whatever goes into the mouth passes into the stomach and is expelled? ¹⁸**But what comes out of the mouth proceeds from the heart, and this defiles a person.** ¹⁹For out of the heart come evil thoughts, murder, adultery, sexual immorality, theft, false witness, slander. ²⁰These are what defile a person. But to eat with unwashed hands does not defile anyone."*

In the scriptural reference above, Jesus was being questioned about what defiles people. Essentially, He explains, it's not what people eat that defiles them, but more importantly what is spoken of their mouths or their actions – because what comes out of his mouth is derived from the Heart. He notes that evil thoughts, murder, adultery, sexual immorality, theft, false witness, slander – all of these come from the Heart. When these things take root in the Heart, they will eventually manifest…no matter what you think, no matter what you feel, no matter what you know to be right; if it is in your heart, it will show because your heart will give life to it.

Few of us have ever done an honest assessment of ourselves. What is in your heart? Not your mind, not your emotions, but what are you holding onto in your heart? Is it anger? Is it hurt and disappointment from a previous relationship? Were you abused as a child? Did people in the church manipulate you? Were you taught to hate, to steal, to lie? Is that all you've ever known?

These things (and much worse) gradually and overtime can take residence in our hearts. Once rooted in our hearts - they manifest in our actions!! Our Words!! Our Attitudes!! It is what's in our hearts that has the ability to defile us; our heart has the potential to be the fertile ground for some of our biggest struggles. That's why it is a component of man that we need to be aware of, knowledgeable about, and gain increased understanding.

Deceitfulness of the Heart

Jeremiah 17:9

The heart is deceitful above all things, and desperately wicked: who can know it?

Jeremiah doesn't wax poetic about the Heart. He is more realistic in his explanation. He calls the Heart "deceitful above all things and desperately wicked" because it is a conundrum. I've told you that the Heart is where some good things reside (faith in God, morals, values, convictions, integrity, Godly strongholds and principles); however, it can also be the residence of doubt, anxiety, demonic strongholds, fear, etc. You can see how this could be deceiving. On the one hand, my heart can lead me to an incredible existence, while on the other hand, it can lead me to great ruin and destruction.

How could something have the potential to be both good and bad, at the same time? How could something that gives life, also be the harbinger of our death and destruction? It is quite the dilemma. What's more puzzling is that these elements can coexist. I can have faith in God about salvation in my heart, but also have a demonic stronghold for depression. I can have integrity about not robbing a bank but have no moral boundary when it comes to stealing cable.

Jeremiah is trying to get us to go against the popular doctrine of our modern times that tells us to "Follow your heart!" It seems like a great idea, so positive and innocent...until it leads you to destruction.

Our heart is one of the most powerful entities that we possess; however, most of our hearts have schizophrenic tendencies. How do we grapple with something that is so potent, yet has the potential to be so unstable? How do you handle something that has the potential to be a force for such good; while at the same time, has the potential to be a force for such destruction?

Sometimes we need our hearts to be purified. And in dire instances, we may even need a heart transplant. David was a man <u>after God's own HEART, yet even he had to examine his heart</u>—Psalms 51:10-13:

*[10]Create in me a clean heart, O God; and **renew a right spirit within me**. [11]Cast me not away from thy presence; and take not thy holy spirit from me. [12]Restore unto me the joy of thy salvation; and uphold me with thy free spirit. [13]<u>Then will I teach transgressors thy ways; and sinners shall be converted unto thee</u>.*

"God Knows My Heart"

We say this and it has become many people's "go to response" when they have done something wrong but don't want to be criticized, judged, or called out on it: "I know I did something bad, but God knows that I'm really a good person – He knows my heart. He knows that I helped an old woman cross the street this morning…and that I paid my tithes…and that I go to church – He knows my heart. Even though I did cheat on my wife, it's ok. Even though I did lie to my boss., it's alright. Even though I did steal paper from the copy room, it's fine. I'm covered because "God knows my heart."

Indeed, God does know our hearts. And that does not always bode well for us!

Jeremiah 17:10

"I the Lord search the heart
and test the mind,
to give every man according to his ways,
according to the fruit of his deeds."

1 Chronicles 28:9 – **David's Charge to Solomon**

"And you, Solomon my son, know the God of your father and serve him with a whole heart and with a willing mind, **for the Lord searches all hearts and understands every plan and thought.** *If you seek him, he will be found by you, but if you forsake him, he will cast you off forever.*

Psalm 139:23

Search me, O God, and know my heart!

Try me and know my thoughts

Romans 8:27

And he who searches hearts knows what is the mind of the Spirit, because the Spirit intercedes for the saints according to the will of God.

We have become experts at fooling people; we've become so good at it that I'm afraid we have even begun to fool ourselves. We speak fond words that hide our true intentions. We tap into emotions to disguise ulterior motives. We give gifts or put on performances to make people think we are someone that we're not.

People have become so exceptional at fooling others that we are shocked when a scandal erupts. The pastor preaches against homosexuality; all the while, he is having 3 different affairs in the church. The politician promises transparency and love for the people, only to find out that he has been embezzling money and stealing from those that elected him / her. When the sports team owner punishes players for not living up to a certain standard; all the while, they don't hold themselves to that same standard.

We've become so good at getting people to believe that we're good, honest, trustworthy, loving, etc. However, we can't fool God. He searches the very thing that we can't hide: our hearts. He knows your motivations. God knows the real you.

Isaiah 29:13 (NIV)

*The Lord says: "These people come near to me with their mouth and honor me with their lips, **but their hearts are far from me**.*

I may not be able to tell if you're sincere or putting on a show, but you and God know. Do you have doubt in your heart that's keeping you from the manifestations of God? Are you saying that you're blessed and highly favored, but in your heart, you believe something different? Are you saying that you trust God, but in your heart, you've given up and are fearful?

What's in your heart matters to God more than what you say, feel, or reveal to other people. This is because what's in your heart is the real you. Because God DOES INDEED know my heart, searches it, and created it - I trust him. I follow God and not my heart. The goal is to subject my heart to God, to allow my heart to be led by God...not people, the world, or what I think.

Double-Minded

James 1:5-8

*[5]If any of you lacks wisdom, let him ask God, who gives generously to all without reproach, and it will be given him. [6]<u>But let him ask in faith, with no doubting</u>, for the one who doubts is like a wave of the sea that is driven and tossed by the wind. [7]For that person must not suppose that he will receive anything from the Lord; [8]**he is a double-minded man**, unstable in all his ways.*

I never really understood this scripture...until I got the revelation of the Heart. So, as noted earlier, we have a conscious mind, and we have a subconscious mind (the spirit of the mind or heart). It is when these two are at odds that we are unstable. My conscious mind knows to treat people a certain way; however, when faced with a real circumstance, my actions may not always align with what I know to do. This dichotomy is often the source of our hypocritical nature. I say one thing.... I teach that thing.... I preach that to my children; however, I do the exact opposite. One thing is in your head, but another thing is in your heart.

You'd think something was wrong with me if I told you that the stove is hot, and the next minute, I'm putting my hand on the stove. It just doesn't add up. Likewise... if someone tells you cheating on your spouse is wrong, and when you look up, they've cheated on their spouses. It doesn't make sense – you're unstable. I don't know what you think or believe.

We have to reconcile our conscious minds and the spirit of our minds – we have to bring the two into one alignment. God hates double-mindedness. In the Book of Revelations (Revelations 3:14-17), God refers to this as being "lukewarm." No matter what you do or how you are – "hot" or "cold" – God wants you to be single-minded. Of singular focus. Then, at least you'll be stable.

Think about this. Paul was once "cold". Paul was once a murderer of the people who believed in Jesus, the Christ...but he was single-minded and devout even in his error. Because of this, I believe that is why he was useful to God. God eventually revealed Paul's misguided zeal and he became a powerful Ambassador for the Kingdom of Heaven. In Romans, Paul even articulates this battle that we face.

Romans 7:17-25 (MSG)

*17-20But I need something more! For **if I know the law but still can't keep it**, and if the power of sin within me keeps sabotaging my best intentions, I obviously need help! I realize that I don't have what it takes. **I can will it**, but I can't do it. **I decide to do good**, but I don't really do it; **I decide not to do bad**, but then I do it anyway. **My decisions**, such as they are, don't result in actions. **Something has gone wrong deep within me and gets the better of me every time**.*

*21-23It happens so regularly that it's predictable. The moment I decide to do good, sin is there to trip me up. I truly delight in God's commands, but it's pretty obvious that not all of me joins in that delight. Parts of me covertly rebel, and just when I least expect it, **they take charge**.*
*24I've tried everything and nothing helps. I'm at the end of my rope. Is there no one who can do anything for me? Isn't that the real question? 25The answer, thank God, is that Jesus Christ can and does. He acted to set things right in this life of contradictions where **I want to serve God with all my heart and mind**, but am pulled by the **influence of sin** to do something totally different.*

Paul does an accurate job of explaining something that most people view as the unexplainable. I know the law (in my conscious mind), but I don't do it. I make a decision (in my conscious mind), but I find myself not doing what I decided to do. I will myself NOT to do bad (in my conscious mind), but that's what I find myself doing.

In the KJV, Paul describes it as a "law in his members," a teaching, a rule. He says that it happens so regularly that it's predictable. The Heart, the unconscious mind, drives our actions. When not filled with God's teachings and commandments, the heart influences the physical body to rebel and take charge. Paul highlights that he wants to serve God with all his heart and mind, but sin has taken root and created a stronghold in his heart, and he does something totally different.

Get These Teachings in Your Heart

Why am I telling you about the heart? What does this have to do with teaching? How is this important to manifesting the miraculous in our lives? I'm glad you asked…

I've been stressing the importance of teaching, but I would be doing you a great disservice if I didn't tell you "where" to put the teaching. In the beginning of this chapter, I used the analogy of a remote control and batteries. Both being in the same room or vicinity isn't enough to operate the remote control. I can even place the batteries inside of the remote control; however, if they aren't positioned correctly, it has the same effect as if I had no batteries at all. Batteries must be placed in the proper chamber with proper positioning in order for the remote control to function.

It is the same with teaching – Teaching is the battery to the miraculous living that we desire. However, if we fail to put the teachings in the correct place, they will not have the miraculous impact and our lives will not function according to God's design. If we have teaching written down, it's ineffective. If we have teaching in our heads, it's not as effective. Our hearts are the remote control; and teachings are the "double A batteries" that allow us to change the channel and volume of our lives. We have to get teachings in our hearts in order for them to be effective and manifest in our lives.

Proverbs 3:1

*My son, do not forget my teaching, but **let your heart keep my commandments**,*

Jeremiah 31:33

*For this is the covenant that I will make with the house of Israel after those days, declares the Lord: I will put my law within them, and **I will write it on their hearts**. And I will be their God, and they shall be my people.*

According to these scriptures, we clearly see that God wants to get His laws and His teachings into our hearts. He wants it to be so deeply ingrained in us that we do it unconsciously. He wants it to be so intertwined within us that it becomes our instinct when under pressure. God wants the teachings in our hearts because what is in our hearts defines us, defiles us, gives life to who we really are and what we truly value. What's in your Heart? Is it the teachings of God? The teachings of television? The teachings of your parents? The teachings of your friends? The teachings of what you've experienced in life?

Is it something you learned unknowingly? Being taught by my dad not to love and trust anyone had taken root in my heart. It came out, no matter what I said or how I tried to act. What's in your heart will eventually reveal itself!

Have you ever said, "This is the last time that I'm going to do _____" (just fill in the blank). No matter what it is, we've all been there. And the next day, the next week, or the next month, you were back to doing the same thing again.

Why is this the case? Is it because you're weak? Because you're a bad person? Because "God didn't take it away from me" like you prayed? No...Oftentimes, I'm convinced that it's because there are certain things that we have allowed into our hearts...or things that we have been subjected to in our environments that have crept into our hearts (addictions, immorality, thoughts of suicide, a defeated mindset, etc.).

How to Get God's Teachings in Your Heart

When questioned about which is the greatest commandment or greatest teaching (Matthew 22:36-40), Jesus responded with two commandments:

1. Love God with **all your heart**, soul, and mind.
2. Love your neighbor as yourself.

He taught that these two commandments were the foundation of every other commandment, teaching, law, principle. So if Loving God with All MY HEART, soul, and mind is a foundational teaching / commandment in the

Kingdom of God, I need to understand what this means. As we noted earlier Jesus told His disciples, "*If you love me, you'll keep my commandments*" (John 14-15). God equates understanding and keeping His teachings with Love for HIM. So in essence, He is saying Understand and keep MY teachings (which is the way to demonstrate Love for God) with all your heart, soul, and mind. Once the teachings are in your heart, they will overflow into your soul, and then your conscious mind — thus impacting and influencing your physical actions / behavior (even how we treat / love our neighbors).

However, I would be negligent (and cruel) if I told you **what to do**, but **NOT** tell you **how to do it**. Yes, it is imperative to get God's teachings, His way of doing things, His perspective, His understanding, His wisdom into our Hearts. One does this by inundating themselves with the teachings of God. Consistently putting the word of God into practice in my life. One has to bombard their physical senses and saturate their very soul with the teachings from God. Fasting and dying to their physical desires and fleshly impulses; and rather, being led, taught, and fortified by the HOLY SPIRIT. In short, the key is *consistency*. Consistently hearing and understanding God's teachings. Consistently implementing God's teachings. And Consistently teaching others God's teachings.

Through our five physical gates/senses, we have to allow the teachings and components conducive for nourishment and growth; while at the same time, guard our hearts – guarding those gates and points of entry in which things that aren't the teachings of God can enter or gain access to my heart. I have to be hypervigilant and aware of what I allow my eyes to see, my ears to hear, my nose to smell, my tongue to taste, my hands and body to touch. I have to be mindful of my conscious thoughts, my imaginations, my will and line them all up with the Word of God: Watching positive things on television and positive life examples...listening to sound doctrine and uplifting conversation...thinking like God thinks...balancing my intellect, emotions, and will with the Holy Spirit. All of these things will contribute to advancing the teachings of God from seeds of external instructions to being rooted deeply and written in our hearts.

Once God's teachings of handling finances are in my heart, I give life to prosperity. Once God's teachings of praise and worship are in my heart, I'm able to go deeper into a relationship with God. Once God's teachings on healing are in my heart, I give life to healing. Once the teachings of treating my fellow man right are in my heart, I give life to the impossible because we are in Unity in God. Once the teachings of loving my spouse are in my heart, I give life to an amazing marriage and relationship.

Think about it in terms of a car and gasoline. We know that a car needs gasoline to function. There are instances where you can have gasoline and the car not be able to function. You can pour the gasoline on top of the car. You can set the gasoline in a canister and buckle it in on the passenger side. You can put the gasoline in the trunk. In all of these instances, you have gasoline. Yet, the car will not function. Until you put the gasoline in the proper designed place - the gas tank - it will fail to function.

Similarly, many of us have and know God's teachings and we are failing. Unfortunately, we have the teachings in our notebooks, but not in our hearts. We have them in our smartphones and laptops, but not in our hearts. We may have them in our emotions, but not our hearts. We need these God's teachings in our hearts because our faith gives life to what is in our hearts. Our convictions are constructed from what is in our hearts. What is in our hearts forms our values, priorities, and principles. If it's not in my heart, it is incapable of governing or setting the climate for my life.

What Satan Fears Most

Your faith gives rise to what's in your heart. The kingdom's teachings make your heart valuable and a dangerous threat to the enemy. I believe this is why Jesus prayed for Peter's faith (in Luke 22:32) because Peter and the disciples were getting teachings that were taking root in their heart. This is what Satan fears more than anything - the kingdom teachings getting in your heart. Let's see what Jesus says about the subject:

Matthew 13:18-19

[18] "Hear then the parable of the sower: [19] When anyone hears the word of the kingdom and does not understand it, the evil one comes and snatches away what has been sown in his heart. This is what was sown along the path.

Jesus told a parable about a sower; later when he was alone with the disciples, he began to explain the parable. He highlighted that when anyone hears the word

/ message / teachings on the kingdom of God - the evil one comes to snatch away what was sown in their heart. He doesn't send some other lower class demon. He doesn't use some tricks or tactics. Jesus says that "the evil one", himself comes to snatch what was sown in that person's HEART. Why? Because he realizes that if God's teachings take root in your heart, you are a threat to him and his kingdom of darkness. Getting the teachings in your heart is just that important!!!

Let me say this.... I don't think this is the "end all, be all" or most accurate representation of the heart/mind dynamic in terms of understanding God's creation known as "man". I don't think that it is something that is so easily understood without God's insight and Revelation. This is the teaching and understanding that God gave to me. I hope that it is insightful and enables you to unlock the "miraculous" life God has destined and purposed for YOU!!!

Let's Be Honest – Self Evaluation:

1. What's in your heart? Are you still holding on to anger? Frustration? Unforgiveness? Are you fearful or doubtful?

2. Are God's teachings and faith in your heart? Are they habitual and instinctual?

3. When you're under pressure or faced with great difficulty, what do you do?

4. What is keeping the teachings of God to take root in your heart?

5. Is there a particular teaching(s) that you realize that you are knowledgeable of, but it's not in your heart? Have you found yourself feeling like Paul: "When I want to do God, I find myself doing the opposite"? What happened? How did this impact you?

Heart / Mind

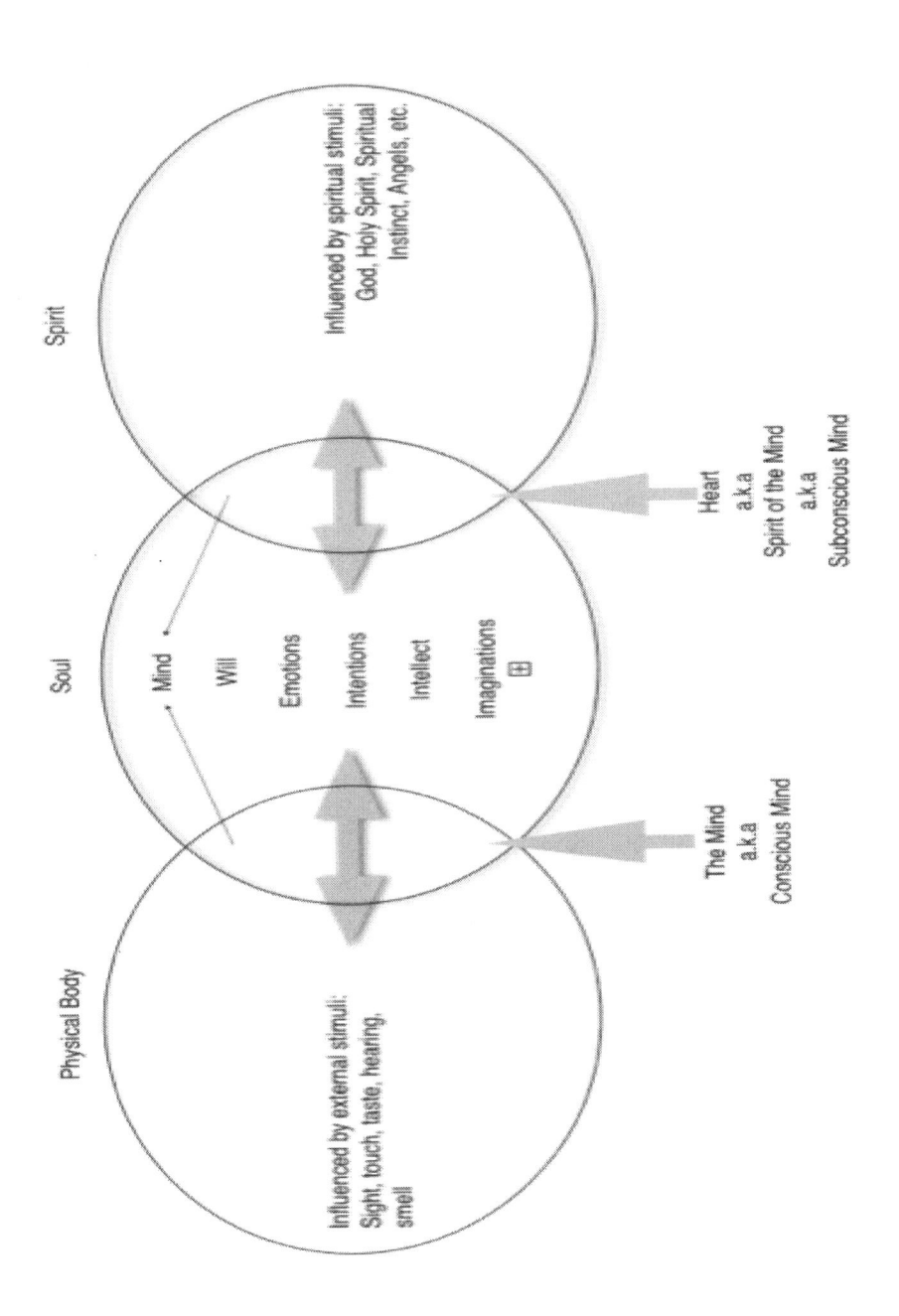

Spirit — Influenced by spiritual stimuli: God, Holy Spirit, Spiritual Instinct, Angels, etc.

Soul — Mind, Will, Emotions, Intentions, Intellect, Imaginations

Heart a.k.a Spirit of the Mind a.k.a Subconscious Mind

The Mind a.k.a Conscious Mind

Physical Body — Influenced by external stimuli: Sight, touch, taste, hearing, smell

Man on One Accord with Himself

Physical Body, Soul, and Man's Spirit:
All become one, like the Father, Son,
and Holy Spirit operate as one.

Mind and Heart:
Conscious Mind and Subconscious Mind
are on One Accord.

Mind, Will, Emotions, Intent, Intelligence,
Imaginations are all guided by
the Spiritual realm and have
positive manifestations in our
actions.

Please contact Art & Legacy Publications for your publishing needs:

Art-legacyworldwide.com

Made in the USA
Columbia, SC
30 November 2024